THE *Movement* OF BONES

A MEMOIR

NOLA PEREZ

This book is dedicated to

The Circle

Able • Eileen • Iris • Lise • Elise • Julie • Suzanne • Patsy • Willene • Cindy Marie • Wendy • Cyndy • Michael-E • Inez • Sandra • Emily • Joani • Donna • Debi • Betty • Julia • Eliza • Dickie

May the circle be unbroken.

and, in loving memory of my Capricorn Sister, Julie,
who read this book in manuscript before losing a courageous
battle with cancer, Thanksgiving Day 2007.

Julie Pietri, 1938-2007

Cover Art

Feeling Blue

by Christina Croft

Christina was born in Germany in 1937, studied graphic design in Darmstadt, Germany, and printmaking at St. Martin's School of Art, London. Along with her husband, she spent decades cruising on a sailing boat with mini art studio. Her multi-colored block prints became a diary of people and countries visited.

She now lives in Queensland, Australia in a large studio/house in the countryside.

Grateful Thanks

... to **Dickie Anderson**, **Able Rae** and **Emily Carmain** for their meticulous reading of this book in manuscript.

... and to **Wendy White Philcox**, whose DNA is all over this book.

"If of thy mortal goods thou art bereft
And from thy slender store two loaves alone to thee are left
Sell one, and with the other dole
Buy hyacinths to feed thy soul"

—13TH CENTURY POET, MOSLIH SAADI

Other Books by Nola Perez

Poetry:
Before Angels
The Continent of Dreams
The Alchemy of Loss
In the Season of Tropical Depression
Precincts of the Heart

Nonfiction:
Excerpts from a Journal
Cruising with the Kir Queen, My Brussels Journal

"We are all longing to go home to some place we have never been—
A place half remembered and half envisioned we can only catch glimpses
of from time to time. Somewhere there are people to whom we can speak
with passion without having the words catch in our throats.
Somewhere a circle of hands will open to receive us,
eyes will light up as we enter, voices will celebrate with us,
wherever we come into our own power..."

—STARHAWKS: DREAMING THE DARK:
MAGIC SEX AND POLITICS

the Movement *of* Bones

CAST of CHARACTERS

The Kir Queen
Miami, St. Augustine and Amelia Island, Florida
The Atlantic Ocean

Paris, France
Catherine, Jean-Claude (aka Joli Prince) and Ségolène
The South of France:
Frejùs, Boulouris, St. Raphael, Marseille
The Mediterranean Sea

New Orleans (before Katrina)
Ms. Julia Jessup

NewYork, N. Y. (after 9/11)
Ms. Julie Pietri • 1938-2007

Several anonymous gentlemen callers

Some significant men friends:
J. D. Beck
Wally Wulff
Walter Griffin

"The Sister Ls":
Elise Braun
Lise Goett
Ms. Elizabeth Perez

Andre of Marseille • 1930-2002
James Alva Baker • 1933-2001
George Derrick • 1922-2006
Corinne Derrick • 1925-2006

Harry Strother Ryder • D. March 2003
Vincent Eugene Ferreira • D. December 2000
Betty Lee Beck • D. February 2007
Larry Dean • D. July 2008

Celebrity cameos by
Gloria Steinem, Frances Mayhall, C. S. Lewis

Prologue

There are many reasons for writing a book. This is one of them:
When I was invited to speak to a book club in Jacksonville, Florida, as a guest
writer (they had selected my Cruising with the Kir Queen, My Brussels
Journal *for their monthly read). There were perhaps a dozen+ women pres-*
ent. During a question and answer session, Evelyn Cooper, one of the group
said to me: "You did not write about your husband's death." And then she
added, as in afterthought, "But that is another story…"

Her comment gave me pause. I had to stop and think for a moment. No, I
had not written about my husband's death because he was very much alive
during our two years in Brussels when Cruising with the Kir Queen *came*
into being. Matter of fact, he loomed large in the cast of characters, as he did
in all my scenarios. Mega man and alpha male of my cosmos in a marriage
that was "beyond beyond," he was alive and well and seated comfortably next
to me in an airplane when we returned to the States from Brussels in the
summer of 1999.

This, then, as I set down my scepter (but never my flute) is the beginning of
that Other Story, as well as certain vignettes in the lives (and passages) of
some fellow thespians along the way—a play wherein, perhaps, we capture the
conscience of the Queen.

• • •

"… *other times feel stunned and lost,*
though living in my own
body and life, presumably,
bewildered and alone

as the knight, kidnapped and released
to a dim world, who said
And I awoke and find me here
On the cold hill side."

—RACHEL HADAS, FROM HER POEM
"THE COLD HILL SIDE"

Chapter One

THE BEREAVED

"Perhaps the bereaved ought to be isolated
in special settlements like lepers"
—C. S. LEWIS

Fall, and the sycamores shed leaves that were light-filled
and green in summer, those branches I touch
for healing as I pass beneath in search of childhood games,
our faded calls fastened in their trunks like druids,
becoming less audible each passing October.

Softly from leprous limbs, leaves drift down,
yellowing the grass, crumpling on cracked sidewalks,
streets of "Red Rover, Red Rover, may I come over?"
"I Spy," and "Hide and Seek," curling and wasting
like the handsomest boy in the sophomore
class, three houses down, who went mano-a-mano
with a motocycle, and the motorcycle won.

We are a tribe of untouchables,
whirling in a downward spiral of molecules
where there is no soft landing, no grassy plain
where we run, arms outstretched
to embrace each other. God takes a handful of earth

shakes it loose, and says to those we love,
Come now, and they obey. For us left behind,
we call each hour by its assignment. In dream light,
we wander caves where other casualties
extend their arms and call us by name. They
mean us no harm. We are the dynasty
of the dying.

"HOME." Where is it? Maybe we need a pair of sparkly red shoes that know exactly where to take us. A magical three clicks of heels, transporting us wherever our gray-haired version of Auntie Em waits with outstretched arms. T. S. Eliot said simply, "Home is where one starts from," and "In my end is my beginning." Once upon a time in a kingdom not by the sea, I was in love briefly (brief in terms of time, not in the duration of a broken heart) with a man who declared he lived in his head. It was impossible to enter his house because there was no door, front or otherwise. In the spirit of that idea, home had always been a state of mind to me, and difficult to determine brute boundaries.

Home was an emotion experienced when crossing certain bridges, inhaling the perfume of salt marshes and tide pools that spelled the little barrier island where I grew up. Driving on the Champs Elysées after long absence, watching the River Meuse flow past a little town in Belgium called Dinant, where my husband and I spent many happy hours; or passing a mystical point of beach on the south end of Amelia Island, which had been my high school peer-group playground. There was no lovelier place on the island than there where the beach turned back on itself to head toward the setting sun. There was always a strong afternoon wind, whipping a cobalt sea into frothy breakers, and time hung suspended in a warp of forever young.

I live by a deep lake, now. I never thought to be a lake person, but this particular lake, surrounded by salt marshes, has enough seasoning in it to satisfy. When the wind blows the water my way, and activates the pine trees and marsh myrtles to tell their stories, there are some elements of that blessed south end of the island I loved in my girlhood. As the sun is setting and I sit on my screened porch to watch it disappear, I am as happy and peaceful as anyone gets. The only component missing is my companion of 52 years beside me. We had that much time in each other's company, despite an interlude of search for self on my part from 1973 to 1983. Deduct 10 years from our union if you absolutely must, but we were never really apart. We could never cut the cord that bound us. So be it: my own personal tale of two cities, tale of two continents, tale of two lives, irrevocably entwined.

• • •

THIS IS also a story about homecoming, an attempt to understand what home means, especially for a wanderer who began her journey on Florida's northernmost barrier island. In the growing-up years, we used to refer to our hometown in its entirety as "Fernandina." Since those days, Beach has been added to the name, and now, more often than not, it's just "Amelia Island." We have become gentrified.

So, where exactly is home, and who was the man I married whose death aroused the curiosity of a woman who never knew him, causing these pages to be come into being? This writer not only grew up on "Amelia Island," she met the man who would become her husband when he immigrated from the South of France, ending up in the most unlikely small town in America. What was unlikely was someone from the huge, bustling seaport city of Marseille coming to seek his fortune in a small, sleepy little fishing-cum-mill town like Fernandina.

Years later, someone asked Andre how he felt, landing in Fernandina after entering the U. S. through Ellis Island, and stepping foot in the grand city of New York. New York met with his unqualified approval, and after celebrating his arrival by consuming a whole box of Hershey bars; he boarded the train to travel to his new home with his sister Sylvia and his brother-in-law, Vincent Ferreira. When the train deposited him on Centre Street, his final destination, Andre said he looked around in astonishment, and voiced a single question to his sister and her husband: "Is this all?" Yes, it was, and it was beyond culture shock.

Andre of Marseille, and the wife-to-be, whose destiny was to be irrevocably tied to his when he migrated to America, ended up being long-time marrieds. They were an implausible couple that found each other from across 5,000 watery miles of the cold, dark North Atlantic. For 52 of their married years, 40-plus were spent away from Fernandina, where they met. They had no real home—just stops along the way, though there were some pretty significant stops. Raising two sons kept them preoccupied with parental duties for 10 years in Jacksonville, Florida.

There was no child on the horizon until 10 years into the marriage, and then a baby on the way was like the sun coming up. The new father was pretty sure of his role, but there never was a more anxious mother-to-be. She was 31 years old, and had never thought of herself as a maternal being. Happily for baby makes three, she worked that out before the deadline. As her doctor brother, Jim Baker, remarked, "There's nothing like a baby for putting your feet squarely on the ground." Her feet were rarely squarely on the ground, so while they were, at least temporarily, it seemed an auspicious time to add another baby to the mix. Son number two made them an even number. The offspring were afforded a rather exotic mélange of bloodlines. Their mother's people were Dantzlers who immigrated from Prussia, and Bakers, classic English/Scotch/Irish. Their father spiced things up with his Roman-Catholic mother from a Spanish family in Alicante, Spain, and his father, a handsome man of the Muslim faith, born in Algiers, Algeria. Major roots!

Andre's sister, Sylvia, was the unintentional means to all ends. Sylvia, a pretty young French girl, growing up in Marseille's *Vieux Port* during the Great War with her sister Marie, and her brother, Andre, went out one evening with her best friend, Yvonne, to an American Army USO dance. She attracted the attention of a saxophone player in the band whose name was Vincent Ferreira. She didn't know it then, but the Ferreiras were one of the oldest and most prestigious families on Florida's northernmost barrier island. Vincent came from a fishing village on the island called Fernandina. She couldn't have known this, because she was from a huge seaport town called Marseille. Now, Fernandina was unique, and Fernandina was old, but Sylvia's town had the corner on old! Fernandina, starting with Jean Ribault's landing in 1562, has a recorded history of over 400 years, but Marseille's origins went back to 600 B.C. when Greek sailors from Phocaea settled in the *Vieux Port* of today. That made Marseille (anciently Massalia) undeniably the oldest town in France.

Young Mlle. Sylvia Perez and her girlfriend, Yvonne, soon began dating the boys in the band. Sylvia paired off with Vincent; her friend paired off with the drummer. They dated in tandem, they fell in love, they married in a double ceremony—Sylvia loves Vincent, Yvonne loves Ralph. There is a charming photograph of Sylvia and Vincent right after their wedding. They are standing before the doorway of the *mairie,* the city hall in Marseille, after a civil ceremony, looking soulfully into each other's eyes. Vincent handsome in his Army uniform, Sylvia in a short print dress Vincent bought her especially for the occasion, looking much like a '40s bobby soxer on any American small-town street. I once asked Sylvia how Vincent proposed to her. When it came time for Vincent to return home to the States, Sylvia said he simply told her, "I don't think I can leave you here." And, he didn't. She followed him to the States on a ship carrying other war brides, bringing Vincent's newborn son (also named Vincent) to their new home in Fernandina. Some time later, there was another son born to the couple: Andre, named for his uncle in Marseille.

It was difficult adjusting to her drastically changed life for the young Frenchwoman. Many of her ways were amusing and strange to her American in-laws. In Fernandina, not many, if any at all, spoke her mother tongue. Sylvia became homesick for her family in France, and asked Vincent if it would be possible to bring her adored younger brother to the States. Would Vincent vouch for him? Those were moot questions, and that is how I met the Andre of Marseille who changed my life forever.

So, Sylvia got her brother, he got America, and I eventually got Europe by way of the American Government. It was my perception during the time my husband-to-be and I were dating, that Andre was one of the most competent young men I had ever met. I felt safe hitching my wagon to his star because his star was shooting straight up. Sparks flew off it like a Fourth of July sparkler, or better said, Bastille Day fireworks. With practically no English language skills, he found work in Fernandina as a plumbing contractor's helper. He learned English, tool-by-tool, coil-by-coil, and sink-by-sink. After that employment ended, he was hired in Container Corporation's pulp mill as a 'hand' on a machine called the broke beater. He worked shift work in a blue-collar job because an immigrant with no U. S. high school diploma equivalent had to start somewhere.

Then, on February 18, 1950, he married a young island woman who had been away in South America all that prior year. They met in the summer of 1949, and were married the following February. When his bride said, "I Do," before a priest at the altar, she knew, given half a chance, the man she was embracing would someday be somebody. That is how it came to pass that Andre's best friend, Jim Baker, walked his sister down the aisle in St. Peter's Episcopal Church, Amelia Island, to bind her life to that of a beaming Andre' of Marseille, resplendent in a navy blue suit, white carnation in his button hole, and, long before Elvis Presley, a pair of blue suede shoes. He may have wanted to shed his French identity in the total Americanization process on which he was embarked, but Andre' of Marseille is the name his wife always called him. Years later, it would be etched in granite on a marker in Fernandina's Bosque Bello Cemetery. Andre of Marseille was an Amelia Island adopted son to the end.

His new wife was ambitious for Andre, almost as passionate about his advancement as he was. It was a misfortune, initially, but fortuitous in the scheme of things when after only two years, their married life was interrupted by a Greetings letter from the American military draft. He was the first married man, (not even a citizen yet) to be drafted into the Army from Amelia Island. Andre went off for basic training in Ft. Jackson, South Carolina, while his wife remained behind. She had no idea what was going to happen next in her drastically altered life, her short-term husband torn away from what had seemed destined to be a predictable Fernandina lifestyle. It was during the Korean War, and after boot camp, Andre was one of only two men in his outfit who did not get sent to Korea. Instead, he was sent to Leiphim, Germany, in the 54th Combat Engineer Battalion for two years. He was there from August of 1952 to July of 1954. Escaping combat in Korea was one of the many strokes of good luck which would befall him. Fate had big plans in store.

In light of the long separation she faced, Andre's wife of two years knew she had to go to work and support herself. She had never held a real job before. She applied to Massey Business School in Jacksonville, and went to live for the next year with Andre's sister, Sylvia, in Jacksonville. It was just one of the ways the Ferreiras took her into their hearts and their hearths. While Nola was in business school that year, Sylvia was learning beautician skills in cosmetology school. The sisters-in-law supported each other, even riding the same bus each morning to their respective classes in downtown Jacksonville. After completing secretarial courses at Massey College, Nola was offered a job in the Administration Office at Container Corporation of America.

She returned to Fernandina in 1953, and rented a small garage apartment on South Third Street. She lived there the entire time of Andre's two-year tour with the Army in Germany, and when Andre came marching home again, Hoorah, Hoorah, he did not resume his job at the mill. With allotment checks his wife saved during his absence, the G. I. bill, and a little help from his friends, Andre enrolled in the University of Florida, Gainesville. He graduated four and a half years later with a degree in civil engineering. That is how he got from nowhere to somewhere, from Amelia to the Champs! One of Nola's aunts, Lillian Ryder, worked in Tallahassee as personal secretary to the then-Attorney General for the State of Florida, Richard Ervin. Lillian was instrumental in helping Andre get established with the U. S. Army Corps of Engineers, so after graduation, into civil service went *"Mon Beau"* with his first good job. That is how the U. S. Government eventually "got" Nola her heart's desire: a life in Europe.

Initially, Andre and his wife settled in Jacksonville where his job with the Corps was situated. They acquired a first house and the two little boys who made them a family. Nola stayed at home with her children as a full time mom for ten years, never regretting a minute of it. Her only regret was that her favorite first cousin, Harry Ryder, her Aunt Lillian's only son, had initially deplored her decision to marry Andre. One of the reasons was that his cousin's fiancé was a man of little means. Another reason dashed the high hopes of Lillian and Harry Ryder that Nola would do them proud, in that Nola put her education on hold to get married. Her future husband pulled her out of her studies at Florida State University with an ultimatum. Leave school and get married—it's now or never. Andre was never confused about what he wanted. He was never confused, period. But, oh ye of little faith! Years later at a 50th wedding anniversary celebration for Nola and her husband in a room overflowing with family, friends and all manner of well-wishers, Harry Ryder, ever his cousin Nola's favorite relative, conceded in public before many witnesses that with no reservations, Andre of Marseille was the quintessential American Success Story.

Andre had a way of becoming bored when he mastered a work situation. It was an energy that defined him all his professional life. He was Aquarius, the water bearer. I was Capricorn, the mountain goat, climbing ever higher. Perhaps we should have switched signs, but as a water bearer I could never have quenched his thirst for success. Dissatisfaction with the status quo moved him up, and up the ladder of opportunity. After ten years with the Corps of Engineers, Jacksonville, a project on which Andre had been working, the new Panama Canal feasibility study, came to an end. The understanding of all who signed on for the study was that if the Canal did not go to construction, they would be required to relocate. The Canal did not go to construction, we had to move, and the relocation choices were Washington, D. C., or Atlanta, Georgia. We chose Atlanta, and lived there fairly happily, if not happily ever after, because after twenty years, once again boredom with the workplace changed Andre's direction from one branch of civil service to another. He took a job with the Federal Aviation Administration, and began traveling abroad on their behalf. He had his sights set on a European assignment, and in the summer of 1990, dream of dreams come true, Andre and I were on a plane headed for Paris!

My husband was the proudest American I have ever known. On his naturalization paper, there is an official photo of an extraordinarily handsome young man with a short haircut that destroyed the wild black curls that crowned him in his youth. Our son Michael inherited these curls, along with his father's confident, easy body language. On Andre's naturalization certificate, it reads that "Andre Perez intended to reside permanently in the United States (when so required by the naturalization laws of the United States) and had in all other respects complied with the applicable provisions of such naturalization laws, and was entitled to be admitted to citizenship, thereupon it is ordered that such person be admitted as a citizen of the United States of America on the tenth day of November, 1954." From that auspicious beginning, little did we dream Andre would be sent to France by the United States Government to represent his adopted country in the newly created position of Civil Aviation Security Liaison Officer, (CASLO), negotiating with high-ranking French diplomats as an American.

In the wake of the disastrous Pan American Flight 103 that crashed over Lockerbie, Scotland, in December of 1988, President Bush created the CASLO positions to be headquartered in the major cities of Europe. Andre applied to be appointed CASLO Paris, and gained the appointment in 1990. His mission was to insure, as would CASLOs in other countries, that proper levels of security were maintained for American airline carriers in foreign airports. Andre's area of responsibility was for France, Switzerland, Tunisia, Algeria, the Ivory Coast and North Africa—a huge load and a big honor for this naturalized American.

• • •

MUCH HAS BEEN WRITTEN by me about our Paris sojourn, principally in a book of poems, *The Continent of Dreams,* which was completed during the four years we lived there. The book, published in 2000, is out of print now, but my memories of Paris will never run off the page. France was a lifetime dream of mine, and proof that some dreams solidify. When my boss of twenty years in Atlanta heard the news that our long and harmonious association was coming to an end, he put his head down on his desk for a few moments, then sprang immediately into action to find my replacement. I had waited extra long to announce that Andre had been awarded a job in Paris because loyalty, and sadness to be leaving my boss of so many years was causing me pain. Aware of my reluctance, Andre finally said to me, "OK, Nola, I've accepted this job—somebody is going to have to go to Paris." It is not that there was any real choice between moving to Paris, or remaining alone in Atlanta. There was the developing realization of leaving all knowns—flying 5,000 miles across the North Atlantic to an intimidating unfamiliar.

I decided to make an appointment to seek advice from my longtime psychic counselor, Frank Rambow, minister in an Atlanta metaphysical church, and a prestigious, highly respected interpreter in the ancient art of Tarot cards. I knew Frank would have wise counsel. "Newness causes fear," he told me. "You will feel fear every time you step into the unknown, but one must hold fear from a position of power, not a position of pain." Frank quoted this, "He who leaps from the head of the lion will pass in safety," meaning a leap of faith—a walk off the cliff, the step down into the abyss where there seems no support. "You came in with the World Card," Frank told me. "Only once or twice in my lifetime did I see someone with the World Card. This is a lifetime of completing things. Things not dealt with in other lives are being dealt with in this one. You are pulling all strings together in this lifetime. Do I graduate, or do I blow it? Am I willing to face the uncertain?"

Of course, I didn't want to blow it. There was never any real question, and Frank Rambow's counsel strengthened my resolve. Frank's final words to me that July afternoon in 1990 a short time before lift-off to France were these: "You came back with the Christ energy. The return is for the Christ initiation, and there are seven major tests on the Christ level. You have an opportunity to complete the second initiation. We are concerned with only four; however, within each one of them are seven and within those seven are seven. Most of humanity is still working on the first one, but if you do this in this lifetime, the third one you earn. It is bestowed on you at death. The energy comes into the body and it is like being electrocuted. Too much power comes in and destroys the body. Death and the power come at the same time."

For me, this was a novel way to look at physical death. Death empowers? What a concept!

Holding Frank's beautiful Tarot Cards in my hands, and turning them over and over, it was difficult to believe where all this was coming from. I didn't feel their energy, but I believed in it—and I boarded that plane, Andre and me, flying toward the CASLO life, whatever that would bring to us. Hopefully, we would find a lot of illumination in the City of Light.

We could have stayed longer in Paris than the four years we were actually there. But during that fourth year, we had to make a decision: go or stay. Our initial tour was up, and Andre and I conferred as to whether to sign on for another four years. For multiple reasons, we began to consider that perhaps it was time to return to the States. We were getting older, and approaching retirement time. Our already small family was dwindling. These seemed reason enough, and finally Andre advised Washington of our decision. As time grew closer and closer to departure time in the summer of 1994, however, both of us began to have second thoughts.

We underestimated the claim Paris had on us. She had dug her nails into us all the way to the heart. There was an escalating reluctance to leave. Caught in Paris' magical net, it became harder and harder to consider being anywhere else. As a fellow expatriate remarked, "Something happens to you here." He came, he saw, was conquered, and he never left. The sad thing for us was that changes were already in place. A new Paris CASLO had already been selected. There was nothing to be done. The cast net was flung far from the Seine—we were destined to reap new experiences in South Florida, its capital city of Miami, probably the most exotic destination in the States you could ever imagine. That part was a plus, however. We could "do" exotic.

In Miami, Andre was assigned the same kind of CASLO mission he had in Paris, but his responsibility was for South and Central America and the Caribbean. We lived on Collins Avenue in North Miami Beach for three years. During that time, I learned to love the Latino aura of South Florida, the wealth of water and warmth, side trips to the Keys, and the eye-catching beauty of an aquamarine sea, so different from my North Florida Atlantic. I attended writing conferences in Key West, rubbed shoulders with the famous, the less famous (my category) and in due time, a chapbook of poems came into being: *In the Season of Tropical Depression*. Indeed, the season of tropical depression was anything but dark for both Andre and me. We had some challenges to face, but our faces were turned toward the sun.

We ended the FAA CASLO years with a two-year sojourn in Brussels—Andre overseeing airports in the Benelux countries: Belgium, the Netherlands, and Luxembourg. He was barely into a retirement so richly earned after forty-three years of Government service, when his health, fragile for some time, began to dramatically decline. My own health held firm, and it was a miracle that I had no clue about my disintegrating right hip joint until there was no longer any necessity for me to be a caregiver. I was able to be there for my beloved Andre in our own safe haven at home until his death, June 7, 2002.

• • •

WE ARE NEVER prepared for the eventuality of losing a loved one even though loss is a given in this life. "This sad, old life," my aging grandmother Clendenon used to say after she lost her husband, John, and her daughter, my stepmother Lucille. Of all the sorrows my grandmother endured in her life, "There is no pain worse than losing a child," she told me. On a faded piece of paper with curling brown edges in her delicate, school-marm handwriting is something I saved for many years. My grandmother did not identify the author, but she wrote this down for her daughter, Lucille, endearingly nicknamed "Tutie" by her: "A bell is not a bell until you ring it. A song is not a song until you sing it. Love is not put in the heart to stay. Love is not love until you give it away." Philosophy—we try our best to deal with heartbreak with whatever words we can find, but words are never adequate for the task.

She also wrote down this rhyme thought to be from Oscar Hammerstein: "When daylight draws its curtains and seals it with a star, I think of you, Little Darling, and wonder where you are." "Just before dark, many days," she added, "I went out to the cemetery to be near our darling little Tutie, and I thought of this."

I read an article by a writer, Frances Mayhall, who lost her husband in 1997. She began writing, she said, with astonishing fluency—sometimes three or four poems a day. "I think it must happen to a lot of people that they really fall in love when someone is dying," she said. "You see what the quality of life is, and how desperate and true it is." Oh yes, I was to experience this particular insight in an acutely personal way myself. "I don't want to get over death," Ms. Mayhall said. "My writing was trying to keep hold of my husband. It was a daily way to speak to him and about him."

I didn't want to get over death, either. I wanted to understand its mystery. I wanted to shout out to the world my deepening realization of what my husband had really meant in my life. The actor, Rob Corddry, who plays a reporter on a television show, expressed this in an interview in *The New York Times Magazine*. He replied to the question, "[Who is your] favorite real-news reporter" this way: "Dan Rather, because you don't realize how much you love someone until they're gone." After Andre's passing, I knew I would be facing this realization. I was expecting it. Many poems were addressed to him. I had so much to say, and could only say it in the way best known to me. One of the Polish poets wrote, "The purpose of poetry is to remind us how difficult it is to remain just one person, for our house is always open. There are no keys in the door and invisible guests come in and out at will."

Gloria Steinem, who married late in life, was asked, "How are you coping with your husband's death?" She replied, "I don't know how to answer that. I'm all right, but only basically. I haven't come to the point yet of coping with death. I'm still coping with the length and sadness of his illness." Yes, and yes again, I related to that. It is as much about the difficulty of the trip as it is about the ending. The reality of the loss kicks in later and knocks the breath out of you. If the most difficult thing we have to do in this life is to lose someone, the second most difficult is to witness their suffering. The images of suffering simply never leave you. They come crashing in at the most unexpected moments to level you with grief, anger, and feelings of complete helplessness.

During the last months of his life, I would look at my husband and try to understand my whirling vortex of feelings. Intimacy had long been denied to us, but what remained of the physical touching became sweeter. The hugs, kisses, sitting beside him on the edge of the bed in the early morning hours, bathing and dressing him, and all the things that had to be done because he could no longer manage them became lovemaking in a new way. In the small hours of the night, he was afflicted with insomnia, as well as an intolerable itching of his skin. We thought this was from the dialysis he was undergoing. His only relief came from a warm shower, a rubdown with lotion, and then a soothing dusting over his body with baby powder. Sometimes there would be more than one shower during a night. My husband kept his sense of humor, though. As we sat on the edge of the bed together in the middle of one of many sleepless nights, my arms around him, he remarked wryly, "That used to be an invitation to sex. Now, it is an invitation for a shower."

Andre jokingly said that he liked to see me on my knees on our bathroom floor, putting on his shoes and socks when he could no longer bend down to do this for himself. What a reversal of our early relationship when he thought of himself, whimsically, as the pure-hearted knight, kneeling before his lady! That must be the reason why so many dear greeting cards he sent to me bore that chivalrous image. "My lady," he called me; however, he disliked the French term *ma femme*, preferring to refer to me as *mon épouse*. For Andre, there was something inelegant about the term "my woman." He preferred to say, "my spouse."

If there are former lives we have lived, my husband and I began our long journey together in the Middle Ages. L'Âge moyen, it has the right ring to it! W. B. Yeats wrote in an essay, "One should say before sleeping, I have lived many lives. I have been a slave and a prince. Many a beloved has sat upon my knees, and I have sat upon the knees of many a beloved. Everything that has been shall be again." Well, I have been a slave and a princess, and many a psychic has told me that my husband and I have been together in many lives, that we were brother and sister at the court of one of the Louie's. The Louie of my choice would have been Louis XI, The Spider King, 1461-1483. He had a reputation for craft in diplomacy, unscrupulousness and treachery. Yes, France has been in the bloodstream many times, literally, in streams of blood throughout history. The part told to me that I did not find agreeable about this pro-posed past life of mine was losing my head due to treason. The Spider King would have been in back of that. But, treason? Gee whiz! I have always considered myself a solid citizen, and liked it even less when told I was once Egyptian royalty, collecting a bagful of bad karma for putting people to death. Who me? I couldn't even squash an ant! I hope all dues have been paid in this year of Our Lord 2007, but as far as having been a crowned head; there is some truth in the fact that when entering a room I expected people to rise! Here comes the Queen? Kir Queen, that is.

What remained, then, after Andre's death was a complete inability on my part to comprehend his loss: the big mystery of where was he now? I had a new, painful awareness of something to which I had paid no atten-tion in the past. I began to observe the lightheartedness of others—all those others, attending their daily rounds, interacting blessedly unaware, so cheerfully as if life lasts forever. I had lost a certain, insulating inno-cence. Didn't they know there was going to be an end to their story and all our stories for that matter? "Don't you know?" I wanted to ask. But, of course, they didn't. Not yet.

"We are such stuff as dreams are made on, and our little life is round-ed with a sleep," Shakespeare wrote in The Tempest. How innocent those who peopled my world seemed to be of my dark secret! Life was fragile, time was brief. There was a different dimension looming—one, which was out of step and out of sync. Andre's life ended with that final breath, the flat line of a hospital monitor, the disconnected respirator and tubes.

I knew about the debilitating loss of control that chips away at self-esteem in a lingering illness, destroying all dignity—witnessed it not only with Andre, but also in the death of my younger brother, himself a physician and caretaker of others. Compounded by the loss of my father as a girl on the brink of puberty (the blood about to flow more ways than one) these deaths felt like a total wipeout of my most important men. I never felt so alone, and more loss was to follow.

This state of mind was followed by a series of health emergencies of my own, the major one being a total hip replacement in February 2004. The hip held out until after the passing of my husband, but by the end of that year, I was barely able to hobble about with a cane. Unfortunately, I had taken a certain medication that shall be nameless which made me feel so good, so pain free, prescribed for my osteoarthritis for some time. It worked like a miracle, but there was a dark side as well. I didn't know the risk, and I didn't care. I just kept on popping pills until routine blood work turned up my elevated liver enzymes. My doctor telephoned me to warn me my liver was damaged.

In the months following with my hip surgery on hold, I underwent a liver biopsy, constant blood monitoring, and the worst part—no painkillers whatsoever. Not until the source and extent of the liver damage was known was even a single aspirin allowed. Fortunately, of all the important organs, the liver has the capacity to restore itself. The liver is one of the good guys! The doctors decided that the medication I had taken over a long period of time was the culprit. A happy ending was on the horizon. I was now pronounced able to move forward with the necessary hip replacement surgery.

• • •

MY HEALTH ISSUES were minor compared to those of Andre whose heart problems had surfaced in the 1970s. Surviving two heart attacks in the mid-'80s, he subsequently underwent emergency quadruple bypass surgery. At that time, we were living in a lovely, old triplex building in midtown Atlanta. Life was good. I had the top secretarial job in my office, and my husband was traveling extensively for the Government in Europe and South America. When he came home from a trip complaining of what seemed minor symptoms: heartburn and an annoying tickle in his throat: neither of us was overly worried. Next day, after a routine appointment with a therapist, Andre's doctor called to tell me he thought Andre was having angina, and should undergo diagnostic tests. Andre was immediately admitted into the hospital.

I will never forget the day we found out about the significant blockage. I stopped by the hospital after work to hear the results of the tests. Andre's best friend, Wally Wulff, was sitting with him in his room. Wally said, "Nola, you better sit down." Then Andre gave me the bad news, and for the first time in his life, my husband broke down and wept in my arms. I remember that crying spell for its brevity—how he pulled so quickly away from me as if tears were utterly disgraceful in a strong man. The next step was open-heart surgery, and happily, the operation was so successful that after recovery, Andre got that coveted job in the FAA's CASLO position that would take him and his willing wife to Paris for four years. He passed his rigid overseas medical examination with flying colors.

• • •

CLARITY is what you seek when trying to understand the dynamics in your life in a period where there is all the time for introspection ever needed. The muddy stuff sinks to the bottom of the glass, and the clear liquid rises to the top. You dredge up things you didn't realize before. The blinders come off. After Andre's death, more and more components of myself, which had lain beyond insight for years, began to rise to consciousness. The catalyst for these self-discoveries was the absence of the main character in my movie and distance from scenarios played out in the past. It was not that I led an unexamined life. It was simply how the impetus for one's own behavior can often be a mystery. In particular, there was a revelation about my attitude toward certain persons in my life who were perceived by me to be controlling, calculating, and insensitive. Was it possible to be host to traits myself I so hotly deplored in others? It never occurred to me to look for the mote in my own orb. Where there are strong feelings over another's "faults," I was discovering the truth that this is a place where you can profitably dig into your own psyche. It never occurred to me how in my marriage, I thought it my absolute right as the wife to make decisions for me, and my mate: where we lived, the furnishings in our house, where we vacationed, and the clothes my husband purchased. Except Andre consulted me as to how he dressed himself to go to his office almost every morning of his life. He wanted me to go along with him when he had his hair cut to make sure it was done to my satisfaction. He was fond of telling people he was "hand-picked." This sometimes came out slightly askew due to his accent (which he never lost and which, he was under threat by me to never lose) as "hen picked." That was a term he didn't know and certainly never, God forbid, intended.

My husband deferred to me, not because it was my right, but because of his innate generosity and his direct choice. The only thing I can ever remember where he adamantly asserted his rights was in regard to the place where we would end up in retirement. He knew my love affair with Atlanta, where we had lived for twenty years, and he knew I would like to return there. But, that was not an option as far as Andre of Marseille was concerned. Twenty years of Atlanta was enough, he said—and he had to be near salt water. So, salt water it was. Not negotiable.

• • •

SHARING with a trusted friend—it's the best! The realization of being overbearing in matters pertaining to my marriage: perhaps my friend in Stowe, Vermont, Elise Braun, could shed some light. She had always been there, my closest friend since high school days with whom everything was discussed. Nothing was sacred between the two of us. We have kept close all these years by letter and telephone. If there was an issue, any issue at all that troubled me, I could always take it to Elise and get wise counsel. It's not because she is at the present time in the Episcopal clergy, it's that she knows me so well. I need to explain less to her than anyone else in the world. Elise's response to my outcry arrived in a letter, written on a "Wednesday." Elise never dated letters except by the day of the week, an idiosyncrasy that I loved. She was a name, not a number! She wrote, "I was touched by your honest self-appraisal about the control factor in your and Andre's marriage. I'm sure it was there, but looking through that, France would never have happened, and that was an opportunity which gave Andre his chance to shine and be an authority, and that was a very good thing for both of you. A lot of what you described was also true of Susan [her daughter] and Jim's marriage. She chose the moves, picked the houses and did all the home furnishings and décor. And, like Andre, that was OK—anything, anything, as long as he was with her. They were happy, Andre and Jim."

Well, I hope so, because I was happy—I was with the love of my life!

•

Personal space has to be negotiated when two or more people live together. I felt I had been thoughtless about Andre's. He was in the beginning stages of poor health when we moved in the summer of 2001 into our new house just off Amelia Island. If there was any inkling on my part that this would at last signify we were home in the best sense of the word, I must have known it on some level. The first thing done before moving from St. Augustine was, we had a sign made to hang beside our front door that read "Casa Massalia." Then, a photograph of the *Vieux Port* went over the doorbell. Full circle, at last: Marseille to Amelia Island, Amelia Island to Marseille and back.

I had a new place of peace and tranquility to create, just as I attempted to do everywhere we ever lived, but Andre was unusually short-tempered in being my helpmate. He had been so willing, always, to hang the walls of pictures his wife designed, place furniture where she thought it ought to go. There is a photograph of Andre sitting on the floor in our flat at 2 rue Lamblardie in Paris shortly after we took possession of our apartment. A picture wall is spread out on the floor around him, preparatory to hanging. He had endless patience in trying to execute my designs, hanging and rehanging as many times as I changed my mind. He had great practice in my trial and error shenanigans, and seemed as much interested as I was in getting it right. His perfectionist wife always knew when a composition was out of whack, even slightly.

In our new Fernandina house, we had a spacious two-car garage for the first time since our Atlanta days. Andre said to me, "Okay now, you have always had our whole house to yourself to do with as you wished, but this garage is mine!" We shook hands on it, I pledged complicity, and some time later when I gradually began trespassing, hauling excess pictures to hang on the walls of his garage, he became furious. Furious, but resigned.

I didn't respect that a garage was important to the man of our house. We had no garage at our condo in St. Augustine. In city life in Brussels we shared garage space beneath our building with all the families who lived in the apartment dwelling on rue Devroye. In the foyer of our building, there was a small monitor with a buzzer that rang into our apartment, transmitting the image of the person seeking admittance. Every Friday evening of memory, my sweetheart, returning from work, could be seen by me on the companion monitor in our apartment. He would be standing at attention as he entered from the garage with a weekend bouquet of flowers in his hand.

Oh, my angel! Here is my affidavit: all the garages in the universe will stay free of my clutter, if you could just come back. But he can't come back, and if the truth be known, he would not want to come back. He is content, measuring infinity with his slide rule, negotiating with Big Power a chair closer to the throne for the underprivileged in purgatory, and making sure the airways are unobstructed for the passage from death's door to the pearly gates. Moreover, his eye is on the doorway (not the sparrow) until his wife comes through it, his bouquet of flowers from celestial gardens ready for her homecoming.

• • •

Andre'S BATTLE to stay well came to the beginning of the end during the three years we lived in a high-rise on North Miami Beach. The Paris years, 1990-1994, had come and gone. We returned Stateside in the summer of 1994 where Andre's work with the Federal Aviation Administration was to continue in South and Central America and the Caribbean, based in Miami. I didn't want to leave Paris. Paris casts a spell from which you never recover. The famous fashion model, Suzy Parker, when asked "What about a favorite city?" replied: "Paris. Because you never know what's going to come around the next corner, because you live in surprises. You know like when you're in love and you hurt a little bit? I always hurt for Paris." Recently I went to see the movie of *The Da Vinci Code*, largely filmed in Paris. The final scene in the movie took place at the Louvre Museum. Sitting in my seat in the darkened theatre, seeing those images of the Louvre, the familiar and well-loved surrounding streets where I had walked so many times, there came over me such a siege of homesickness, my tears began to flow so that it was an embarrassment when the lights came up.

•

Despite my reticence, Miami turned out to be not at all like returning to the USA. Happily for me, (who went out kicking and screaming from my entrenchment in a beautiful, second-story flat in Paris' 12th arrondissement) our arrival in Miami Beach was the perfect place for reentry. Why? Because there was little of the fabled reverse culture shock about which we had been warned in State Department departure classes. Miami was a foreign country in and of itself. Miami was its own unique planet, and the adjustment turned out to be from one beautiful, interesting place to another.

My husband and I camped out in a motel on Miami Beach's Collins Avenue for several months while searching for a place to live. We spent many days on the prowl in our car. I remembered a complex of three high-rise apartment buildings seen while driving over a bridge. Drawn to its swimming pool and recreational area on the Intercoastal waterway, there was that unmistakable recognition, that feeling of "I could live here!" When out on search expeditions some time later, we drove across many bridges searching for those particular apartments, and failed to find them. Then, riding on a bus one afternoon on our way to Aventura Shopping Center, *voilà!* There below, the pool and recreational area of the buildings reappeared, residents lazily enjoying themselves in the sun. We had first seen the apartments from the higher perch of a bus window, not our car. That's how the ninth floor of the third building overlooking the intracoastal became our home for the next three years. A friend, visiting our new digs for the first time, looked down on the waterway below our little balcony: our personal vantage point for breathtaking sunsets and extravagant yachts gliding by. "So much is happening down there!" he remarked.

One of the things that intrigued me most about living in the Intracoastal Towers was being part for the first time of a largely Jewish community of retirees from "up North." I acquired nurturant Jewish mothers who treated me like an adored daughter, not realizing I was as old as, or older than, many of them. I cultivated the charade. My youthful appearance was an asset and an enjoyment to me. In the large downstairs lobby with its huge potted plants and 1950s mirrored walls, less active residents of the building would line up against the walls in their wheelchairs for the morning amusement of watching neighbors depart and return. It was a place to pick up mail from their mailboxes, and to chat and gossip. It wasn't necessary to be Jewish to belong in their world. As an honorary member of the clan, I was completely accepted, and on Jewish special celebrations; such as Hanukkah, I was wished, "Have a good holiday!" and I never failed to say, "The same to you."

And then, there were the Latinos! Be sure to have a copy of Berlitz *Spanish for Travelers* on hand to negotiate around Miami. I got lost in *Cinco de Mayo* territory around *Calle Ocho* one day, trying to find a doctor's office. It's not your ordinary Eighth Street. It's not like cruising across "the" bridge to Amelia Island all the way to the stoplight at the Episcopal Church. When I got out of my car on *Calle Ocho* to ask directions, I had only my rusty Caracas, Venezuela, language skills from 1949 to help me out. Despairingly, I inquired, *"Habla usted inglés?"* "Do you speak English?" And nobody, but nobody did in that part of the world.

I gained notoriety at Intracoastal Towers as a result of wee-hours fire alarms. Andre traveled extensively, and more often than not he would not be at home at night. Occupants of our building were often unceremoniously awakened in the middle of the night by a loud alarm and revolving yellow ceiling light in each apartment, calling us to evacuate. I would gather up my poetry collections and head down nine flights of stairs, heart in mouth, a lifetime of writing clutched in file box and dossier. When we were all downstairs in the lobby, milling about, waiting for the All Clear to sound, the treasures in my arms were the subjects of much amusement. Never mind the family fortune—save the poems!

There were so many things to love about Miami and life in a highrise. Dawn power walks on Collins Avenue to an intensely colorful sunrise over an aquamarine ocean. South Florida clouds of unbelievable

purity, thick as cream, stacked up in a flawless blue sky. The lively neighborhoods of Aventura, Surfside; the restaurants and celebrity watching
on South Beach and Lincoln Avenue. Bayfront's live music and wonderful food: flank steak, fried plantains, black beans and rich, dense Cuban
flan. No wonder the old folks migrated there. It's the Fountain of Youth!
St. Augustine, move over...

•

The first symptoms of Andre's congestive heart failure began when he
returned home from a weeklong business trip to one of the South
American countries for which he was responsible. He complained he had
suffered heartburn after a dinner he attended while he was away, and he
still did not feel well. This continued through the weekend, and I
thought it was just stress until he began having chest pain and difficulty
breathing. After a frightening Sunday when we were constantly on the
telephone to confer with my physician brother, Jim, in Winter Haven, I
drove my husband to the emergency room at Aventura Hospital. He was
admitted to the hospital, and a cardiologist on duty examined him. He
was given a breathing tube, and put into intensive care. Overnight, he
seemed to be much better, and he was moved to a regular hospital room.
When I arrived at the hospital the next morning and found he had been
moved, I felt a surge of great relief. Back in the comfort zone, I was sure
we were home free. My relief period, however, was short-lived. Andre
became agitated with the nurses who did not want to bring him a bedside
commode. When it was finally brought to him, his efforts on the commode caused him to feel chest pain again. There was a sinking feeling in
my heart; realizing things were not as good as they seemed earlier. As I
sat with my husband, my arms around him, one of the nurses was ready
to scold me for being on his bed. Another said, "Let her stay—she calms
him down." My husband was never notorious for being easy to handle.

When the cardiologist arrived on his rounds that morning, he told us
he suspected Andre had a leaking heart valve. He wanted Andre to be
transferred by ambulance to Mt. Sinai Hospital for a diagnostic procedure. I was thankful that my brother Jim got into his car and drove in
from Winter Haven that next morning to meet me at Mt. Sinai. It took

Jim longer than anticipated to get to Miami, and I ended up on the phone with him, giving him directions and guidance to the hospital. My brother was already beginning to be affected by the memory disorder that was to come. It was mid-morning before Jim and I got to the hospital, and a chagrined doctor met us in the hallway and wanted to know why we had not gotten there earlier. We were already anxious about our late arrival. We knew the procedure would already be over and the results in. When we saw Andre in the recovery room, however, he was as in-charge as ever. He was kibitzing with the recovery personnel, and seemed in good spirits. The bad news was, he did have a leaking heart valve. His mitral valve had failed, and his doctor had scheduled surgery to receive a mechanical heart valve as quickly as an operating room was available.

•

It was afternoon before we were allowed into the intensive care unit where Andre had been sent to await surgery. One of the most horrific moments of my life was watching my husband struggle to breathe. It seemed to me that none of the hospital staff were paying any attention to his alarming condition. A nurse brought a tray of food, and in spite of his protests she removed his oxygen tube. How could he eat if he could not breathe? I still see him as he lifted himself up in the bed on his elbows, chest heaving, tears running down his cheeks as he strained for air. My brother walked over to Andre's monitor and pointed out the big question mark ? on the screen for oxygen in the bloodstream. When I saw this, I panicked, and ran out from the room screaming for help. "My husband cannot breathe—Do something!"

At this point the whole floor came alive, and people rushed into my husband's room. What would have happened if we had not been there to take care of business? This was the prestigious Mt. Sinai Hospital ICU care unit? We were quickly ushered out of Andre's room. We stood outside, waiting until we were permitted to reenter, and when we returned, my husband was on a ventilator. It's an image I will never forget; seeing a loved one's suffering is one of the most intolerable things in the world. Someone's surgery had to be bumped because of my husband's grave condition, and Andre was in the operating room first thing next morning.

•

Our sons, Anthony and Michael, flew into the Miami airport next day. They arrived at the hospital where they joined us in the surgical waiting room. It was a long, frightening wait; an interminable period of time passed as we waited to be told Andre's condition. Doctors came and went, spoke to other families gathered there, but no one came for us. Finally, there was a phone call to the desk summoning us to come up to the surgeon's office on the next floor. I was so apprehensive, I ran, not walked, and left the guys behind me, feeling that since the surgeon had not come to the waiting room to talk to us, the news could only be the worst. To my vast relief, it was only that this particular surgeon chose to speak to the family in his office rather than in the waiting room. Andre's surgery to implant a mechanical St. Jude valve was successful, and he was doing fine. How appropriate the valve was named in honor of St. Jude, the patron saint of hopeless causes! I had had many moments of feeling helpless in what looked as if it might turn out to be a hopeless situation.

Andre's recovery at home was a long one, but nothing mattered to me except that he got well. We marked our February 18th, 1997, wedding anniversary by having dinner in his bed with seafood takeout from a nearby restaurant. When he was finally well enough to move about and leave the apartment, we celebrated in style by having dinner at Lemon Twist, our favorite restaurant in Miami Beach, run by a former disk jockey from Marseille. Entering Lemon Twist felt like putting your feet again in the South of France. Small wonder it was our favorite restaurant. The walls of the restaurant were painted colors of country houses in Provence, ochre and brick-red. French antique furniture and decorations filled the intimate, one-room dining area with its European-style bar running the length of the room. Waiters spoke French, there was a fine French wine list, authentic French cuisine and when the bill came, it was brought in a cigar box along with small complimentary cups of a potent lemon liqueur. Serendipity!

•

Andre, once back in his stride, was ready to be done with the warm climes. We had spent three years in Miami, and Andre very much wanted a final European assignment before retirement. He wanted to finish up his career overseas, and he had in mind applying for the CASLO job in Brussels, if medically cleared for overseas duty. I had my misgivings, but Andre wanted to go, and he got the job. Then began the arduous medical tests for clearance, and the funny thing is, I was the one who had health problems. While Andre was in the hospital, I developed adult onset asthma. It was a stress thing, I was sure—if Andre couldn't breathe, neither would I. Our doctor who was to write off on the clearance for Belgium shook his finger at me, and warned, "You better get well!" I did not, however, keep my husband from that Belgium adventure. I got better, and Andre got his heart fix: new job, new valve and all. He was able to finish up his distinguished work career for the Federal Aviation Administration in the way he wanted.

We were on our way to Brussels in summer of 1997, and lived there until the summer of 1999. Shortly after arrival, and once settled into our apartment on rue Devroye, I was poised for the batch of new poems changed circumstances usually brought me. Strange—no poems were forthcoming. Had the well dried up? I began to carry a notebook and pen tucked into my pocket on morning walks and excursions, praying for the muse to join me. Soon, I was writing copious notes about what I observed. These notes were typed up, and they grew and grew into what became during two years of Brussels life, a nonfiction book, *Cruising with the Kir Queen*. Quirky title, some observed, but I thought it was apropos! I had sampled enough Kir Royales in countless cafés all over Europe to be genuine royalty. Champagne and cassis were always to be found in my *frigo* like milk or orange juice.

Unhappily, my misgivings in Miami that Andre was not as fit as his physician had pronounced him to be turned out to be prophetic. While we could have remained in Europe for many more years, Andre was slowing down. We spent more time in doctor's offices than we wanted, and it became more than clear it was time for my husband to retire, spend his days fishing and playing golf—the things he loved most. He just didn't retire soon enough, but his life had been rich and fulfilling beyond all expectations.

•

We returned to the States in the summer of 1999, with the expectation of retiring in Miami, remembering our happy days there, except, of course, for the mitral valve experience. Coastal south Florida and the Keys certainly met Andre's Number One requirement for salt water. But, as Thomas Wolfe observed, you really cannot go home again. Never thinking that would apply to Miami, or that in the short space of time we were away in Europe, the ambiance we had enjoyed before would have changed so drastically, it was with astonishment that we found this was so. There was somehow a harsh energy; a frenetic quality we had either not noticed, or had not cared to notice in our initial enthrallment with the subtropics. At any rate, something was awry.

Within two weeks' temporary residence in an oceanfront hotel, our room piled high with the contents of five bags of luggage, plus the air-freight shipment that had been delivered to the hotel, my beloved and I looked at each other and agreed that Miami was simply not going to work. Perhaps we had changed as much as we thought the south Florida environment had, but there was no doubt in our minds that we should move on. My husband said, "Let's drive north," and drive north we did, loading up our new Dodge minivan, and the old Buick car that had served us faithfully in Belgium. Our ragged little gypsy twosome, plus belongings, looked like the exodus in *The Grapes of Wrath*. Everything but the dust and Henry Fonda!

We went as far as St. Augustine, Florida, just fifty miles south of my hometown, Fernandina, on Amelia Island. We had talked about St. Augustine in the past as a possibility of someplace we might live, and it must have been right because almost upon arrival, we had a consensus that here was where we would drop anchor. We had friends, extended family close by, and Andre's sister, Sylvia, lived in nearby Jacksonville.

Andre and his sister were close in the way my brother, Jim, and I were close. We were more than siblings because, lacking the nurturance of a mother, both Sylvia and I became surrogate mothers to our younger brothers. We practically raised them. We were the significant women in their lives, and for that reason I always stepped aside for Sylvia when it came to Andre. "You were there first," I would tell her.

There is a very special bond between siblings who have been together through a difficult childhood. We came from significantly dysfunctional families, Sylvia and I, although the Fernandina therapist who loomed in my future, Dr. William Ross, remarked that there are no functional families. He ought to know, but our two families, Sylvia's and mine, were surely less normal than most.

It was beginning to seem that home meant "people." St. Augustine was a comfort zone in that regard, plus the Nation's Oldest City had copyrighted "quaint." It had endless charm: a college town with all the perks of lecture and concert tours, an active arts and literary community, and an international ambiance that appealed to me after my years of living in Europe. Our close friends, Wendy Philcox and her husband, Chris, lived on historic St. George Street. Extended family of the highest order, they offered us temporary housing in a nearby apartment building which they owned. They allowed us to move in with no contract, which was exactly what we needed at the time while searching for a permanent home. Their beautiful old building, once known as The Barracks, now the Lakeside Apartments on Cordova Street, was originally built in 1893 by Henry Flagler to house a hundred workers who were working on what was to become the magnificent Ponce de Leon Hotel. Things seemed to be falling into place at last. Perhaps this was the way it was supposed to have been. Man proposes and God disposes, as the saying goes.

•

I was happy there in that apartment building on historic Cordova Street beside Maria Sanchez Lake. Spanish conquistadors probably once camped in this neighborhood. Andre completed his pre-retirement assignment for the FAA by driving to Craig Field in Jacksonville every weekday. We liked the small town aspect of St. Augustine: its family concerts in the park, and the Christmas season's Night of Light ceremony in which the whole town came ablaze with tiny, sparkling white lights. The holiday parade of gaily decorated, lighted boats, special Spanish festivals celebrating St. Augustine's history, and springtime Blessing of the Fleet were annual city ceremonies, steeped in tradition. Ceremony was very big at our house.

Early morning walks took me deep into the historic district. My energy level was at its best, and I was polishing my book for publication. Horse drawn buggies filled with tourists passed by my living room windows as I worked on the final touches to *Cruising with the Kir Queen*. We could happily have stayed there in that fine old building with its memories and stories. If only the walls could have talked! But we knew we needed a larger space, and it happened that Wendy's mother, Marie White, one of our closest friends, was a realtor. Marie and her husband, Carol, lived in Jacksonville, and had been in our lives since the early 1960s. They were more family to us than our family. Marie stepped in immediately to help us go house-shopping.

In the fiery heat of the summer of 1999, Marie drove us around St. Augustine looking at possibilities. We looked at numerous houses and condominiums in town, but nothing seemed quite right. Then, we ended up across the San Sebastian River where there was a new condominium complex right on the marsh. Being on the marsh was of interest to us island Indians who must be near water, so we stopped in at the sales office to take a look at their offerings. When entering a place for the first time, there has always been a sense as to whether or not I could live there. The property manager at Vista Cove took us into a small condo which had yet to be completed. We walked through the front door into an area destined to be the main living area. It opened out through glass doors soon to be installed to a porch the full length of the room, just a few feet from the marsh. A cool river wind blew in to meet us as we entered. That breath of fresh air seemed an omen of good fortune, and the view to the marsh was so stunning, I had that sense of homecoming. We signed on the condo the next day, but it was fall before construction would be completed. We still had happy time to spend on Cordova Street.

In the meantime, our household belongings in Miami, which had been in storage for two years arrived by truck, and thanks to Wendy and Chris, we had an apartment in which to receive it. Unfortunately, however, our furniture had been stored in a warehouse that had no air conditioning, and many of our things were ruined by Miami heat. We simply sent them back on the truck, and the drivers were not opposed to accepting them. Shopping for new furniture was unexpectedly on the horizon, and it was good to have time to accomplish it before our condo was ready for a move-in.

•

Finally, the condo at Vista Cove was ready for our occupancy. It was barely completed before our furniture was to arrive, and, early in the morning of move-in day, I went in to clean up after the construction crew. There wasn't time before the furniture truck arrived for a cleaning crew to come in. I hastily vacuumed and polished the pretty new wood floors so that movers could set down the furniture. That should have been an omen that things were not going to go as smoothly in our condo life as we anticipated, and little did we know our time there would be ridiculously short. In two years time, we would be putting the condo up for sale, and the surprising reason was rediscovering just how strong our attachment really was to Amelia Island.

It was an hour and a half drive to Amelia Island. Sometimes, as often as two times a week, we found ourselves in the car headed for Fernandina. Andre, with his passion for golf, was invited to join a golf group comprised of old island friends called "The Lemonade Boys." One of the first things he did when he began playing golf with his longtime buddies was to buy a white golf shirt and have "The Lemonade Boys" printed on it. He was proud of his acceptance back into friendships he had formed years ago. He belonged somewhere once more. Home, once again, equaled people.

In the first February of our condo period, Andre and I celebrated our 50th wedding anniversary. The party was planned with the help of my close friend in Fernandina, Betty Woehle, to be held at the Fernandina Woman's Club. She contacted the caterers, bartenders, and did all the decorations, and it's a good thing, because just as the invitations were in the mail, Andre fell ill with a bad virus. He had to be admitted to St. Augustine's Flagler Hospital. The day of the party dawned, and Andre had told his doctors that if they did not release him for our big event, he was going to tie sheets together and go down the side of the building. He finally got permission to leave the hospital just for the celebration, with the stipulation that he must be readmitted the following morning.

We were staying overnight in the beach house I grew up in on South Fletcher Avenue—now a bed and breakfast establishment. It was back to point of beginning for us because when we were first married, we lived in one of the apartments in the downstairs of my father's house. Did it feel odd to be a guest in my father's house? In revisiting the place in which I had evolved from child to adult, an odd unfamiliarity haunted me like a layer of emotional dust. The child was still there; the adult was a stranger in a strange land. Even so, a flood of memories assailed me each time I crossed the threshold of the house of my childhood. I go back where it is always summer, and a bright cloudless sky is blue beyond all imagination. The ocean that lulled me to sleep every night is North Atlantic navy, and it carries the scent of salt, the muted roll of white-crested waves through flung-open windows. The cicadas sing an oratorio in the hammock; sometimes increasing to a deafening volume, almost as if they know their time is near. It is the sound of home, heard by one as well in the pines at Cassis, France, as I stood transfixed by their music on my way to a swim in the Mediterranean.

There's a shimmery mirage in the black asphalt of South Fletcher Avenue. Wild blackberries invite invasion in the prickly brush behind our houses. In my father's house, the clock is stopped at three o'clock of an August afternoon, and no one will ever grow old.

•

The clothing I packed for our anniversary evening had been carefully chosen: a long red skirt with a side split, and a matching red jacket. When dressing a little too hurriedly for the party, I put on the skirt, and it promptly split up the side almost to the hip. No time to sew it up! No panic. I got into the car and drove to the nearest consignment shop where I explained my predicament, and the kind sales ladies helped me put together a new configuration. I bought an ankle length black dress with spaghetti straps, a pretty pair of black pumps, and over the dress went the red jacket. It worked, and we had our grand party, hospital or no hospital. We cut the wedding cake and danced the first dance of the evening to a DJ rendition of "The Lady in Red." In honor of the occasion, Betty Woehle, so instrumental in making our special evening beautiful while recovering from cancer surgery and intensive chemo, took off her turban for the first time and showed her mettle (and her medals) to our guests: a shorn head, a brave heart, a true friend.

• • •

WE NEVER took into consideration when we decided to purchase a condominium the restrictions that kind of communal living imposed. Andre, rarely one to compromise in almost any area of his life, grew tired of rules and regulations. When told by the condo Gestapo in no uncertain terms that he could only have a certain number of plants at his doorway, it was the final straw. Andre was outta there, and I was right behind him! In the summer of 2001, as much as I had resisted a return to Amelia Island that is exactly what happened. For my part, however, this change of mind and venue had a lot to do, not with the path to the golf course, but the path to Rome—a fork in the road on the highway I had been traveling all my spiritual life.

• • •

BECOMING CATHOLIC! In the beginning, there was my father's Methodist Church on Centre Street in Fernandina where my two brothers and I dutifully went to Sunday school. My father Nolan insisted. He was predictable in his churchgoing, showed up two times a year at Christmas and Easter—whether he needed it or not. We children were always packed in the car to attend the cool early morning Easter sunrise service on one of the brick parapets at Fort Clinch, the historical fort on the island. Now, Fort Clinch has become a popular state park. Then, it was simply our playground.

It just so happened that, beginning with my mother sending me to the only show in town: kindergarten under the Sisters of St. Joseph at St. Michael's Academy, I fell in love with the Catholic Church. I was enthralled with the beauty of its liturgy, ceremonies, pageantry, and mystery. I felt a yearning I kept to myself, as the Roman Church was not an option for a member of my Protestant household. Margaret Sanders, my very best childhood girlfriend, came from a devout Catholic family, and since my grandmother, Dosia, lived at the corner of Sixth and Date, cattycorner to the Sanders home, I spent a lot of overnights and sat often at warm, nurturing family suppers in the kitchen at Margaret's house. There was no religious observance at all in my own family life, and I couldn't help but notice the difference in Margaret's family's strong religious faith, their piety, prayers at meals, holy water at the door. When Margaret would come to the beach for a weekend at my house on Fletcher Avenue, she would pack her little bag for after school Friday, and my father would deposit her at the door of St. Michael's Church on Sunday morning. Although just a young girl, I wanted Margaret's faith for myself, but there was no way it was going to happen early-on, due to my family's resistance. The Calvinist flag waved over our firmament!

So, I did the next best thing. In my teens, my family was in complete disarray due to my father's sudden, untimely death in the summer of 1944. My stepmother, Lucille, was young and unprepared for such a tragedy. She was preoccupied with grief, her unexpectedly changed life and circumstances. No one in the traumatized household was particularly concerned with what path either I, or my brother Jim, were on. As long as we showed up for school and were generally to be found where we were supposed to be, no one bothered about what we did (or didn't do.) I drifted toward the local Episcopal Church, where I found companionship and a sense of stability in my unstable life through an institution that wasn't in disarray. It was structure when I didn't have any. It was the rug beneath my feet.

Attraction to the Episcopal Church also began early on. When I would stay over from the beach at my grandmother Dosia's on Sixth Street, I walked home, as many school children did in those safer, more innocent days. The route, for me, was down the sidewalk on Centre Street toward town, past the city water tower with its low wall where boys sat at lunchtime and made catcalls to us girls, past the Keystone Hotel to turn left at the corner of South Sixth Street. Few will remember that on one side stood the old Ritz movie house and, on the other side, a splendid frame house occupied by the Lockwood family of Lockwood's Drug Store fame on Centre Street, both locations no longer there except in memory.

St. Peter's Church was directly on my path, and the rector was often outside the rectory with a basket of salt water taffy to offer to the passing children. Perhaps this kindly priest never achieved sainthood, who knows? But, he is remembered by this schoolgirl some sixty years hence for a simple, sweet act of generosity.

Later on, I followed some of my Episcopal girlfriends into the young people's choir at St. Peter's. There were choir robes that dressed us all alike (call it the uniform of acceptance and belonging), lighted candles we carried for processions through a darkened church, lovely chants and hymns from the big blue hymnal. Moreover, St. Peter's seemed as mysterious and alluring as any church I had ever attended. I loved the Evensong services at which we sang, and choir practice under the tutelage of white-haired organist, Ms. Elizabeth Carroll. We began our choir practices by singing A E I O U, over and over in unison in an ever changing higher key guided by a note from Ms. Carroll's organ. It was to train our voices, not just warble a hymn. Elizabeth Carroll was *serious* about her mission.

Wanting to be singled out as possessing an especially pretty voice, I let that be known. Ms. Carroll called me into the church nave one afternoon and had me sing for her. She didn't think I had the goods, but it didn't darken my desire for being an Episcopalian. Solo singer or not, Canterbury was the closest possible road to get to Rome without family resistance. Even though some members of my clan were unable to understand my yearning for a liturgical church, they allowed me to go my way, and at fifteen years of age, then-Bishop Juhan confirmed me into the communion of the Anglican Church. It served as my home, rock of ages, at a time when my own young life was in turmoil, and for many years thereafter. I will always be grateful. "Mother Church"—how appropriate!

•

My husband, Andre, was a cradle Catholic. I have a lovely studio portrait of him as a young boy on the occasion of his first communion. He stands beside a high backed-chair with a prayer book in his hand, a white ribbon tied on an upper arm. He had been an altar boy in his youth, serving at Mass, and his family records can be found at the Paroisse

Saint-Charles on rue Breteuil in Marseille. When he came to the States, he was not a practicing Catholic. He must not have been for some time because he was perfectly content to be married in the church I attended: St. Peter's Episcopal Church. There was a bit of fallout that came our way from some in the local Catholic community because Andre married outside his faith.

While living in Europe (four years in Paris, two years in Brussels) I often attended Mass at Catholic parishes in our neighborhoods. In Brussels, we lived across the street from the college of St. Michael and its adjoining church. Brussels was the city of St. Michael, and the main thoroughfare that ran past by my street was boulevard St. Michael. No wonder I took the archangel's name for my holy name when received into his church. I have a close friend, a woman, whose name is Michael-Earle Carlton. Michael, apparently, can be generic. When choosing my saint's name at Confirmation in the Catholic Church, I checked to see if it had to be the name of a woman saint. The answer was "No," so I am now known in the heavenly spheres as Michael. That ID should get me through the pearly gates without being carded.

•

When we returned to the States in 1999, settling first in St. Augustine, I began attending the historic little Episcopal Church there. I felt like a fifth wheel in that parish! Not through any fault of the friendly folks and the beautiful ambiance of their church, it had to do with me and a cross-roads in my life where one of those directions veered toward Rome. On impulse one day when I had dressed and gone downtown to attend the Episcopal services, I found myself crossing the park, and through the doors of the Catholic Cathedral. The first time my neighbors in the pew took hold of my hands while saying the Lord's Prayer, it was all over. I was hooked. It felt like family, like homecoming. I attended Mass regularly from then on, though not able to participate fully—make my communion. There came a day I no longer wanted to be an outsider. I told Andre about my decision to begin taking instructions in the Catholic faith. He was bemused, but not in opposition.

I attended one RCIA (Rite of Christian Initiation of Adults) class at a private home in St. Augustine, but somehow that meeting was off-putting. It wasn't quite right, even though the leader was a caring, charismatic person. In a state of indecision about continuing the quest, and just about on the verge of giving up, I spoke to Iris Ward in Fernandina, one of my closest friends from high school days. Iris, about as Catholic as anyone gets besides the Pope, was a convert to the Church in her teens (as I had been to the Episcopal persuasion) and she made me promise to come over to the island and meet with her priest in Fernandina, Fr. Mark Waters. Iris later became my sponsor, and there never was a better one. Iris, may she have an extra star in her crown when she crosses over, devout though she was, never said a word of reprimand when Andre and I were married outside the Roman church. Her strategy was to invite my new husband to go along with her to Mass at St. Michael's from time to time, and wait, however many years it took, for Andre to come Home, bringing me along with him. Or, was that vice versa?

• • •

SO, I went to see Iris's priest one summer afternoon at his office on Broome Street in Fernandina. His dog Chauncey met me at the door, and promptly rolled over on his back in delight. It was quite a welcome. Father Mark loomed over Chauncey in the doorway, and re-Marked that his half-grown pet was yet a puppy. Then, Chauncey and his master led me into "their" office. One hour with Mark Waters that day, and I was a done deed—in love with priest, puppy, and Church. As I was later to learn, there never was a cradle Catholic so much in love with the beauty of his faith, its traditions, its ceremonies, as was Mark Waters. The Masses I later attended with Mark as celebrant assailed all the senses. He brought us together through his reverence for ceremony and tradition—together in the moment, as a gathering of Christians was meant to be. It was sensual, uplifting, and unifying.

Leaving his office that day, I admired the icons on his wall. "I have an icon of St. Michael in my bedroom," I offered. Father Mark said, "Nola, you are a Catholic! We just need to formalize it!" To that end, my husband and I made the hour and a half drive from St. Augustine to Fernandina once a week from then on to St. Michael's parish hall for the entire year it took to complete RCIA classes. It was a year of unimaginable joy. Such a rich, creative RCIA experience, I don't think, has ever been, and I was a receiver of its bounty. There was laughter, and not only laughter, but also tears and personal revelations shared by the persons in our group of "how we came to be here." What shared pain, what questions, what questing! It was a forging of friendships never to be forgotten. We became family, brought together in the birth pains of mutual longing, mutual need, and intense desire.

At the following Easter Vigil, in the company of my RCIA class, and in the company of angels, I was received into the community of St. Michael's Catholic church, where I had always belonged. It was full circle from kindergarten to consenting adult. Never having attended an Easter Vigil Mass, it was one of the most emotional, moving and beautiful experiences of my life, and I will never forget my very first one in St. Michael's Church, Fernandina. When those who were to be confirmed were called to come and kneel at the altar while the Litany of the Saints was being sung—every saint in heaven asked to pray for us—it happened that I was on my knees in the exact center of our little row of supplicants: our little string of beads soon to be fastened in heaven. Kneeling in front of the three priests who were celebrants at that festive Mass, I was close enough to have touched their beautiful robes. It was overwhelming. It was as if in that moment the roof of the church fell away and the whole company of Heaven, the Archangel Michael himself, and all those saints we were invoking came down into St. Michael's sanctuary, Amelia Island, on Easter Even, 2002. Joyful, joyful!

• • •

COMMUNITY, then, on many levels, was the reason we finally came home to Amelia Island to live. Andre's golf group made up of his friends who called themselves "The Lemonade Boys," was his greatest pleasure. The people in my RCIA class were my new family. We were together for a whole year, getting to know each other intimately, sharing our lives and our concerns. Old friends on the island welcomed us back, included us in gatherings and other social events. It was anything but easy, that second move, but we did it.

Our realtor, our friend and Ferreira family member, Dorothea (Ferreira) Stillwell, helped us find a house we liked in a community called Marsh Lakes. The house was situated only a few feet away from a deep lake with a beautiful view of the water, and it was a one-story house with no stairs to climb. In the following year it turned out to be well suited for the care of the invalid my beloved was to become. There was a very large walk-in shower and roomy master bath and bedroom. My bird-loving husband had a literal aviary paradise in his new front yard, and the first thing he did was set his binoculars in the window by the bed. His next mission was to shop for, and plant a fig tree beside the lake so that he had his bit of Provence outside his bedroom window. All manner of wading birds came to roost on neighboring docks, and in season, there was a wood stork invasion at dusk of epic proportions. Winging in just before dark, as if by communal consent, hundreds of snowy wood storks blanketed the trees around the lake, settling in for safety and reconnaissance during the night. One evening shortly after we moved into our new house, while bustling about in the kitchen, I looked past my husband sitting in his comfortable chair in the living room to see our idyllic vista of the lake beyond. I couldn't help exclaiming, "I love this house!" Yes, it felt good. It felt right.

• • •

HOW THEN to speak of dying in the midst of all this life? Andre chose to stay here for a difficult last year before it all ended because he did not want to go. He had congestive heart failure, and eventually his kidneys failed, and even so, my son, Anthony, said, "He didn't want to leave you, Mom." Andre endured constant hospitalizations, four hours of dialysis three times a week, a necessity for strictly monitoring fluid intake and making sure certain foods high in potassium were omitted from his diet. Sleepless nights at home, trips to emergency rooms and confinement in the ICU became the norm. Some hospital stays would be as much as two weeks, and I would sleep on a cot in his room. Andre had a lot of anxiety and fear of bleeding, and a lifelong aversion to knives. One night after he had a procedure, and I was sleeping in his room, privacy curtains drawn around my cot, he woke me, saying he felt wet. He was bleeding badly, and I ran out into the hall in my pajamas to summon a nurse. When she came in, I helped her stem the bleeding while she called for extra help. What if I had not been there? This was the reason Andre's bedside was always my place when he was hospitalized.

At home, falls from muscle weakness and night emergencies that resulted in 911 calls were routine. He would come home from dialysis so cold from the procedure that he would doze in the car in the warmth of summer afternoon sunlight before entering the house. Leaving the kitchen and garage doors open while preparing supper, I could watch him as I worked, and get him into the house and into bed when he was ready, piles of blankets on him until he regained his body warmth. I never believed the day would come when dialysis would no longer serve him, but his potassium level mysteriously went off the charts. The dialysis technicians and I would check what foods he had eaten each day to make sure nothing that could cause this problem was slipping past. There was no accounting for it. And, the day that I lost him dawned like any other day. I had no clue it was our final twenty-four hours.

• • •

ON THE DAY Andre died, we drove to St. Augustine. His sister, Sylvia, who lived in Jacksonville, accompanied us. There was an errand to take care of at the St. Augustine Courthouse having to do with the sale of the condo in which we had lived. Halfway to St. Augustine, we had to pull over and stop the car because Andre was experiencing an intense itching on his body, something which had never happened in the daytime before. That problem up to this point had only been troublesome during the night, but before we left to drive to St. Augustine, the dialysis clinic called to ask me to telephone them on the way home because Andre's potassium level was being checked from the previous day's blood work, and there was a concern about it.

The courthouse business taken care of, we drove to a restaurant to have lunch. My husband had been very subdued, and as he took himself laboriously out of the front seat and unfolded his walker, he remarked that he did not really care to have anything to eat. He was simply not hungry. With a pang of apprehension, I asked him if he would just like to return back home. He said, "Yes." We stopped at a fast food place for Sylvia and me to have a sandwich, and a drink for Andre, and then we drove Sylvia to her house in Jacksonville. She says she will never forget how as she was walking to her front door, her brother opened the car door and called her back for an embrace. We didn't know then, but it was his adieu to his sister, and they exchanged the last words they would ever have.

•

I called the dialysis clinic on the island while driving across the Dames Point Bridge to return to the island. Andre's potassium level was off the charts, and I was instructed to take him to the nearest hospital for emergency dialysis. I drove to Baptist Hospital, and my husband was admitted to the emergency room. He was so anxious, he would not allow me to leave the ER, even to go to the bathroom. Even as ill as Andre was that day, I was in denial as to the gravity of it. One of the demeaning things about this kind of illness was a loss of control over certain bodily functions. Andre deplored it, but to me he was the beautiful man I married and nothing diminished that.

While lying on an examining table, waiting to be taken to a room, Andre needed care. I asked the emergency room nurse if she would let me do what needed to be done because my husband felt more comfortable in my hands. As I was attending him, he said to me, "Nola, I am tired." Had I heard, had I listened to the tone of his voice, I would have known he was telling me he was ready to go, but I still believed in forever. I never thought to lose him.

After a couple of hours, we were assigned a hospital room. Andre was so agitated, he asked for a sedative. I asked that he be brought some food before dialysis because he had eaten nothing all day, and the dialysis treatment would take four hours. A tray was brought with a sandwich and some tea. My husband began to eat the sandwich, and asked for something to drink. I gave him the glass, he drew on the tea through a straw, and when he did that, he inhaled a bite of sandwich into his air passage and he began to choke. He sprang up to the side of the bed, tried to speak in a strangled voice, and then just bent his head, unable to breathe or talk. I screamed for help, an emergency light began blinking outside his door, and hospital staff swarmed into the room. They laid Andre back down on the bed, and someone asked me, "Who are you?"

"I am his wife," I said. I was immediately taken out of the room, and ushered into the nurse's break room and left, terrified, and completely alone for what seemed like hours. Finally, the hospital chaplain came and took me to a private room. She said Andre was in the ICU, and I could see him soon. I told the chaplain I wanted a Catholic priest called immediately. When the priest came, we went in together to see my husband, and the priest gave him last rites. I called Sylvia and my nephew, Andre Ferreira. The three of us spent the night in the ICU waiting room.

I notified my parish, St. Michael's, on the island, and they contacted Father Bob Napier, the associate priest who was very close to our family. It happened that Father Bob was on the St. John's River nearby the hospital on a cruise on the boat of some friends of his. When Father Bob got the message on his cell phone, they docked the boat, and Father Bob in shorts and sneakers came to the ICU waiting room to speak to us. He stayed a while, and then he had to go. As he left, he said to us with an anxious glance, "I hate to leave you here."

•

It was a long, anxious night in the waiting room, looking in on Andre from time to time. He had not regained consciousness since the choking episode, and we were told his heart had to be shocked several times. Next morning, as we waited for our sons to arrive from Atlanta and Houston, Andre's cardiologist came into the waiting room to see us. The cardiologist said, "We are having to shock his heart and administer medication to keep your husband alive, and how long are you going to do this?" That was my first realization that Andre was not going to survive, and a decision would have to be made about life support. I told the doctors there would be no decision until my sons were there. I heard in my head our primary physician's remarks in his office one day on Amelia Island when he was caring for my very ill husband. He told us there would be no life support in the event of a crisis where there was no hope of recovery. I nodded my head in agreement, thinking it would never come to that. Talk about denial!

When Anthony arrived at the hospital, and we all walked toward his father's ICU room, the floor sprang into a flurry of conferences and phone calls to the doctors. My son said, "I know what Dad wants me to do," and that was to speak with three of Andre's most trusted doctors, and if they all agreed there was no chance of recovery, we were to discontinue any life support. And, that is what was done. There would be no more medication keeping my husband's heart going, and he would be allowed to peacefully die. The ICU nurses attending Andre told us, "It will be several hours, at most."

What I knew was, no one was going to tell Andre of Marseille when it was time to die! He lived for seven hours more that day while Anthony, Father Bob, Sylvia, my nephew, Andre, and I never left the room. We prayed over my husband, told stories around his bedside, laughed and cried and kept watch.

Then there was that moment when Andre stirred restlessly in his bed. I sprang to my feet and exclaimed, "Something is happening!" As we stood there, my husband blew out a final breath as if he was blowing out a candle. The heart line on the monitor narrowed to a straight line, and it was over. Lex Hixson described that defining moment in his book *Coming Home:* "One more deep breath and no more. There was no struggle, no other signs of death, only the next breath that did not come."

The nurse rushed in and checked Andre's pulse, shined a flashlight into his eye, then she said as she bent over him, "You fought real hard, didn't you, but it was time to go." She knew that he heard, he heard…

We all held each other and wept. Sylvia had turned away from her brother's bed, crying alone. Father Bob motioned to her, and he took her into his arms. Then we left Andre while the nurses disconnected all the tubes that had kept him alive. After that we each had a private moment with him alone in the room before going back to the island to do all the painful things that had to be done. I had never before seen someone die. It was so amazingly peaceful.

Before we left, the nurses who attended Andre told the five of us that in all their years on the ICU floor, they had never seen a family support a loved one through his final hours in the way we did. It was a comfort to hear that, but we were completely numb and disbelieving of what had just occurred in our lives, the implications of which would touch us forever and ever.

So it was that on June 7, 2002, I lost my beloved. He fought a valiant battle because he did not want to go, but his health problems were too many to overcome. "The only thing you can count on is that everything will change," states an old Chinese teaching regarding the essence of life. For the longest time after my husband's death, I could not accept that. My state of mind was expressed in a paragraph taken from *A Grief Observed,* the book written by the English clergyman, teacher, and writer, C. S. Lewis, who lost to cancer the adored wife he married late in life. I have paraphrased it, "If A is not, then he never was. I mistook a cloud of atoms for a person. There aren't, and never were any people. Death only reveals the vacuity that was always there. What we call the living are simply those who have not yet been unmasked."

This is how my husband's death colored my life, or better said, rendered it black and white. The pleasure of living eluded me. People seemed just so many masses of atoms. I was a card-carrying member of the community of the unmasked, not to mention, "dethroned royalty."

• • •

"And well before
I have dressed or brushed out the braid of my hair,
a woman with my own shadow
has showered and chosen her earrings, bought groceries
and fallen in love, grown tired, grown old."

—JANE HIRSHFIELD, FROM HER POEM, "THE GALLOP"

Chapter Two

CARLOS' WAY

For Dr. Tandron

Good Sir, you left your mark on me!

Your heavy metal in my hip,
your rubberized fingerprints needing
no forensic expert
to identify the genius touch
x-rays cannot capture.

It's between us two,
that ominous whir of saw behind the door
beyond which peered a face
summoned by gurney knock
like some under world or
nether world keeper-of-the-keys.
Enter, says he. Pain
being the password,

And there inside, the competent
strangely dressed beings
about their business, all.
Their mysterious, preparatory
business. Me,
the matter at hand.

So, now I am repaired.
A mummy in drag,

dragging feet through hospital halls.
Your robotic woman
waiting to take control
of her life.

THE TURN OF THE CENTURY. That phrase brings up an image of old photographs in sepia tones, such as one of my mother (born November 14, 1900) a fox fur around her shoulders, a string of pearls around her pretty neck. The expectancy for 2000 was for a brave new world, an exciting advent of all kinds of wonderful new beginnings. Instead, for our family, it was a time of grieving. It began with the death of my brother-in-law, Vincent Ferreira, who died on December 30, 1999. He died at home under the loving, watchful care of Hospice. All our family, along with the Hospice aides, stayed near to him during his final days. It was sorrowful, but it was also a privilege and a joy.

I am a train person who loves the sound of their passing—their organ chord signaling the approach of crossings. All life should have such warnings! There is something about that sound that stops me (not the train) in my tracks. Something happens to me when hearing that music, that lure of "going somewhere," its glamour and excitement. I could get on a train, and travel forever—I love it so much. Some of my poems talk about attachment to trains. So, my great, good luck was to get a train-man in my family through marriage. Vincent was a trainman with the CSX for fifty years. When my boys were little, he took each one on one of his trips. It is part of the folklore of our family: going with Uncle Vinnie on a train trip.

How did I happen to become the lucky sister-in-law of Vincent Ferriera? He was a U. S. Army veteran of WWII—a recipient of the Purple Heart, and he served as staff sergeant with Company C, 713th Engineer Battalion of the U. S. Army. While he was in Europe during the big War, and more specifically in France, he played an instrument in an Army band. It was at a USO dance in Marseille that Vincent Ferreira ran into a special French mademoiselle. He fell in love with her, they got married, and Vincent brought his bride to Amelia Island. Later, Vincent sent for his wife's brother to join the family in Fernandina. The rest is history. Mine!

Vincent came from a huge musical background. He and all his four brothers played instruments and their mother, the piano. Together, they formed a family musical ensemble, and played at various events around town. Vincent's son, Andre Ferreira, named for my husband, inherited the music genes. He is an accomplished musician who taught music and chorus at Jacksonville schools. It was such a pleasure to attend Andre's school concerts, to hear beautiful choral arrangements, see how orderly and composed the students were under his baton. He is retired from teaching, now, but he may not be able to stay away from music very long. Music is who he is!

•

While my brother-in-law was dying from cancer at home under the compassionate care of Hospice, I had an epiphany. I crawled into Vincent's bed one night when we were visiting, and laid myself down beside him. Taking his hand, I said, teasingly, "Big Vinnie, don't tell any-body I got in bed with you!" In all seriousness, he replied, "I won't tell." The dear man—he thought I meant it...

Holding my brother-in-law's hand in mine, it occurred to me what an immense role he had played in my life. If it had not been for Vincent Ferreira falling in love with Sylvia Perez and bringing her brother over from France, my path would have gone quite differently. Big Vinnie gave me my husband, my children and therefore, my wonderful life. He brought Andre Perez over from Marseille, vouched for him, and was instrumental in his becoming a success. Lying close beside my brother-in-law, I whispered to him exactly what he meant to me, thanking him for his place in my life. Then, I told him that those who loved him on the other side were waiting to welcome him home, and when he was ready, it was all right to go.

We returned to St. Augustine that evening, and just as we entered our condo, the phone rang. It was a call from Jacksonville that Big Vinnie had died shortly after Andre and I left. His funeral service was held in St. Peter's Episcopal Church in Fernandina, and the eulogy was given by the

Hospice minister who had been with Vincent all during his illness at home. I don't think I have ever heard a more moving, loving and heartfelt expression, especially from someone who had known Vincent such a brief time. This minister ended his eulogy with the image of a ship moving away from one side of the life experience to another, sailing to where Vincent was lovingly expected on another shore. Hospice does an incredibly loving work, caring for the ones we love who are passing on, and, not only that, they will be there in our time of need.

•

My brother-in-law, Vincent, belonged to one of the most important old families on Amelia Island. The Ferreiras were indeed, "First family of Fernandina." Vincent knew my father when I was just a child, and my mother, as well. He related things about my parents that made me happy. I had no one else to tell me these stories. He told me how beautiful my mother was. "Your mother was a real lady." He told me he saw me many times, being carried in my father's arms as he went about business in town. Young Vincent worked at a filling station on the corner of Centre and 8th Street—an establishment my father often visited. Vincent also delivered groceries to summer people at Lang's Cottages on the north end of the beach. Lang's Cottages, our tidy little row of small frame cottages with screened-in porches facing the ocean, are no more, now. They are among the mourned "monuments" of many of us native islanders. Vincent told me he once made a delivery to one of the cottages when my mother (divorced from my father) came to the beach for a brief visit. She came for the main attraction: her mother, still living on Fernandina's 6th Street— the grandmother left to raise me—and, only as a side show, my brother Jim and me.

In William Faulkner's book *The Sound and The Fury,* Candace Compson (said to be Faulkner's favorite character) sends her daughter, Quentin, home to be raised by her grandparents. "Imperious and enthralling," Candace is described. That could describe my mother, and beautiful, as well. Poor Quentin—she had some shoes to fill, and so did I! There was no mother in my book while I was growing up, but there was a lot of sound and fury.

I did inherit the best two grandmothers on the planet. Here's to the grandness of grandmothers! My children had a mother, maybe not the best mother in the world, but a pretty good mother, as my friend, Elise Braun, described her own mothering. My children did not have grandparents. Both sets of my grands had passed on, and Andre's mother, 5,000 miles away, never had the joy of knowing my sons.

My brother-in-law, Vincent, and his wife, Sylvia, were so much more than uncle and aunt to my Anthony and Michael. They were surrogate grandparents, and maybe this is the reason my second-born, Michael bore Vincent's name. Our little family sat around my dining room table in Sandalwood in Jacksonville for a ceremony before Michael was born. "Let's name this child." My brothers, George and Jim were present, their wives, Corinne and Gay. Vincent and Sylvia were there. Names were placed in a hat, and Vincent was the name that was drawn. I was happy about that, although one of my brothers had his issues. To me, Michael Vincent was a proud and lovely name. I loved my brother-in-law—and was honored to be able to be with him in the last hours before he shipped out. Big Vinnie will be on the welcoming committee that comes forward when the wind fills the sails of a splendid galleon, maybe one with Neptune on its prow, his trident pointing to another shore. I have a ticket to ride, but not yet. Not yet.

• • •

AFTER LOSS, there's the effort to make some kind of sense out of your life again. There was depression, meltdowns, sitting in a therapist's office, wondering what you were doing still here in time and space when the ones you most loved were gone forever. What helped me considerably was a deepened relationship with my husband's sister, Sylvia; the only part of Andre I had left. In tandem, my sister-in-law Sylvia lost a husband, I lost my beloved Andre, and two brothers, as well. In the aftermath of these deaths of our most important men, my sister-in-law and I clung to each other as we never had before. After Vincent and my husband passed away, we told each other that at some point that we were going to go away together, take a sabbatical from sadness. We considered the possibility of a cruise, because one was coming up for several church parishes, and I had seen it in St. Michael's Church bulletin. "Romance on the high seas," we joked with Sylvia's son, my nephew Andre.

That is exactly what we did! We signed up for that eleven-day cruise to the West Indies through the auspices of local Catholic parishes. It seemed a great idea to travel with people we knew from my own St. Michael's Church, along with several other parishes in Jacksonville and one from Palm Coast. The ship was a lovely little Italian ocean liner with mostly European staff and an Italian captain. Our day began each morning at sea with a "Sainte Messe en Anglais," at 7:30 A.M. in the Junkanoo Point Lounge. The M/S/C Italian Cruises ship Melody turned out to be a perfect choice for a respite from cares on shore. The trip was from 13th to the 24th of January 2003, with stops in San Juan, Antigua, Grenada, St. Lucia, St. Barts, Tortola, and ending up in Nassau, Bahamas. It all seemed so exotic and carefree.

Did we find romance on the high seas? Well, we had our moments. On our first formal evening at dinner, I was immediately drawn to the knowledgeable wine steward at our table, a handsome Bulgarian. A European man could always turn my head. His name was Kaloyan, which I later discovered was the name of a twelfth century tsar, described as "The hottest tsar." The ship's Kaloyan, his namesake—surely the blood of the Bulgars also boiled in his veins! "Coco," as his mother called him from childhood, made sure there was an unflagging supply of white wine for my glass. It was good for my soul to be found attractive again, and by someone years my junior. Kaloyan's respectful ways and professional demeanor impressed me. We took advantage of the few moments we had while he refilled my wine glass to have a conversation. Mindful of the ban against fraternizing with the passengers, and under the watchful eye of the head waiter, Kaloyan whispered, "I will keep as close as I can." I would look up from my dinner plate and from my dinner companions to find him stationed nearby for a few minutes, just to catch my eye.

Like all vacationers, especially Sylvia, and me as the first-timer on a cruise, we took a lot of photographs around our table at dinner every evening. In one particular instance, Kaloyan draped his arms about me for a photo shot. The cruise mate with the camera was slow to pull the trigger, and Kaloyan, his arms around my shoulders said, "Take all the time you want!" A little moment of intimacy all the more exciting for being *interdit!*

•

One evening, I came to dinner resplendent in sequins for an after-dinner theatre show. Kaloyan was already at our table, and met me with a quick kiss on the cheek. "Before the headwaiter comes," he said, having been warned a time or two for too much attention to this particular passenger. One of the ladies at the next table laughed and said, "I saw that!" Yes, it was noticed that Kaloyan stayed as close as he could. There are enough eleven dollar charges for a split of white wine on my credit card invoice to prove it!

Making sure Kaloyan told me in which lounge he would be working the next day at noon, I would have my lunch there. In between his taking orders and serving beverages, we had more time to talk than at the more formal dinner hour. His father, Kaloyan told me, had a vineyard on his property in Bulgaria and bottled his own wine. That is where Kaloyan began his education as a sommelier. "One day," Kaloyan said to me, "We will go there." I just smiled at the absurdity of it even to think our fantasy romance would continue, but I folded my napkin and lifted my glass to the temporal time when "Nola got her groove back" as a friend later remarked! I didn't need two aspirin and/or anybody to call me in the morning.

Other than my preoccupation with the Bulgarian, what did I like best about the ocean voyage? Simply being at sea for the first time in my life, I suppose. Sylvia and I had modest accommodations consisting of twin beds with a privacy curtain between them, a small living room with a television, and, of course, just adequate shared bath area. Sylvia had access to the only television when the curtain was drawn at bedtime, but I had a porthole window beside my bed where I could see the ship cutting through the ocean as it sped toward our next destination. I loved waking during the night, getting to my knees beside the little round window to watch the ship moving smoothly along, feeling the exhilaration of being suspended in time and space. It was a heady feeling, healing salt water therapy. Often there were sparkling lights outlining shapes in the distance of small islands we passed in the night, and sometimes another ship passing by. I was, after all, on my own personal ocean—the one that raised me on Amelia Island. If the earth is our mother, the ocean is our grandmother.

•

When I returned home, Kaloyan and I kept in touch briefly. He would call whenever he was in port, but he was very limited between sailings, and our conversations on the telephone were hurried. We toyed with the idea of meeting at some point. He was planning a month's sojourn in the States between cruise obligations to visit friends, but he never made landfall at my doorstep, and we never tasted wine in a vineyard beyond the ship. It was only a movie, and we were running out of script. The End was flashing on the screen. It was all fluffy icing, sugary and satisfying, but—no layers underneath, much as I wished there were. But I had other things to think about: hip surgery, looming on the horizon. It was time to come back to terra firma and deal with the Boooooooooooones.

•

As time for my operation drew close, I suddenly found a sisterhood who had undergone the procedure ahead of me. I was inducted into a community of Hip, Hip, Hooray survivors. When the news circulated through the tom-toms that another island Indian was headed for the operating room, they came forward with such support and encouragement, I felt I was joining a select and secret society. I was going to sit in the circle and pass the pipe. I was going to get the T-shirt! It would go great, the smoke signals said. I would be better than ever after my surgery, but in any event, I was up for it because losing pain was the priority.

There was no other option but the surgeon's knife. My body parts were wearing out with no warranty. There was not even a grace period. I was now reduced to using a cane, and even one with a snazzy ivory ram's head was no consolation. I absolutely refused to take a cane on my ocean trip even though my doctor, Carlos Tandron, advised me to. Well, that didn't fly! (or cruise) because I knew I couldn't shake a leg with a stick in my hand, much less do the quickstep. But, dancing days were over for now. Dem bones, dem bones, dem dry bones was wearing out—now hear the word of the Lord!

• • •

SURGERY MINUS ONE. My son Anthony and I checked into the Radisson Hotel on Prudential Drive near Baptist Medical Center, Jacksonville, on the night before the hip operation. We celebrated having everything in order for my big day by going out for a feast at my favorite restaurant in Jacksonville: Bistro Aix in San Marco where we wined and dined ourselves as if it were the Last Supper.

Next morning I showered, scrubbed my body hard with the antiseptic soap which the hospital had supplied, dressed myself and went to meet my son in his room. It was still dark outside when we made our way to the hospital. My son was allowed into the small, curtained-off space where patients are prepared for surgery, and wait to be called for. I was past nervous—just numb, ready to get it over. It seemed forever before the gurney came, but at last, it arrived and wheeled me briskly down the hall. The door of the surgical sanctum sanctorum loomed ominously before us, beyond which something could be heard which sounded suspiciously like a buzz saw. Please—hold the special effects! There are no mighty oaks here, just a limb or two.

Then, I found myself in a room bustling with activity where, ready for my close-up, was my surgeon, Carlos Tandron. He was dressed out in his scrubs, dictating into a machine. "Hello, Nola," he said while his production staff went busily about their task: me. I was no movie star, though, just another body in the butcher shop, lamb to slaughter, set out on a cold slab—body rigid with fright, jaw locked in dread. My therapist, Dr. Ross, defined anxiety as not knowing. He got that right. In those moments while waiting for Morpheus to take over my body, relax my jaw, and plunge me into blessed oblivion, I considered the information someone gave me that new artificial parts are tried out on the patient in order to fit just the right sized ones as he/she is lying on the operating table. Heads were to be bent over my carved-up body, assembling the pieces of the puzzle for my new hip like a shiny new pair of shoes... and then, Nirvana! The drugs kicked in. I slipped into dark and dreamless corridors where I did not drift, but dove down deep into welcoming darkness.

• • •

SURGURY PLUS ONE. I awoke in my room at Baptist Hospital,

Jacksonville, to discover a huge, wedge-shaped foam block had been placed between my legs. Mercifully, there was little pain. People came and went, brought gifts and flowers. In my drugged state, I talked to visitors and callers on the telephone as if I had any real clue as to what I was saying. Later, there came that moment of horror, realizing I was incoherent, creating dreamy scenarios from a state for which there was no abbreviation. My friends had listened politely—too courteous to show they knew I was not in my senses. There were moments, waking in the middle of the nightmare hospital night when I did not know where I was. Several times in my sleep I knocked my call box out of reach onto the floor beside the bed. Unable to get out of bed, and no way to summon help—what a predicament! At one point with the call of nature upon me and an embarrassing accident imminent, I pounded the metal bars of the bed with my telephone receiver, calling out as loudly as I dared. It seemed no one came for hours. Helplessness. I didn't sign up for that!

I was consigned for seven interminable days in my room in Baptist Hospital, waiting for an opening at Brooks Rehab, the interim facility to which I was to be transferred before going home. No one was sure there was going to be any room at the inn, and when I had just about given up hope, there was a break on the horizon. A place for me had been found. In short time, I was packed up along with my belongings for the trip across town to Brooks. A gurney arrived and wheeled me downstairs into an ambulance. It was at least the bumpiest ride through Jacksonville streets outside of a Tilt-A-Whirl carnival car of my teen-age years, before I was strapped to a rolling bed and taken up to Room 341 in Brooks Rehabilitation Hospital to begin the second phase of my hip replacement journey. The Riverside wing of Brooks was to be my home for the next eleven days.

• • •

REHAB LIFE was an endless cycle of long, identical days filled with appointments with physical and occupational therapists. Mercifully, you were administered enough meds to get you through. Nights, however, were unspeakable—protracted, wakeful and full of pain when the meds wore off. It was necessary to sleep, or better said, attempt to sleep in one position, only on the backside, and at times, to call for assistance for pit stops or to replenish the painkillers. I took so much dope, I thought it might be necessary to go to the Betty Ford Clinic for rehab after the rehab, but no one could possibly get through the hip surgery process without the drugs. Recovery is tough work, and not for sissies.

On some occasions with so many patients needing medication before therapy, I did not get mine delivered in my room in time. I rolled myself in my wheelchair up to the nurses' station, and made sure I was not forgotten. Sometimes there were several wheelchairs waiting in line at the station. One morning as I rolled up to collect my pills and a bottle of water for my trip downstairs, the cute Oriental nurse on duty sang out, "This is the Riverside Drive-By Pharmacy!" Some fun was to be found in the daytime hours at Brooks, if not in its endless nights.

There was an amusing choreography for getting patients to their therapy appointments. Either someone came to your room for you, or you wheeled yourself, if you were able, to the elevator doors where everyone queued up for the downstairs descent. Once below and out of the elevator, patients in their wheelchairs were stacked in orderly rows in a holding pen until the therapist assigned to them came to collect them. Each wheelchair had a bin attached at the back containing the patient's papers, and in large letters the last name and cell number of each of us good children, graduates of the bone factory. Kinder care for surgery survivors. Boot camp for bones.

In therapy sessions, we were shown how to get in and out of a mockup automobile, negotiate a curbside, climb and descend stairs, maneuver in and out of a shower stall, and function in the kitchen. We were taught to store food on easily reachable racks in the refrigerator and pantry, store utensils, pots and pans on counter tops, and how to slide items from one spot to another while in a wheelchair. One of my favorite sessions was baking day when I was rolled into the kitchen and told to choose a box of something to mix up and cook in the oven. Looking over the various boxes of grocery store mixes, I decided to make peanut butter cookies with the aid of my pretty occupational therapist, Tiffany. I got to keep the cookies I baked, hot out of the oven. I shared some later with Henry, my physical therapist. Henry said, "Next time, make them chocolate chip!"

• • •

LONG HOSPITAL NIGHTS. Bedtime was dreaded. Imprisoned on my back, I would wait until the last possible moment before asking for the evening pain meds. Those, I knew, if I calculated the spacing exactly right would guarantee me several intervals of sleep through the night. During the wakeful wee hours, dialogues with the night duty nurse and her aides got interesting. There were a couple of aides who became very special to me. One was Mary, and one was Susan. The best personal advice I took home with me came from Susan, who when we discussed losing our mates, told me she was forty-five years old and had been widowed at twenty-five. "I got a new man who loves me," she said. "I kissed a lot of frogs, honey. Find you a man who loves you," she advised, "not one you love, but one who loves you and everything will be all right." Well, I knew from experience that with partners, there was usually one who loves more than the other. If anyone ever got it balanced on both ends of that seesaw, it was a wonderful thing, but I had pretty well decided that all things being unequal in the game, it was best to be the wide receiver.

Mary, an older lady, wore an American flag in one lapel and an angel pin in the other. She could always be depended on for a hot cup of coffee first thing in the morning, cream and sugar already stirred in, brought to my bedside when I was ready to begin my day. So many mornings, pain would wake me at five o'clock. As I got better and more successful at the ordeal of getting bad leg first, then good leg off the bed and into the bathroom for a pit stop, I would then hit my call button to summon Mary. "What you want, sweet thing?" Mary would say over the speaker, and then, "Pain pills coming right up!" after which she would appear in the doorway with my coffee, night nurse Lindsay in tow with her little cup of meds. I could usually count on them to stay for a chat. Lindsay reminded me of a friend I met when I lived in Belgium, who now lives in Singapore. "Well, I'm from Belgium!" she giggled because, of course, she wasn't. She told me, "Singapore is my favorite place to visit because they have good music there." Mary asked, "Now, how would you know that?" Lindsay replied, "Because it's SING-a-pore, or maybe not—maybe Sing-a-POOR," to which Mary, exiting the room with a toss of her head, retorted tartly, "Well, in that case, you should go there." Why was this zany repartee remembered after returning home? I don't know—these two were just funny and affectionate with each other during the time my world was just those four walls.

The best company provided besides the omnipresent television impaled on the wall, which flickered all night long with color and noise for the dark hours, came in the form of Safet, a male nurse. The minute he entered my room, my antenna went up. He had an accent, something which always gets my attention. He was maybe Egyptian, I thought. "My name is Safet," he offered. "In Arabic, it means Clean of Heart." Well, not only had I always been a sucker for foreign men, my poet friend, Lise Goett, maintains I am a pushover for the pure of heart. Midnight at the oasis, kids, and zing went the strings of my heart! Safet, going about his nursing duties, hardly imagined he was my prince of the pulsating palms, not to mention the nuts I would have cracked with my teeth, and the dates I would have peeled for him. Yes, Lord!

The postscript was that I didn't get whisked away to a desert tent where Safet ravaged my imperfect body, but after eleven long days of rehab at Brooks, I was finally permitted to return home. It was sad to leave Safet with the keys to my heart, Lindsay and her magic potions, and Saint Mary of the Coffee Cup, but I knew the hip would heal, and so would my heart. My task now was to stay well. There was work to be done. Even with the medical problems inherent in my family which left tangible and intangible wounds, I could help myself so much more than my mother did. Maybe we do become our mothers, as the poet, Anne Sexton wrote. But, I reject that. I will rule my unruly bones and predilection for spirits (any kind to put you under and out.)

Mother, so formal—never known as Mom, Mama, or any of those loving diminutives. Never my close one: you were the feminine counterpart of Sylvia Plath's father. You were the Bell Jar; I, the mouse that swam and turned the cream to butter.

•

Your own walls are never more welcoming than when you have been away, especially when the absence was a command performance. I remember when my poet friend in Atlanta, Walter Griffin, underwent bypass heart surgery. He told me of his emotions, returning to his little house in East Point, Georgia—how grateful he was to go through that front door again. Recently, after spending the night in our local emergency room—and this was not related at all to hip surgery—I found myself in the ER with an IV in my arm for five hours. When I was liberated around 3 A.M., I drove myself home and literally did a swan dive into the big, comfortable bed in my own bedroom, pulling the covers over my head. Believe me, safe haven had never seemed so precious!

That I was elated to be home after the hip surgery experience was a gross understatement. On one of the first mornings in my own bed, I awoke to light in the bedroom windows, grateful for having slept late. For me, any hour after 4 A.M. would be considered late. I went into the kitchen to make coffee, and glancing out toward my screened-in front porch, I saw the lake was as still as, well, a lake, and the cool morning light was so compelling, I could not resist it. I was out the screen door, down the steps, and seated in my yard swing a few feet from the lake with my coffee cup in my hand. As I sat there watching the birds cavort in the aviary bliss of my pine trees, marsh myrtles, and delicate ferns lining the lake, I looked up where the wind was moving in the pines, and said aloud, "Your cathedral, Lord! Who would want to be any place else?" Good heavens, was I actually, at last, living in the moment?

In a letter from my friend, Elise, who lives alone, as I do, in Stowe, Vermont, Elise wrote of a recent visit from loved ones, how she did indeed desire their presence in her home, yet, simultaneously, she missed the luxury of her solitude. When I answered her letter, I told her about watching a documentary on television of Woody Allen's tour of Europe with his Dixieland band. On the last evening of the tour, Woody was standing out on his hotel terrace with his wife, and he asked her if she would be glad to be back in New York. His wife replied in the affirmative, and Woody, looking out over the rooftops of Paris, made the comment, "When I am in Europe, I want to be in New York. When I am in New York, I want to be in Europe. I don't want to be where I am at any given moment." I sat straight up on my couch, raised my fist in the air and shouted out, "YES, Woody!" He was a compatriot of the country of chronic dissatisfaction. And, I thought I was the only one.

One less than perfect moment shared with my husband while living in Paris occurred when the two of us were sitting in the most idyllic setting one could imagine—a sidewalk café on boulevard St. Germain in the cool of the evening. It was the Latin Quarter, place of my heart. As I sat there sipping my kir, Andre his beer, I suddenly had this intense, unaccountable longing to be on the Normandy coast in the little fishing village where I had happily stayed so many times in the past. I remarked wistfully to Andre, "How I wish I could be in Honfleur right this very moment!" He looked at me in chagrin, and scolded me so heartily for wanting to be someplace other than there in his company, that I excused myself to go for a good cry in the toilettes. Longing, for me, was the name of the game.

Another time, when we lived in Atlanta and had been vacationing in Europe for a couple of weeks, while driving toward the border of Belgium I was taken by a sudden desire to go home, be on the little island where I grew up. I said to my husband, "What do you say we cut our trip short and go to Fernandina for a few days at the beach?" He was incredulous. Imagine wanting Florida, always at my fingertips, when one could be in France. I was never satisfied. My head was never where my feet were!

• • •

STALKED by a cardinal! On the first occasion, this prince of the pretty birds flew across my line of vision as I was approaching a stop sign in my neighborhood. There was this red flash which caused me to catch my breath in excitement. Next day, he was sitting on the For Sale sign in the yard across the street from my house, the sign as red as his feathers. This bird picked his camouflage carefully! It's difficult to disguise a cardinal. Then, the following day I discovered him perched atop my mailbox. Time to talk, I decided, so my sweetest voice reserved for cats and cardinals called out, "Pretty bird! Pretty bird!" He cocked his head, and looked my way. When I told a friend about my cardinal, she asked, "Who do you think it is?" My thinking was, if my husband flew around in our neighborhood, he could conceivably be a cardinal, but a sea hawk would be more his style. He once joked when we were standing on a balustrade high up at Mont St. Michel in the French countryside that he was going to come back as a seagull, assigned to the midnight watch. Andre was a man who loved birds. He was an avid birdwatcher, and his binoculars still stood on the nightstand by his side of our bed, that side of the bed I never slept on. That side of the bed was still His.

•   •   •

RED LIKE ME. The cardinal kept returning. It was uncanny. He was in the pines beside the deep lake at the front of my house, and he seemed to consider my mailbox his special perch.

Often he would be in my next door neighbor's palm tree, bouncing husk to husk down its rough trunk before taking flight. His most favored spot, though, seemed to be the large bottlebrush bush across the street from my house. In the bottlebrush among its red blossoms, he was safe should a hungry osprey venture in. I tried several times to wheedle the cardinal closer in my yard by offering him a rice cake from my pantry. Later, I would go back outside and sweep the untouched rice cake off my driveway. A wild bird cannot be cajoled. My husband never could.

•   •   •

IN A MOVIE, *On the Waterfront*, for example, when Marlon Brando tended pigeons on his rooftop, his charges brought him messages. But they were trained, not cajoled. They had a job to do. In my neighborhood, one large gray dove in particular seemed to be bringing me messages. Even if he didn't have a white band taped to one leg like Marlon's couriers, he seemed much more than just any old ordinary dove. More than once, returning from my daily round of errands, there he was at the very peak of my rooftop, striking a pose as if he had aspirations to be a hood ornament on a fancy vintage limo. Master of the universe, owner of all he surveyed, wanting to be noticed, and was. It so happened that at that particular time, I was cultivating a friendship with a gentleman in my neighborhood. We had enjoyed a lunch or two and a glass of wine in the afternoon *chez moi* or *chez lui*. We attended a party together, and had a few more outings, after which something in me stalled—keys in the ignition, preventing the friendship to go forward. I wasn't ready for the next level. Not yet, maybe not ever. Some sort of sixth sense was kicking in, but I needed help making a decision. I wanted to get it right, out of all respect to someone interested in me. In my opinion, that should never be taken lightly or as a given—always treated as the gift it is.

One evening Mr. X, I shall call him, had arranged for us to go out to dinner. A close friend of mine, a man, dropped by unexpectedly close to the time we were to go out. I called Mr. X and asked him to delay our hour of meeting. It was not very well received. Then, when Mr. X came to my door, and we headed out toward the driveway, my personal dove was on the walkway directly in our path. He didn't budge as we approached, and it was necessary to step around him to continue on our way. I commented on the bird's strange behavior, and as we passed by something even more extraordinary occurred. The dove flew up over our heads, and perched like Poe's raven over the door on the driver side of Mr. X's car. He did not budge until Mr. X reached for the door. Never was there exhibited such bizarre bird behavior! I pay attention to signs: remembering an evening on Sea Island, visiting friends. Three of us were sitting on a low wall outside a beachside restaurant, having a nightcap as a shooting star swept dramatically across the horizon and fell into the sea. It was clearly a sign, sent for me, from sources beyond our limited understanding. Similarly, I took the messenger dove's counsel in regard to Mr. X that early evening in my driveway to be precisely, "Not this one, my dear!"

• • •

WOOD STORKS. I inherited a batch of them along with my house in Marsh Lakes. One morning heading from the bedroom of my house toward the washer with an armful of laundry, I was so struck by the splendor of the morning and the peace in my front yard broken only by birdsong that I dropped my burden on the floor to step out on the porch. The wood storks were flying out at 6:30 a.m. Rise and shine stork-time. They were about the stork business of the day. They flew out mornings with the same sweet, slow rhythm with which they flew in at dusk, all seeming to choose approximately the same low altitude, as if guided by a compass. I was lulled at night in my bed in my room by the lake with a lullaby for serene sleep, visualizing our stork community, quiet and stilled in their half-circle around the lake. White guardians of the dark, they celebrated a snowy holiday (all banks closed) in an enviable show of strength and democracy—cohabitation in a kingdom where there is no need for a king. Washington, take notice.

There was always a veritable bird paradise in my front yard. There were bitterns, an occasional ibis, noble herons, including the little green heron, a shy and low profile bird that likes the edge of the lake, and stately gulls, of course, from the nearby ocean. The wind brought the scent of the ocean, and sent the sedentary lake rippling my way like the living thing it wanted to be. Thinking about it, in addition to growing up at the edge of the sea, I have always lived in a river town and never had much admiration for a lake. But a lake is good. So there you have it! History. Ocean, alpha; Lake, omega. We can change, we can change.

• • •

FOURTH OF JULY, Nature's style. "There go the fireworks," I hollered to no one in particular, standing in the doorway of my porch as the sky exploded with lightning and the thunder crashed loud and near. I hurriedly stepped inside, but not before "Hooray!" said I, "God's fireworks. God's special effects!"

I watched the storm approach from behind the safety of my glass doors. The pines warned of ferocity, told of it in their bending and thrashing. The wood storks and gulls told it in their frenzied circling over the lake, mad with excitement. Drug of choice! I hoped as I stood in my doorway with a second glass of Chardonnay, that the 4th of July revelers at the beach had time to escape, time to cover the hot dogs and potato salad, protect the sparklers, on hold until dark. God is no respecter of holidays. Every day is Independence Day to Him. Then, the lights went out. My computer went on override. The cable television screen broke up into a hundred jagged squares of color, froze in time and space like my breathing, my heart, before the uncontrollable fury of a summer electrical storm. It seemed an interminable amount of time before the storm subsided. The nocturnal froglets did not wait for darkness to glorify God with their national athems. What do they know of red, white, and blue? Green is their color, and they have been born into Freedom.

• • •

"...roar all you
want and nothing will be disturbed; you can
drip with despair all afternoon and still,
on a green branch, its wings just lightly touched

by the passing foil of the water, the thrush,
puffing out its spotted breast, will sing
of the perfect, stone-hard beauty of everything."

—MARY OLIVER, FROM HER POEM,
"THE POET WITH HIS FACE IN HIS HAND"

Chapter Three

A WEATHER ADVISORY TO THE ANOLE ON MY PORCH

Here we are, the lizard and I, at the eleventh hour
before advent of rain. The clock strikes twelve for me
in my rocker, and the anole in his cling to the screen,
convinced of entitlement to common terrain.

Beware! we're warned by radio advisory: the storm's
not a watch, but a sighting now, from which all
must scatter from the wrath in its path. Seagulls,
with their acute antenna, tell us something's
afoot, (or a-wing) they say, circling the lake

and over the ocean, seconded by motions
in my Mediterranean fig, spiraling like the storm
into beanstalk proportions. As for the anole and me;
he, on the screen, and I, in my chair—we are loathe
to leave our private lair of emerald grass, (called for
St. Augustine of Hippo I ask?) Of the saint's
attributes: pen, child, dove, shell and pierced heart,
I am the pen, and the doves sit in peace
with the osprey, anhinga, and the marbled godwit.

Little lizard of the Gulliver gall, your blood-red
balloon, billowing throatily in my direction,

is that a flirtation, or a battle call? Save your fire
for the menace we face. May it heed your acrobatics
as it threatens our space. You came by banana boat
to my table d'hôte. I know how to swim,
you know how to float. So, come, funnel cloud,
for all we care! My downsized dinosaur
and me? We're not that easy to scare

CUBAN ANOLES, those brash little guys that immigrated uninvited to the U. S. can grow to alarming proportions. They live in abundance in my yard, around my house, and to my dismay, on it. The biggest ones are a dark spotted brown, give you a baleful stare, and it is said, have been known to bite. Horrors! I can tolerate the critters if they keep their distance and do not invade my personal space. There is a gap under my screened-in porch door, however, through which, if a plastic yard bag is not stuffed securely in the crack, it is Open Sesame for anole invasion. These devious critters like to decorate my porch walls, and send out smoke signals to their community if there's no plastic bag to deter them. Y'all come! And, they do. They consider me an interloper on the porch. When I open the door from my living room, they scuttle for safety just out of reach and fix me with a defiant stare. Invariably, one of them chooses to hide behind the picture of old St. Augustine that is hanging on one wall. He (or she) has the audacity to suppose I don't know that ruse, even as I am muttering threats like, "Your days are numbered," or "Just you wait. To the moon, Alice!" I turn to a broom, my weapon of choice. Anoles are incredibly fast, but their adversary (me) can be faster, not dealing death, just pursuing with a broom—the mad sorceress of Village Drive, sweeping them out the open door and into the grass. Their turf, literally. Why don't they know that?

One of their numbers being chased by my broom managed to flee into the living room. He had the good grace to be one of the graceful little green varieties, but invited into my salon? Never! We battled around the furniture for a while until I was able to brush him back onto the porch and out the door. In the process, he lost his tail, but better his tail than his head. A tail can grow back, but the head runs things, or so they say. Someone should have told me that in the flaming youth of my middle age!

• • •

CLUTTER. I seem to attract it. When moving into a virgin space, it was never long before it began to look like the one just left. Once there was a magazine cartoon where a child, sitting on the floor was surrounded by an untidy collection of playthings. Her mother on the telephone was explaining to a friend, "Everyone says she has the clutter of someone twice her age." That could be said about me. Yesterday I took an entire morning to attempt to make some sense and order out of the chaos in my office. Books falling out of shelves, every surface littered with papers, pictures in frames, work in progress needing to be dealt with, one way or another. Opening my file drawers and feeling hopeless at the task of cleaning them out, the better plan seemed to slam them shut and concentrate on the easy exteriors: bookshelves, desk and table tops, the couch with its battery of folders lined up like sergeants, giving commands. At lunchtime when I had created what I imagined was a new, improved space, looking around, and seeing that my disorder had been simply rearranged into a new configuration—despair set in!

It was the same feeling as when we first moved into our new house in Marsh Lakes. My nephew, Andre, my husband's namesake, was helping clear away debris in my garage. In confusion at one point, seeming to be going in circles, I stopped transferring boxes, took a deep breath, and inquired of my nephew, "What am I doing?"

He looked at me calmly, and he said, "You are just moving things from one side to the other. That's what you're doing," he said, in his musical way. Well, on a scale of any kind, count me in need of a sense of direction. There is this though: maybe I like the mess. There are plenty of reasons to stay messy, say some experts—the creativity, discovery, and peace inherent in chaos being some of them. Maybe it's time to succumb to the inner slob. As if I had any choice in the matter.

• • •

THE BACK YARD of my Marsh Lakes home has been my front yard because that is where a lot of my time is spent. Having a yard again seemed really strange to me after living right off the street in apartments in Europe, a high rise in Miami Beach and a condo in St. Augustine. When Rosemary Daniell, my writer friend who lives in Savannah, moved to a house in the suburbs after many years of living in-town, I wondered why the move? She said, "So I could have a yard." What is this yen for ownership of a yard? Is it so you can say if you have a mind to, "Git off mah land!" So that you can dig your heels into dirt that belongs exclusively to you? Plant cabbages and carnations? At this point in my life I had thought to be downsizing, not adding a yard. Be that as it may, I not only added a yard but I placed a swing in it. Shades of the rockers on my grandmother's wraparound front porch in Bainbridge, Georgia! More baggage!

• • •

The back yard that is not the back yard, but the front, proved full of surprises. One morning, standing on my screened-in porch, I encountered more than just the usual community of wood storks taking off from their roosts, and wading birds posing on toothpick legs on our little docks before morning maneuvers. The lake on which I live is not a huge lake, but it is deep enough for canoeing, paddle boating, and modest fishing. Since the lake is stocked, fishermen must throw back any fish that are caught. The fish are for recreation, not dinner. And, speaking of dinner, I was not in the mood to be a hot potato on a cold-blooded reptile's menu, so imagine my consternation, when slowly cruising past my neighbor's dock there appeared the quite unmistakable head of a good-sized alligator. In disbelief, I ran for my binoculars, and sure enough, an alligator it was, taking over his watery position with alacrity, lifting as I watched, half his body to the surface. As he slowly swam past, lo and behold, there followed a second alligator. There went fantasies of a lawn chair out on the grass in the dark of the moon for a cool summer night's reverie!

Now, an alligator in the lake is one thing, but a fish in a tree? My neighbor, John Givens, cornered me in my yard one morning. He remarked that we live in a very strange neighborhood, and if I did not believe him, he had something to show me. We walked together under one of his tall pine trees, and he pointed out to me high in the top of the tree, a most unusual sight. There, imprisoned in the fork of a branch was stuck a very large fish. Some aviary aviator/feathered fisherman dropped his prize while piloting it home to Mama. However could he explain it? A fish out of water, and a bird out of dinner!

• • •

VARMINTS. William Safire wrote an article called "On Language" in *The New York Times Magazine*. He calls varmint a gem of dialect out of the Wild West. "In hundreds of cowboy movies, the man in the white hat—from William Boyd to John Wayne—scowls at the rustlers and the gunfighters and excoriates them with varmint, the meanest, dirtiest, most lowdown word permitted by the prim self-censorship office then run by Will Hays." Since cowboy movies were major in my growing-up years, this must have been why I thought of the invaders of my territory by that moniker. Some of them were, in my opinion, the meanest, dirtiest, most lowdown critters in my small universe. Who would have imagined the pests one would fall heir to when deciding to live by a lake? Slithery garter snakes surprised out of their cool, quiet haunts in the shrubs, bumblebees in my bottlebrush, the army of anoles scuttling up and down the house walls and windowpanes (making whoopee and lots more squiggly babies to replace them) could be tolerated.

Dirt daubers and I, however, are another matter. We have a personal, private vendetta. Whatever combination of building materials is used to construct the supremely ugly, indelible black nests that suddenly appear in the cleanest, coolest, highest reaches of the exterior of my house, the chemistry could be used to make bomb shelters. It is indestructible.

Daubers are incredibly sneaky by nature. They try to outwit us. My therapist laughed when I mentioned this in one of our sessions. He said, "Someone is going to ask you, Nola, just how long have you felt that dirt daubers have it in for you?" All I know is, these critters have surreptitiously constructed a castle behind the bench in my entryway, well hidden from eyesight. They also left an unsightly glob behind an ornament over the bell at my front door. This is not my idea of a "Welcome Friends" sign. But what these pests like best is to start a housing development as high up as they can get, so that it takes a tall ladder that must be hauled out of my garage to knock it down. After trial and error, what is the best nest cleaner for that disgusting black spot from hell? Hose off as much as you can, take a Tuffy and a spray can of soap scum bathroom cleaner, the stronger and more evil-smelling the better, and scrub, scrub, scrub. I now have a Post-It on my kitchen cabinet. In huge print, I have lettered DIRT DAUBERS! It's a reminder to make routine daily inspections of my premises anywhere the winged devils may nest next.

• • •

NEVER IN MY LIFETIME had a roof rat and I crossed paths. I didn't even know what a roof rat was. One morning while going out to the curb to bring in my garbage can, instead of going through the garage, I went out my front door. When returning to the house by the same route, I happened to glance back over my shoulder. I saw something that stopped me in my tracks. It was like seeing King Kong striding purposefully over the nearest sand hill. High up where walls joined in my entryway was this enormous black rat with the longest tail in history hanging beneath it. At first I thought the rat was dead, but in fact it was just clinging there, working on some private project I had a bad feeling about. I slammed my front door quickly, but it was noon before I was able to get back home from running errands and deal with the rat. In the meantime, I described my visitor and his long tail to a woman who was standing behind me in the checkout line at Publix. She identified the critter as a "roof rat" and she warned me it might be trying to get into my attic where it could do a whole pile of mischief.

When I returned home, the roof rat was still there, exactly where I had seen him earlier. Same spot, same action. I immediately telephoned one of my neighbors for help. He advised me to call the City. I did that, and was transferred several times before ending up with someone in Animal Control. "We don't do roof rats," I was told. The rat might be rabid, I was cautioned, but more likely just thirsty. And, Oh Yes, be sure not to antagonize it, as roof rats could be nasty when challenged. "Go out and purchase a trap, leave it in the entryway," was the advice.

At this point, in light of the 911 hysteria heard in my voice, I was given an exterminator's phone number. A prompt call to the exterminator's office got me a promise someone would come to my house immediately, if not sooner. The sheer terror on my end put two guys on my doorstep within fifteen minutes, asking, "Where is the roof rat?" "Right behind you," I said, pointing. "Well, so he is!" one of them said, and asked for a broom or a shovel. Broom in hand, one of them approached the rat. "Close the door," he warned.

From the safety of my house, I watched through a glass pane in my door as my rescuer knocked the rat with the broom. It fell to the floor, and scampered off into the bushes. How simple was that? And, it was easy to see what Mr. Rat had been up to. It had managed to displace a board in the ceiling large enough to poke its head through, and had been close to making landfall in my attic. There is a song Maurice Chevalier sang called, "Thank Heaven for Little Girls." I say, Thank Heaven for Little Boys who grow up to do battle with windmills and roof rats. They saved the sanity of this Lady of the Lake. It cost me ninety dollars, but I would gladly have thrown in my chastity. On hearing that, my friend Dickie Anderson said, "What chastity?"

• • •

MIDDLE OF NIGHT is that time when you are alone with your self, that odd identity you are trying to decipher, stranger than any stranger and Higher Power, whatever you conceive that to be. Returning to consciousness at two o'clock, crushed with the weight of my dreams, I saw the bedroom windows opening out to the lake flooded with light as if someone had turned a searchlight toward my bedroom. Full moon, it was, and the very idea brought buoyancy to every part of my being, brought me to my feet and out the glass door onto my screened porch. There in a bright rectangle of moonlight cast on the tiles, I raised my arms to the sky in awe of the consummate beauty of the night. "Lord," I said to anyone who was listening, probably only the froglets who stopped their songlets at the sound of my voice, "You have made the most beautiful of worlds!"

How nature heals us since only hours ago, undressing in my bedroom, a sudden storm of tears for my lost life, lost husband, lost children grown away from the innocence of childhood overwhelmed me. I packed it all in at one time. Grief for my beloved workplace, glamorous cities in which I lived, lost youth, vitality, and what I had believed was my indestructible optimism. Now, thanking God for the beauty of the present, what would have been missed in this moment had I opted out? Surely the frosting of ghosted grass, the outdoor swing lit with carnival light, almost rocking itself back and forth with moon power. The world beside the deep lake bathed in motionless night-lit beauty.

Thinking about the carnivals of my small-town childhood set up in a grassy field across the road from the high school, I remembered the taste of cotton candy, candied apples, the pied piper smell of fragrant popcorn. The pop-pop of rifles at conveyor belts of plastic ducks, but most of all, the swings whirling toward the stars, my young self with the wind in my face and the magical night of a full moon around me. With the night, its moon burn, carnival memories and satiated beauty of the moment, I walked back to my bedroom, drinking great gulps of the gorgeous light, spilling through my windows.

• • •

HURRICANE SEASON! Barely approaching the middle of storm season, we bore the brunt of three storms in two weeks time, the worst being Hurricane Charlie, and the most recent one, Frances, still upon us. This monster storm turned cartwheels over the entire state of Florida. Like a giant spider, ceaselessly spinning, she covered us in her web from border to border. It was an incredible sight to see on the television screen.

On the morning after the storm arrived on Amelia Island, I rode my stationary bicycle in my garage, business as usual. Pedaling my bike, going nowhere fast, I thought about the movie, *The Wizard of Oz*, and that glorious character actress, Margaret Hamilton, as Miss Elmira Gulch riding her bicycle through the sky in the wake of a Kansas cyclone, then morphing into the Wicked Witch. I never recovered from the childhood spell of *The Wizard of Oz*. I loved the illustrations in the Frank Baum book and the movie, first seen at age nine in the old Ritz movie house across from the Methodist Church on Fernandina's main drag, now known as Centre Street. I took Glinda, The Good Witch, for my make-believe mother, not having one of my own, and, to this day you can find My Lady of the Glass Globe all over my house. Glinda encased in a snow globe, Glinda on a greeting card, Glinda atop a jewel box in her gossamer pink gown, crystal ball, silver crown, her beatific smile a maternal blessing for this motherless chile.

Although my little island was not enormously affected by Frances, except in terms of pelting rain, high winds of tropical storm strength, and power loss throughout our county, it was still a tense and harrowing period for all of us since Frances made landfall. Statewide, two to ten billion dollars worth of property damage occurred, six million households lost electricity, and 230,000 residents of nearby Duval County were without power. The end of hurricane season was devoutly to be wished, not only for a return of tranquility to our lives but because it would bring with it the magic month of October and my departure on a three week trip to Paris. France!

PARIS! The city of my heart where I spent the happiest four years of my entire life—most particular place of my heart, and husband yet in good health. The trip came about when in May of 2004, my friend, Catherine Fabre, found me online after our ten years of separation, and sent a message to the e-mail address of the Amelia Book Island Festival web site, subject "Looking for Nola Perez." Her communiqué read, "My name is Catherine Fabre. I live in Paris and I met Nola Perez there years ago. I would like to find her mail address because I would like to meet her again. Could you please send her my coordinates?" Then, after months of a spirited e-mail correspondence between Catherine and myself, I accepted her invitation to visit Paris in October.

I was Going Home! For me, Going Home had a more joyous connotation than Coming Home, as much as I loved my island origins.

• • •

"We have to learn to trust our hearts like that.
We have to learn the desperate faith of sleep
walkers who rise out of their calm beds
and walk through the skin of another life.
We have to drink the stupefying cup of darkness
and wake up to ourselves, nourished and surprised."

—EDWARD HIRSCH, FROM HIS POEM,
"FOR THE SLEEPWALKERS"

Chapter Four

CATHERINE, THE CÔTE D'AZUR; THE ANHINGA ON MY DOCK

At the edge of the dock he perches
in his shadowy beauty, as dark as Lucifer,
at the edge, always, where he lives.
Facing east to the rising sun, wings outstretched
like Christ crucified, his tubular neck twists

snake-like, as he warms in Jesus light.
He does not live in the temporal light I love,
its gift-wrapped, pulsing, transforming reflections
through windows from the lake, igniting
a thousand candles through leaves'

obeisance to breeze like whispered messages
of Chinese fans. Beak preening feathers
are his morning ablutions, preparatory to flight—
wings wide to the sun, a mighty stretch
in his neck as he drinks in warmth

like Catherine in the little cruiser on the breast
of the Medìterranée, offering body to sky,
 eyes closed, legs dangling over the edge,
face lifted to the sun, its Côte d'Azur blaze,
storing light for the gray Paris winter.

Catherine, in her solitude, the water bird
in his. No child, no anhinga offspring,
neither cheers nor clapping hands, just this lone
observer drawn to window and boat
for the pleasure of prayers.

THINKING of my friend, Catherine, and an upcoming trip to Paris, essentially trying to go home again, revisiting and reclaiming my old life in Europe without the man I most loved. Can one do that—go back in peace to a place where you were happy—where the woman you once were accompanies you every step of the way? Memories, the only thing we can keep, break through the dikes into the low country of reminiscence. You meet your old self on every street corner. Joan Didion wrote, "I think we are well advised to keep on nodding terms with the people we used to be, whether we find them attractive company or not."

The She I used to be is not always good company; mistakes were made, but there was no problem with being on nodding terms with myself of Paris days. I stood in a daze in the cool afternoon light of the Place de La Concorde, watching myself, years ago, walking past the Hotel Crillon on my way to work at the American Embassy, seeing myself sitting on a park bench at lunchtime, a circle of pigeons around my feet. Our history goes with such haste into God's archives, if, indeed, you hold him accountable for your existence.

• • •

THE OLD DAYS: Paris the dream and Paris the reality meeting head-on in the summer of 1990, when Andre and I stepped off a plane at Charles de Gaulle Airport. Dazed after the long flight, and awed at what was happening, it must have been akin to what my husband experienced when putting his feet the first time on American soil. We were met at the airport by the then-FAA representative from the American Embassy, and whisked away to our temporary home, a hotel in the Latin Quarter on boulevard St. Germain. Our quarters were a large, roomy suite located in the front of the hotel; between a little café we were to frequent many times and some trendy shops. For two long months that hotel room was home. When I was blue, missing Atlanta, missing my two sons, missing the old life that had defined me (and that was a time or two) the bathroom was the only place of privacy for a good cry. In particular, it was the cry room after a frightening experience in the Luxembourg Gardens. On a hot August day, Andre and I had lunch in the gardens, and had claimed two chairs in a cool spot under shade trees, near a lovely little rectangular pond. It was Sunday. The gardens were full of feast-day visitors. My husband had his chair tipped back against a tree, and suddenly, he said he was dizzy. As I rushed to him, his eyes rolled back into his head in a most alarming way, and he passed out. Not knowing what to do, I accosted a couple walking on the foot path, and asked for help. My French was minimal, but enabled me to say my husband was ill, and an anxious "Please help me!" They did not halt their walk, simply motioned behind them, and indicated I should call a policeman. I was distraught, scared out of my wits, and unsure of how to find the police on the grounds.

At this point, mercifully, Andre regained consciousness. He seemed groggy, but okay. I went out of the gardens through one of the large gates to find a taxi stand in order to get transportation back to the hotel. It was not a long walk to the taxi stand, but I knew Andre could not manage that. There was a stand with a taxi waiting at the curb just outside the garden gate. I stuck my head in the taxi window, and pleaded with the driver to meet me to the gate because my husband was sick. He shook his head in refusal. It was out of the ordinary. No, no, Madam—no way! Then, I saw Andre approaching us, walking very slowly. He had seen what was happening, he said, and that I was in trouble. When we got into the taxi, I began to cry, half anxiety, half relief. A subdued taxi driver, realizing he had been insensitive to our emergency, drove us to our hotel in meek silence. Andre went immediately to bed for the remainder of the day. His terrorized wife took to the bathroom for the first, but not the last breakdown of the trip.

•

During the next couple of months, thankfully we had projects to keep us occupied. There was a whole new life to organize. Because there was no room at the inn at the American Embassy, we had to locate our own space for the CASLO office off the Embassy grounds. We found a one-room efficiency for rent by a dentist, Michel Rinieri, in a building over the Monoprix store on avenue Charles de Gaulle. Dr. Rinieri had his own office and living quarters on another floor. We had yet to know he would bring us a lovely friendship with Catherine Fabre, his live-in (married in the French manner) significant other and their precious small daughter, Ségolène.

Avenue Charles de Gaulle is the extension of the Champs Elyseès which stretches to the part of Paris known as Neuilly sur Seine. We liked the location, but Andre's "office" was small, and for some time, the only furniture we had was a chair and a telephone. The carpet was a splendid royal red, and the windows opened to busy traffic on the avenue. My image from that first office of the Paris CASLO was my husband in his official capacity, sitting in his only chair, bent in conversation over the telephone. Me? I sat on the floor, and was the gofer for lunch and errands.

We had so much clothing and personal effects in our hotel room in the Latin Quarter, that when Andre mentioned this to Dr. Rinieri, he offered to put a rack of my dresses in one of his closets. Catherine was away at that time, and when she came home, she was nonplussed to find she had acquired a strange woman's clothing. It was an odd start for a friendship between Catherine and me that would remain strong even after Andre and I left Paris.

Eventually Dr. Rinieri had another suite available on an upper floor. There were two rooms, a bathroom, and a small alcove in which the doctor placed a marble top-table and two little chairs. A tête-à-tête in an office? How very French... In the beginning Andre had no secretary. That is where I stepped in, and glad for the opportunity. It was a huge adjustment for one who had always been in the workforce to suddenly find herself unemployed, even worse, designated a "trailing spouse." Who me, Proud Mary? I didn't take kindly to the step-down. Therefore, it felt good to be going to work with Andre each day.

Furniture was delivered, computers and a proper desk. My responsibilities were setting up the new office, the CASLO files, taking telephone messages, and typing letters and memos. Twenty years as a secretary in

Atlanta served me well in this capacity, and also during a year in which I took a job in the Administration Office of the American Embassy. When Andre finally did acquire a secretary, my good man tried to get me paid for my year's work. Unfortunately, because of government regulations, this did not happen, but seeing my husband in a new light and learning about his job, was gratification enough. It must have been love!

The constant in my life, however, was poetry. An Atlanta grant from the State of Georgia for a body of new work meant there were responsibilities to honor. I had a book to write. Since a large portion of my free time was spent browsing in the fabled Shakespeare & Company book store, it occurred to me to approach George Whitman, the legendary proprietor of the bookstore, to get my name on his reading list. George has a motto, "Be not inhospitable to strangers lest they be angels in disguise," and he is fond of Mother Teresa's "It's a nice day to go to heaven." Well, I thought myself already in heaven in Paris, and George was not particularly hospitable to this stranger. He was a bit gruff and impatient as I knelt down to talk to him beside his big desk in the middle of his ground floor store, surrounded by what he loved best: books. He did not allow for my determination, however. With some degree of irritation, he finally agreed to a poetry reading on the sidewalk in front of the bookstore. "Solo?" I asked, incredulously. This exceeded my expectations! "Yes," he said, making a notation in his schedule book for the following week.

My poetry debut in my new life in Paris took place at the auspicious address of Shakespeare & Company, 37 rue de la Boucherie, kilometer zero. The afternoon of the reading, George bustled around, placing chairs in front of the store, alerting passersby on the sidewalk and browsers in the store there would be a poetry performance. A small group began to gather. They were small in number, but attentive. After the reading, a scholarly-looking young man approached me, saying he liked my Jim Morrison poem. He was with a literary magazine, we exchanged contact information, and I began to feel my writer life in Paris was going to be a success. And it was.

George later allowed me and poet friend, Lise Goett, to have a reading and reception in his upstairs library. Our invited guests, and those shoppers in the store who cared to come, climbed steep, narrow stairs to the small, intimate library with floor to ceiling bookshelves. There in dim, yellow lamplight that seemed to be the stuff of poetry, Lise and I read in tandem. A yearly tradition was in the making, culminating in a Valentine's Day reading on February 14, 1994. We two Paris poet friends left our legacy: lamp lit poems, followed by wine and appetizers to the buzz of animated conversation and laughter from happy people who were warmed by our words.

•

The Embassy leased us a car, a new, squeaky-clean bright blue Ford, European-style, but it was clear the car was for business. Becoming a pedestrian for the first time in my life, my goal was to teach myself the métro system—become a "mole" as Andre put it. In a small, red notebook with alphabetical pages, directions were written down every time we used the train. Soon, there was a whole notebook of entries, such as, Isle St. Louis from the Embassy: take Direction Vincennes, exit Palais Royale, take Direction Villejuif, and exit Pont Marie. Everyone has to work out how to get around by train. Mine was a schoolgirl's solution in a time of sophisticated automation, but it worked for me.

After navigating Paris was a little easier, the métro became a way of life. It was even fun. My particular line, Balard, which went into the heart of town from our neighborhood in the 12th, ran underground with a change at Reilly-Diderot. When going to my friend Lise Goett's apartment, the train ran above past the grassy pyramid of the Palais Omnisport de Bercy, which was a sports arena (don't know how they mowed it—Gulliver-sized clippers?), the Ministry of Economy and Finance building, and passed over the Bercy viaduct. Overhead trains were how you saw Paris neighborhoods. One passed by apartment building windows close enough to take a peek inside. There's a little of the voyeur in all of us, and it was titillating to peer into other people's lives. I was beginning to be at home in my adopted city and my new life—it felt like paradise. If the historians are to be believed, Lutèce, which became Paris in the V century, was already paradise, loved and protected by gods and men alike. It had been paradise for a long time, and no war has ever dared disfigure the City of Light.

How fortunate our search for housing in Paris took us into the 12th arrondissement, and the quarter known as Daumesnil. At one point, Andre and I were about to give up in despair of finding the right apartment, and moving out of our cramped lifestyle in the one-room hotel. We looked at a lot of options, but it was not until the FAA secretary at the American Embassy, Mireille, took us into her confidence. There was a splendid apartment she knew of in the 12th that had been reserved for an American diplomat from Washington. He had cancelled his plans to come to Paris for an extended stay, and the apartment at 2, rue Lamblardie was available. We went immediately for an inspection, and it was gorgeous. The entire second floor flat would be ours in a building built by the architect of Paris 1925, Maurice Boutterin, who won the Grand Prix of Rome. This was a yearly prize from the French Academy of Architecture, which was founded 1671—the Grand Prix of Rome, in 1720. It is interesting that the strategy of teaching design independently from construction preceded the establishment of structural engineering as a distinct profession. That was for me: form over function, every time. My husband, the structural engineer, BCE from the University of Florida: what did he know?

We were shown the apartment by the *concierge*, accompanied by the architect's daughter, Maria-Catherine Boutterin. The apartment had belonged to her father, Maurice, and she had lived in the apartment herself. It was protected by the City of Paris as an historic monument. It had not been in use for some time, was in need of new carpeting, wallpaper and window sheers, which were later supplied under the supervision of Mme. Boutterin. Andre and I looked at the apartment in the company of our friend, Marie White, on her way back to the States after visiting her daughter, Wendy, in Italy. Wendy and her Italian boyfriend, from Florence, joined us. We all agreed our place of peace and comfort in Paris had been found.

The apartment was in the shape of a ship with the prow being an elegant, *large salon* (living room area). The *salon's* set of three glass double French doors each let out to a small railed balcony overlooking an enormous *rond point* (roundabout), Place Felix Ebouié. It was almost as spectacular as the one which centers the Arche de Triomphe. In the middle of the *rond point* was a very large fountain surrounded by life-size iron lions spouting streams of water from their mouths. You entered the apartment from the hallway with its *grand escalier* (stairway) and the ubiquitous tiny elevator in its belly which stopped at each floor. Floor to ceiling dark-wood ornamental doors led into an antechamber, which was the heart of the house. The ceiling to floor glass doors opened to the salon, *salle à manger,* (formal dining room), the master *chambre,* (bedroom) and a rectangular *galerie,* which led to two more bedrooms and a large bathroom. The bathroom windows opened out to an interior communal courtyard. In the morning the courtyard brought succulent smells of baking bread and pastries from the *pâtisserie* on the street level. We only had to go downstairs for our daily baguette, right out of the oven.

•

It had not been my intention to work while in Paris. I would create poems for my new book. My friend, Elise Braun, wrote me, "This is your work now." I did not work for a time, other than helping my husband during the year he had no secretary. Something quite unexpected happened to put me back in the work force for another year. We bought a French television for our apartment on the economy at the Bazar de l'Hotel de Ville, or BHV as it was commonly called. We had PX privileges on a military base where we could have purchased an American brand, but that required a large transformer to work on the French current. Additionally, it was a long drive to the PX, and we still had not been assigned a car.

We stood outside a taxi station with our new television in its box for a long time before a driver would agree to transport purchase and people to Daumesnil. Getting around with no car was not the easiest thing in our new world. Plus, we did not know it would be necessary to pay French taxes for purchasing a television. Apparently, sales of such appliances are reported to city government in order to assess taxes on the proud new owners. When Andre received a notice of taxes on the television, he ignored it. There was another notice, maybe two. Then, we received a polite letter, telling us if we did not pay the tax, police would break in our apartment doors, the television confiscated, and we would be responsible for the damage.

This was our first inkling of The Problem. The Problem was Andre's French citizenship. He was subject to all the laws of France, and his American citizenship was not recognized and honored, nor was his position with the American Embassy. High level Paris officials told Andre the only way he could rescind his French citizenship was to go to the National Assembly and formally request to be released. In that case, he was told, he would be persona non grata in France. France does not forgive relinquishing one's citizenship.

What to do, what to do? After conferring with officials at the Embassy, it was decided that I, solely an American citizen, would go to work at the Embassy as if I had been sent from Washington, making Andre the trailing spouse, and the two of us a tandem couple. While in Atlanta. I had taken the Civil Service examination on a hunch, thinking that if it became necessary to go to work for the government, my Civil Service rating would be a plus. After submitting my resumé and being interviewed by the RSO (Regional Security Officer) application was made to Washington to obtain a Top Secret Security clearance—my red badge (of courage?) This would get Andre off the hook with the French government as far as his citizenship was concerned. God only knows what that government investigator in the States dug up regarding my personal and professional life, and it gives me pause to think what information may be in my files in Washington. My friends in Atlanta reported to me they were grilled by the investigator. Andre's close friend, Wally Wulff, who had been an air traffic controller during the time Andre worked for Airway Facilities, told me, "Nola, he asked a lot of *very* personal questions." I got the clearance, and wasn't deported or jailed for being a subversive.

I went to work at the American Embassy for one year, first as a fill-in secretary for the Admin Officer, Rusty Hughes, whose secretary was on home leave. I liked the job and my new boss, Rusty, but did not like working for the State Department. I worked briefly for the political officer, and hated it. There were stiff security precautions, rules and regulations, inspections of your desk in your absence by the Marines, checking if sensitive papers had been put away. It got to this free spirit! What finally ran me off were all those safes and learning their combinations. Severe performance anxiety set in when faced with a locked safe that had to be opened every morning. Picking up the mail each day in a secured location meant dealing with even more combinations. In a panic one day, I called Andre from his office at Neuilly to come and work the combinations for me. I needed to obtain mail for several different departments. That was pretty much the end of my unholy liaison with State Department employ. Life was too short for sweaty palms...

Although some may disagree, the poet, or at least this one, was never cut out for the political life. What I did do in my four years in Paris was immerse myself completely into another culture and make many French friends. To this day, we remain close. The poems in my Paris manuscript, *The Continent of Dreams*, resulted in being named a finalist in The National Poetry Series. My poet friend, Suzanne Noguere, in New York City, was a finalist that year, as well. Suzanne wrote to me, "Nola, this was the year we almost made it." I felt we made it, though. To be a finalist in that particular competition in any year is not a bad thing. It took stepping off the edge of the cliff. It took Paris to get me there. No regrets. No way.

•

When reminiscing about life in Paris, so many encounters with special people come to mind. One of them is my crossing paths with Pamela Churchill Harrison. While Andre was attached to the Embassy as CASLO Paris, Pamela Harrison was appointed American Ambassador to France. My sons had visited their father and me a number of times during our four years, not easy with 5,000 miles stretching between us. If I had any heartache during that time, it was the separation from my sons. I loved that our son Anthony chose to propose to the love of his life, Sally Stafford of Tifton, Georgia, in Paris during our time there. It was a short walk from our apartment to the Bois de Vincennes and the zoological gardens. It was there that Sally consented to be Anthony's wife. If it is not exciting to declare your uncaged troth to the love of your life before an audience of caged lions and tigers, I don't know what is.

When we had been in Paris for two of our four years, our son Michael left Atlanta and came to live with us. He worked in the Embassy in the video shop, but he didn't have to learn combinations to any safes, as I had to do. One of the perks of being Embassy family in a foreign country is being invited to holiday receptions at the Residence. One of the downers when returning to the States after a tour is that you can no longer expect to be invited to the Ambassador's home at Christmas, Fourth of July and Thanksgiving.

Just before Pamela Harrison reported in for her responsibilities as Ambassador to France, there was a great spread about her in *Vanity Fair* magazine. I clipped out the article, and was much taken with the photographs of Mrs. Harrison, on her way to being Ambassador Harrison. Upon Mrs. Harrison's arrival in Paris, there was a grand reception at the Residence. Andre, Michael and I attended. There was a beautiful salon where most of the festivities took place: a receiving line to welcome the new ambassador, a jazz musician at the piano, and the gardens in back of the residence for strolls in the late afternoon of the party. Michael and I were standing in the salon after the introductions were over, and Mrs. Harrison passed by us, just like any old ordinary guest, on her way to the appetizers table. We followed her in, and Michael engaged her in conversation while we were serving our plates from the buffet. He told Mrs. Harrison he had seen the spread in *Vanity Fair,* and how fine he thought it was. It was mighty fine that Mrs. Harrison took the time to respond with some chitchat to Michael, just as if he were one of her most important guests. It spoke well of our new Madam Ambassador.

When I think of Pamela Harrison, however, I recall an incident one Christmas at the Residence in a very crowded salon. I gave up the luxurious brocade chair in which I had been sitting to someone who needed it more than me. There were no more seats to be had, and without thinking of protocol in such a formal setting, I sat down on the floor at the feet of my friends. At one point Mrs. Harrison passed through the salon, and she gave me a very meaningful look as if to say, one does not sit on the floor at a gathering in the Residence of the Ambassador of the United States to France. I have never been chastised without a word being spoken in such an effective manner in all my life. A lesson learned in the Etiquette School of the American Embassy.

• • •

PARIS REDUX. At last, at last, the ticket was purchased for my three-week visit with my old friend, Catherine Fabre, and her Jean-Claude. I was going home! My bags were packed and repacked with much thought of what I should carry. There would be no one but me to haul them around the airports. Fortunately, security was not as intense as it would become after the World Trade disaster. Still, there would be no helpful FAA husband to assist in guiding me through airport snarl-ups

My frame of mind was one of joyous expectancy, waiting at the Detroit airport to board Airbus 50 to Paris. It seemed time had simply melted away since the last time I was an overseas traveler. Great airport: clean, efficient, and sophisticated. Red elevated tram, fun to watch it whiz by. All those bored, affluent American faces in the waiting room until the call to board for Paris, and all those interesting Gallic faces. Three or four obviously French gentlemen inspected me, and were inspected back. I was glad to be there in the unfamiliar airport, glad to be enroute. A favorite venue for me is to be on hold, in process, not found in any previous condition of life. Everything expectancy, anticipation: how delicious!

In a very crowded plane, I had the good fortune to be in a comfortable aisle seat. It was a party atmosphere in that football field of an airbus. To the strains of classical music on the PA system, stewards bustled about in the aisles, helping stow luggage overhead, joking and laughing with passengers. Two young teenage girls were seated next to me in middle aisle seats. They were part of a contingency of American students on their way to study French language abroad. I was impressed that my neighbor had out her Larousse dictionary, and was working on her papers while all around us; other passengers waited dinner, watched movies and played video games.

My clock was on Paris time, now. Five-thirty A.M., 50 degrees in Paris, 70 percent chance of rain. When tipping my glass of red wine and waiting for dinner, the omnipresent pretzels appeared to accompany the Cabernet Sauvignon, which had already produced a pleasant buzz. With the help of the grape, survival of the seven hour, fifteen minute ride seemed a pleasant prospect in spite of cramped quarters, artificial hip, and knowing X-rays showed my other "good" hip was showing deterioration. No way to escape the bones! I was on my way for a three-week sojourn in Paris and the South of France, visiting Catherine and her "Joli Prince" whom I had yet to meet. All of our circumstances had changed drastically: me, a widow, Catherine no longer with Dr. Michel Rinieri, and Ségolène, now 15, had been only a toddler when I left France in 1994.

• • •

A PLEASURABLE SENSE of familiarity enveloped me when I stepped into Charles de Gaulle airport. So much time had been spent there during the four years Andre worked with the FAA. Catherine, Jean-Claude, and an old friend from Paris days, Edmond Joubert, met my plane. It was as if no time had passed in our lives. Such is the special joy of reuniting with certain old friends with whom there is no need to pick up the threads. That patchwork quilt is there, needing only new material.

We drove into Paris in Catherine's car, a little Twingo, and to my utter delight, the apartment in which they lived was located in the center of Paris within walking distance of the Champs Elysées. Catherine prepared lunch, a ceremonious meal (no potato chips and cold cuts), which was to repeat with the same stylish grace every time we sat down at table. I slept that night for thirteen hours straight in the pleasant new chambre which had been prepared especially for me. Fresh flowers had been placed in my room: daisies, lilies, and a purple orchid from Elyfleur, Catherine's flower shop on the ground floor of the apartment building. On my pillow, I found a small framed photograph of my late husband and myself along with a note, which said, "Sleep well," surrounded by hearts. In French, the note continued, *"On veille sur toi, ici et au ciel. Mille Mercis d'être parmi nous. Love xxxx."* That is to say, "You are watched over here, and in heaven. A thousand thanks for being among us."

Sleep was dreamless that night, knowing I was safely in Paris and in the hands of loving friends. "Try to have nice dreams," Catherine had e-mailed me before I got on the plane in Jacksonville. Remembering dinner parties long ago in my apartment on rue Lamblardie, she added in her quaint English, "For example, you cook me the most extraordinary turkey you used to cook and we all (only with loved people, let all the malevolants on the doormat by mercy) are again together, and Nola, don't forget my artichoke with garlic and mayonnaise. Thank you, Nola, I'm no longer hungry. We sit on chairs around you and you recite and tell, and rue Lamblardie dozes in summer's heat." I think my friend, Catherine, has the soul of a poet, and it's for sure some of my colorful misuse of her French mother tongue must have seemed as odd as the English in this little vignette. For sure, she is special and important in my life and remembers beautifully some of our happiest moments together in my Paris apartment in the 12th *arrondissement!*

• • •

CATHERINE had regaled me with e-mails for weeks before my Paris homecoming with tales of activities around the making of a new bedroom in the house for my imminent occupation. The bedroom in progress had been, up to this point, Jean's office, a project which was completed only just the night before my plane landed in France. Droll messages addressed to *Ma belle et bonne Nola* told me the history of my new bedroom. Closets were cleared, office supplies and machines hauled to Jean's new office location downstairs in a room on the *rez-de-chaussée,* or ground floor. What the French call the first floor would be considered the second floor in the U.S.A. A new bed had been purchased, along with new draperies. I was to christen the bedroom as its very first occupant, hereafter known as Nola's room for all second comers. When I opened the door to Nola's room, it was elegantly appointed with a beautiful damask bedspread and many pillows. Matching heavy damask drapes held back with a tasseled cord could be drawn against noise and light from the street outside. I christened the new room not with champagne, but with a happy, long, dreamless sleep of an overseas traveler.

The next morning the bedside clock alarmed me by showing how late I had slept. Opening my door cautiously alerted Catherine I was up, and, beaming, she came to meet me, bearing a cell phone in her hand. "Your phone," she said, as she ushered me in to a setting at the breakfast table made just for me. Jean was below in his office, the house daughter already off for a Sunday visit with a friend. Catherine had been waiting for me to put in an appearance for breakfast. The plan for our day was already in place.

When I finished breakfast we were to have a museum outing—a very Sunday thing to do. The Musée Jacquemart-Andre Paris Institute de France was showing an exhibition called Trésors de la Fondation Napoléon, An Intimate Look at the Imperial Court. This was the first time this exhibit was ever shown at a museum. This interesting museum was once a private residence of extraordinary grandeur. The exhibit was comprised of works of art and historical objects from the First Empire belonging to the little Corsican and his Josephine, married in 1769, before he began his Italian campaign. The highlights of the exhibit for me were highly personal: Corsican folksongs on the loudspeaker, the funeral trappings and drapery of Napoléon, his *masque mortuaire* (death mask,) Josephine's jewelry and elegant toiletry articles. Of special interest were the *necessaire dentaire de* Napoléon that indicated that in an epoch when hygiene was very rudimentary, the Emperor was extremely careful with his personal dental care. Obsessive/compulsive? Most probably… Who of consequence isn't?

Of many paintings I inspected in the exhibit, topics were mostly religious or pastoral scenes of country festivities and outings. There were a couple of images that stood out above the rest. For me, it was the figure of St. George on horseback, battling the dragon—a bright green dragon, red trappings on the horse. This was the sort of medieval subject, which always struck my fancy.

In my mind, St. George knocked off a little of the heroic air of St. Michael, the Archangel, my hero. Or maybe it's that he's a knock-off of St. Michael. Look out!—there's room for only one Prince of Angels "up there." Another mesmerizing painting was a scene in which the crucified Christ, fresh from the tomb, pays a late night rendezvous to the bedroom of one of his disciples. The disciple, propped up in amazement on his pillows listens to a gesturing Jesus, who, seated in a chair in semi-profile is dramatically backlit.

• • •

I REVELED IN my uncharacteristic laziness of sleeping late in Paris. A nine o'clock rising would be unheard of in my ordinary life on my ordinary island. I usually had breakfast only with Catherine; Jean already off to his office below, and Poupette already at school. That choreography worked well because I shared with Poupette her personal little bathroom with its small shower and basin. Poupette could do her morning ablutions in an unhurried manner. As is customary in France, the toilet was separate from the bathroom, and this was so for Poupette's space. However, in this particular household, Catherine and Jean's master bathroom contained a toilet, as well as his-and-her wash basins and mirrors, a luxuriously large bathtub, and extra elbow space in which to dress and comfortably move about. This was unheard of in an apartment which was not in a modern building, but in one of the beautiful old edifices on avenue de Wagram. One of the omissions in French bathrooms (particularly in the older hotels) was ordinary washcloths. Absence did not make the heart grow fonder when my brother, Jim, on his first visit to Europe with Andre and me years ago, asked in exasperation, "Don't they believe in washcloths around here?"

After sitting with me at breakfast, Catherine went downstairs to work with the accountants of her florist shop business for a couple of hours. I wrote in my room, sent e-mails while outside my bedroom windows, Avenue de Wagram was busy with Monday commerce. I tidied up the very small part of my physical world 5,000 miles from Amelia Island. The rearrangement of my belongings on closet shelves, contents of drawers in the small dresser near my bed gave me some semblance of creating order in my new delightful, unorthodox daily routine. Although there may have been a certain mild discomfort at being without the comforting embrace of routine, it was juxtaposed with enjoyment at having none of the "usual suspects" in my morning lineup.

In one of those moments of morning leisure, I amused myself by making a list of the cast of characters for *The Movement of Bones* (my book title which Catherine playfully referred to as The Booooooooones.) This idle occupation caused me to recall watching a video some years ago, Bill Moyers' "The Power of the Word." Poets reading on this video included Sharon Olds, Octavio Paz, William Stafford, and that gorgeous big Irish lug, Galway Kinnell. Galway Kinnell read for some of his students a rhymed poem he had written as a young man, and he ended with saying that although he wrote that poem a long time ago, he still liked it. He remarked, "I remember writing in the right hand margin of the page while sitting up all night, all rhyme words for blump; every word blump in the language, and then I would try to get a line that would get hump, lump, blump—any of those words—and as soon as I got one that made sense at all, I put it in." Galway was laughing here, a self-deprecating laughter, and he said, "First of all, I wondered if hump was what I wanted to say at the end of that line. I spent a lot of time doing that, and the other thing is, is that a suitably adult activity? I don't think so!" Well, sitting in my chambre in Paris with cool October light streaming through the tall bedroom windows and composing a tongue-in-cheek cast of characters for an unfinished book, is that a suitably adult activity? I didn't think so, either, but that is what this poet did while an hour of her precious life lifted off into infinity.

• • •

AFTER FOUR WHOLE DAYS in Paris, my French language was slowly reasserting itself. There were many errors, but at least I could carry on a decent conversation with Jean-Claude, *the homme de la maison.* Catherine and I conversed half in French, half in English, according to the mood of the moment. Paris, of course, spoke to me with her own special language, pulling at my heartstrings with great emotion. I was beginning to assimilate myself into the rhythm of my French family's household, feeling very much the fourth leg of their table, and pleasuring in an energy so different from my solitary life at home in the States.

Something amusing happened one morning when Catherine took some of my clothing to launder in her washroom, which was off from the master bath. On impulse, I gave her a bottle of cold wash detergent brought with me from home, thinking this would be better for my special-care clothing. Catherine used my detergent in her machine in the same manner as she would have used her own product. It was laundry culture shock, to say the least. The washing machine boiled over with a thick white mousse, which flowed out like lava onto the bathroom floor. Catherine and I spent a very active hour dipping foam out of the machine and off the floor and pouring it into the bathtub. A barefooted Catherine then washed it away with a hand-held shower hose. Barefoot Contessa, indeed! Bubbly morning, indeed, and the champagne was still in the *frigo!*

• • •

PARC MONCEAU. A park like any other, except this one was in Paris, where an arrogant city pigeon, rich in entitlement, inspected me gravely as I sat on a bench under a tree, then he drew near, pecking vigorously around my feet. The sky was half-blue, half-gray, and if I knew one thing about Paris, it was that the weather could change in a heartbeat. A cool wind in October spoke of impending rain, and I checked around me for cover where I might go when needed. Another pigeon thought I looked amenable, and approached the bench. He wouldn't know a Manhattan pigeon hawk, if he saw one. I pleasured in the comfort and content of the plump birds waddling around me. They were as peaceful a presence as cows in the Normandy countryside resting in the grassy meadow with their feet tucked under them like cats. Within a few feet of me, a covered carousel of small cars was whirling around and around. If the cool wind blowing leaves my way indeed delivered rain, perhaps I would leap into the police car, the little tank, or better yet, the gilded carriage fit for a princess. I had forty euros in my pocket, and not a care in the world. Cares were five thousand miles away across the pond. It was enough to be in the company of unhurried people before rain in a park in Paris. Young mothers pushed baby carriages, old couples sat close together for warmth on benches; two women walked and conversed under a red umbrella. One of the old couples exited their bench as the rain came, and slowly walked away. I pulled the hood of my jacket over my head and considered my options. A coffee in a café might be the answer, but I was outside in the rain in Paris, the carousel kept turning, and what else could matter.

• • •

CATHERINE AND I were invited to lunch at the home of her friend, Maryline, and then we were to visit a museum together. Maryline's grand, spacious apartment full of art treasures was located very near the Arc de Triomphe. She displayed a collection of sculptures in her living room which were the work of a famous Paris junk-artist who made his pieces from things people had abandoned or threw away. One amazing work was made of metal objects, a baby's bathing basin which looked like a small washtub out of someone's yard, a wheel, and some old artifacts. There was a bunch of ancient 75-rpm records, one of which actually played on a turntable when the automated sculpture began operating all at once, whirling and cranking crazily.

Maryline's lunch menu was creative, yet quite formal, as the French are wont to do: Egg *en gelée*, toast points with *tapenade*, carrots *rapée* (my son Michael's favorite vegetable when we lived in Paris), lentils with other vegetables, and for dessert, a chocolate cake with stewed fruit from a friend's garden. No ham sandwich or iced tea at this table! You must linger long over meals in France, and so we did that. Conversation, much more than food, is always the main ingredient at any European table, and good manners are critical! It's an assessment of how well you were brought up.

After lunch, Maryline suggested we see the Baccarat crystal museum, a twenty-minute walk from her apartment. We set out on foot, and I felt absolutely giddy to be on those streets I had walked so often in the past, crossing the Champs Elysées which was as familiar to me as my home town on Amelia Island. For the first time, but not the last, I had a strange contradictory sense of Andre's presence while at the same time being acutely aware of his absence.

Baccarat Gallery-Museum was situated in a private mansion located at 11, place des Etats-Unis. This beautiful edifice was once home to Viscountess Marie-Laure de Noailles who made a salon in this place of pomp and tradition and threw magical parties dedicated to painters, writers and musicians. Living in that period, perhaps I would have been among the poets. More likely not in that social milieu, but what a pretty fantasy! In the museum's historical collections, there were such things as the famous singer Josephine Baker's tableware ordered in 1947 for her marriage to the conductor, Joe Bouillon. There were temporary exhibitions where I very much admired a large crystal sculpture, curling back into itself with voluptuous round curves and displaying rainbow colors from every vantage point. The entire exhibition area was shrouded in a magical atmosphere of semi-darkness punctuated by theatrical lighting. There was a most extraordinary canopy in one of the exhibition rooms painted by Gérard Garouste. The canopy is painted in the symbolic colors of blue, green, black and red for air; essential water; the earth, a mixture of oxide, sand, silica and lead; and fire necessary for the melting of the raw materials. We were told he drew inspiration from the Athanor, this philosopher's secret hearth of constant temperature condemned to spread only when in contact with art, in this case Baccarat crystal creations, no doubt.

On the subject of Josephine Baker (my own *nom de naissance* being Baker, no relation, unfortunately) the story has been told that Ms. Baker made biscuits in her Paris kitchen totally in the nude, and could be found with her beautiful black dancer's body dusted with white flour. That image inspired a poem I wrote in French which I will not try to translate, knowing the language is probably mangled:

> *Josephine, ma belle, belle noir,*
> *Qui fait la cuisine avec grand expoir,*
> * c'est facile de reconnatre les sens ou le cu,*
> *quand on fait la cuisine à la nu.*

And, there you have it! It even rhymes.

Thank you, Galway.

• • •

IT WAS THE THIRTEENTH of the month in Paris when Catherine, Maryline and I did our walkabout to the Baccarat museum. Thirteen is a number of which I am wary. Good things have not seemed to happen around number thirteen. Years later after the Paris trip, I was seeing a psych therapist, Dr. Ross, who happened to be Jewish. I mentioned I would be flying to New York City on a Friday the 13th, and I said, partly in jest (except everything you say to Dr. Ross is taken dead serious) "So, keep the plane in the air for me?" He gave me a look askance, and asked me if I had a thirteen phobia. "You should think differently about the number thirteen," he said, "because it is very lucky in Jewish religion. Your Savior was a Jew," he added, and, "The number thirteen is lucky for a Jewish boy because it is an important rite of passage. It is when he becomes a man, enters into the adult world with his Bar Mitzvah."

Did that information help me? Yes, it did, but not on that day in Paris when it precipitated the meltdown I had known would come at some point in my return to Paris without Andre. At every street corner on our way across the Champs Elysées and down the streets to the Museum, I found him there in all the little cafés and special restaurants we used to frequent, the wine bar off the Champs, places where we had parked our car. That evening returning home to Catherine's apartment, I sat in my chambre so lovingly prepared for me, and looked at the gallery of my family photographs which Catherine had placed on a table against the wall. Andre looked out at me from a photo I had taken. In the picture he sat in a chair outside in a Belgian summer garden, smiling at me with that special warmth and look of love I knew so well. Suddenly I missed him so overwhelmingly, I broke down. When Catherine came to my door, I fell into her arms and sobbed and sobbed. Next morning, Ségolène told her mother she had a dream about me during the night, and that I was crying. My grief had slipped through the cracks!

• • •

MA BELLE CATHERINE says she does not cook. However, for each meal of the day, including afternoon tea, she set a lovely formal table for the four of us in the dining room off her small kitchen. She may say she does not cook, but she was a genius at preparing fresh fish in the microwave, shrimps and scallops in a white wine sauce, roasted chicken, arrangements of luscious French cheeses, cold and warm vegetables, fresh breads, fruit, cookies, and yogurt. French yogurt was special. Not our low fat kind, it was made with real cream, and my favorite was prune. I was amused that Catherine stored her fine cheeses on the kitchen window ledge between the double glass panes to the street. Perfect Paris refrigeration!

On the evening of the 15th of October, some of my old Paris writer friends were invited to come to Catherine's apartment for a soirée. Catherine made such a beautiful repast: a salad of mâche—my favorite greens in the whole world—a crab casserole, a vegetable, delicate tea sandwiches, eight different cheeses, pain aux noix (walnut bread), a rich chocolate cake to die for, and, *bien sur*, Kir Royales for the Kir Queen and her court. Members of our former workshop, the Paris Poetry Groupe, which we organized in the 1990s, brought gifts. Norrie brought wine; Gwyneth, a book of her poems published in England, Florence, a copy of her *Poèmes Française-Anglais*, poetry written in English and French and illustrated with her own original drawings. Nothing in these old friendships seemed significantly changed despite the passage of time. It was as if we simply went out one door ten years ago, and reentered another, embracing each other as warmly as ever.

As we sat in the salon catching up on our lives, Catherine, the perfect hostess, served canapés and champagne with an easy grace. After a time, we all gathered in a circle around the dining room table for a late supper, the main dish being conversation. Good talk is always on the table on the Continent. There are very few obese people in Paris! At the end of the evening, I thanked Catherine for entertaining my old friends. I remarked that she had outdone herself. She never heard that expression before, and found it amusing. In trying to remember how to say it, it was too colloquial for her and she would end up with something on the order of, "You did out? Yourself?"

After I returned home to Amelia Island, I made a large hand-lettered sign for Catherine, which read:

Catherine, You Outdid Yourself!

When she received the sign, Catherine wrote me in return, *"J'ai accroche' dans ma chambre 'You Outdid Yourself!' Quand je suis fatigue, je le regarde et ca me donne le courage pour continuer."* In English, "I hung 'You Outdid Yourself!' in my bedroom. When I am tired, I look at it and it gives me the courage to continue."

· · ·

THE PARIS POETRY GROUPE has disbanded now, by necessity. None of the five members of our workshop group are now living in Paris, except Florence Cousin. Florence was present at Catherine's gathering for some of my writer friends, and she invited us for lunch at her apartment the next day. Florence lives on rue Montparnasse over Le Mandarine, a Chinese restaurant we often frequented in the past. Florence's apartment was where our Paris Poetry Groupe had its weekly workshop meetings in the mid-1990s.

Catherine and I caught a cross-town bus, and sat ourselves down in the very back where we promptly became so deeply engrossed in conversation that we almost missed our stop. A highly annoyed driver prompted us off in a very loud voice, much to the amusement of the other passengers who were laughing as we hurriedly, with some degree of embarrassment, disembarked. What *déjà vu* greeted me as we took the tiny elevator up to Forence's third floor apartment and entered into the long, narrow hallway leading to her living room! It was there--at a big round table, the birthplace of many poems, nurturing meeting space for a good glass of wine and some munchies where one French Canadian and five American expat writers gathered to take turns discussing our literary efforts.

Our core group first came together at Susan Ludvigson's day-long poetry workshop in a private home in Paris sponsored by WICE, a Paris non-profit educational and cultural institute. After Susan's workshop, we continued to meet, helping each other and doing readings around Paris. We held readings at Florence's brother's art gallery on the Left Bank, at an intimate little bookstore called Tea and Tattered Pages, and notably, a reading under the auspices of the American Embassy on the Embassy premises. We were four women and one man for whom it was a fruitful writing time and a time of fine friendships.

All in the Paris Poetry Groupe have kept in touch since those Paris days, particularly Lise Goett and me. We met again on Amelia Island in October 2002, when Lise came as an invited author to participate in the Amelia Book Island Festival. She and I read together at the festival on a program called "Two Friends from Paris Read Poetry." Florence Cousin continues to write and paint in Paris. Lise Goett went back to the States to acquire yet another Master's degree at Columbia University, and her first book, *Waiting for the Paraclete,* won the 2001 Barnard New Women Poets Prize. Elline Lipkin went home to get an MFA in poetry from Columbia University and a doctorate from the University of Houston. Her first poetry collection, *The Errant Thread,* won the 2004 First Book

Award from Kore Press. Karen Teenstra still writes, but always claimed she was more interested in writing than in publication. She is married, and lives in Washington State. Jack Mosely, the sole fox in our Gallic henhouse, married his French sweetheart, Claire, and was accepted into the Creative Writing Program at the University of Iowa. He now practices medicine, his other vocation, in the Meskwaki Tribal Health Clinic in Toledo, Iowa. *"Tout change, tout change—ça grandit,"* he wrote to me. My Paris manuscript, *The Continent of Dreams*, made the National Poetry Series, and was published by Sulphur River Literary Review Press in Austin, Texas. Our little circle, disbanded only in body, not in spirit, has done well. We are still connected, and held close in the arms of Paris, *notre amour!*

Now, once again happily ensconced at the round table at which we sat so often to workshop poems, Florence served Catherine and me a lunch of mâche, foie gras, pâte de campagne, thin slices of ham and good French bread. Ah me! Food, glorious food. Catherine and I encountered a little more excitement than we needed when leaving Florence's apartment. We were prohibited from taking the bus back home. There was a parade of demonstrators on strike, marching down the middle of the street. Police were everywhere, and we quickly went underground to catch the nearest métro train.

And the food, glorious food, went on and on, because in the evening, Catherine, Joli Prince and I departed for dinner at the home of their friends, Michel and Michelle Feijoz. They lived in a very modern apartment building on its fifth floor. They gave us a tour of their premises complete with a balcony from which one had a glorious view of the Eiffel Tower. Somehow it seemed improbable to me that anyone could live and look out their balcony windows at such a celebrated sight. From my seat at the Feijoz's dinner table, I could see every hour on the hour how the Tower lighted up its 20,000 twinkling lights like a fantasy Christmas tree of preposterous proportions. I recalled my very first visit to that famous Twiddle Stick! It was my maiden voyage to the City of Light, and like all tourists, Andre and I were taking in all the monuments. On our trip to the Tower, we took the elevator to the second level where I found I had not the courage to go any higher. When it was time to descend, there was a long waiting line for the elevator. It seemed a good idea to expedite things by walking down the stairs to the ground. I failed to realize that the stairs on the outside of the tower are completely open. I happened to look down for the first time and saw the dizzying drop in the space between each step—the enormous, sickening distance below— my sea legs (or air legs) refused to function. I saw down on a step, and refused to go further. I told Andre he would have to send for the gendarmes! I did eventually make it down to the safer first-level terra firma. Surely I am not the only wimp who ever had terror firma on the scary stairs of the Tour Eiffel...

• • •

I RECONNECTED with as many persons who had been important to me during my four years in Daumesnil as I had time. One of these was Candace Nancel, who with her husband, Frederic, had been often in my apartment on rue Lamblardie. I called Candace, and we arranged to meet for lunch near the American Embassy. It was interesting that when I first met Candace in the 1990s, I was working at the American Embassy, and now she was.

I caught the autobus from Catherine's apartment on avenue Wagram to the Place de la Concorde to meet Candace outside the splendid Hotel Crillon. She knew a special place for lunch, no hamburger and chips for these uptown girls! A sumptuous lunch of several courses ensued in an enclosed arcade, giving an illusion of lunching *en plein air* on the beach at Nice or Cannes, perhaps? Of course, we had a glass of wine or two, as working people in Paris do not consider that to be drinking on the job. Wine is food!

After lunch, Candace wanted to take me into the Embassy E Building on rue Saint Florentin (the old Talleyrand Hotel) where she was working on coordination of a restoration of certain of the interiors. She wanted to show me what she was doing. Pausing at the Marine guard station at the entrance for an obligatory security check, I found I had left my American driver's license in Catherine's apartment. I did have a photo credit card, which I presented. The stern-faced young Marine refused to accept it as identification. Candace argued fruitlessly with the Marine. She said, "Her husband used to work here!" Not only that, but I did, and I had a

!?*@#&!*! Top Secret security clearance somewhere in a Washington file drawer. It was still no go. The Marine was an immovable object. Resignedly, I said, "Candace, he has his orders." I was prepared to leave, but Candace flew up a flight of stairs to consult with higher powers. When she came back, the Marine got a phone call, and I was admitted to the building. Never underestimate the power of a woman, indeed!

• • •

PILGRIMAGES. I had two of them on my itinerary. The first one was a return to our old homestead in the twelfth *arrondissement,* to have lunch at my favorite neighborhood restaurant Les Fleurs, and visit with the patron and his wife. The second pilgrimage was reserved for a mission in the South of France. Catherine chose a day for "quest one" when she was not too busy with flower shop affairs and could go along with me. The two of us walked to the Champs Elysées where we descended to the métro and caught my old home train line: Direction Vincennes with a change at Reuilly-Diderot for Direction Balard. This put us out to climb the stairs that surfaced at Daumesnil, Place Felix Ebouié with its circle of beautiful iron lions spouting streams of water into the large fountain in the middle of a rond point. Home! My heart turned over in my chest! My apartment building at 2, rue Lamblardie was directly before us as we came up from underground. How could those people walking around on the sidewalks of my old neighborhood that day fail to feel my excitement, and have no clue that ten long years had passed since I stood among them?

Catherine and I were past ready for lunch. We went immediately to Les Fleurs, only to find that on the sidewalk in front of the restaurant, there was no longer that familiar sculpture of a golden sheep outside the door. That didn't bode well. What! No golden fleece for this daughter of Jason? Instead, there was a golden snail, and stepping inside we were informed that friends, Jean-Michel and his wife, the old proprietors, had retired to their home in Saint Malo on the coast. Everything must change, I thought, but happily the quality of the food had not. The sumptuous lunch we ordered was personally delivered to our table by the chef in his white coat and toque in honor of an old neighbor's return after so long an absence. We had a salad of mâche (what else!) with murderously good foie gras, then salmon, and a tender white fish under a mound of fluffy puréed potatoes. You could call them mashed, but those *pommes de terre* weren't even a second cousin to boring old mashed! Since we were celebrating a homecoming, we ordered a half bottle of fine red wine to accompany the meal. For dessert, the chef treated us to an extraordinary chocolate cake of almost pudding-like consistency, covered with chocolate sauce and prettily decorated with vanilla hearts. Soul food in a northern city for a southern girl and her Parisian friend!

After lunch, we walked across the street to my old apartment to peer through the ornate glass doors into the foyer of the building. It had not changed. In that foyer years ago, I began writing a poem while waiting for my husband to bring the car around for a trip to Brussels. My footsteps were there. My fingerprints were on the doorknob. My heart was up the stairs on the second floor, trapped forever. I felt at that moment as if I had been freeze-framed all these years, that my life had been stopped mid-air since I departed Paris, kicking and screaming, in July of 1994. Catherine and I waited around rue Lamblardie for a while, hoping someone now living in the building would come by and allow us to enter with them. It didn't happen. I no longer knew the code that would open the door, and even if we got in, the new *guardienne* wouldn't have a clue who I was, except some crazy American interloper. We had to abandon the quest, and move on to the next. I had promised my son Anthony in Atlanta that I would walk down to the nearby Bois de Vincennes and take a photograph of the place where he had proposed to his future wife. I will never forget how nervous my son was that day. He had gone to great pains to purchase a beautiful emerald ring not meant to look like a traditional engagement ring. He had conferred about his choice with a jeweler friend of Sally's who knew her taste. He wanted to get just the right ring. He was going to present the ring to Sally and ask her to accept it on the premise that he was standing by, ready for marriage whenever she was. Andre and I had planned a gathering in our apartment that evening with some of our French friends. Catherine and Michel Rinieri (her then-significant other) who knowing Anthony's intentions, had bought two beautiful crystal wine glasses to give to the couple. Catherine stuck her head in my front door that evening with a big question on her pretty face. The answer I was glad to give her was that Sally had said *"Oui!"* So, the little no-occasion party in my living room on rue Lamblardie turned out to be a major celebration of my son's happiness. The one woman in the world for him had accepted his proposal.

Catherine and I walked down the dozen or so blocks from Lamblardie Street to the forest, its lake with majestic black and white swans, rowboats to rent, and pleasant walk paths with little bridges over the water. After a walk around the lake, skies began darkening with imminent rain, and it seemed prudent to abandon outdoor activities for the comforts of home. Since we were on foot, we decided to return and catch the train back to the center of town. Well, as bad luck would have it, the train we were on stopped in its tracks continuously because of an unspecified problem on the line. No one had any idea when the problem ahead would be cleared up, or how long we could be in transit. Finally, we descended from the train and began walking toward Paris Center, yet a distance away, with few taxicabs to be seen navigating the street. When we were just about at the point of despair of ever finding one, Eureka! A chariot, more welcome than Cinderella's, was waiting for a fare at a taxicab station. Our cabby took two damsels in distress, and deposited them in front of the massive wooden doors to Catherine's apartment on avenue de Wagram.

• • •

AT LAST, AT LAST, it was time to head out of Paris for a week in the South of France. Catherine and I would drive in her little car to Boulouris, where she and Jean owned adjoining apartments in a vacation complex in walking distance of the Mediterranean. Jean would join us on the weekend. Ségolène invited a school chum to join her for the school holiday, and would arrive by train a day or so later. I was excited about going south where I knew the weather would still be lovely in October. Before I came for my visit, Catherine had sent me this as incentive from Boulouris, (not that I needed one): "I have done NOTHING but breathe air, sea, wild plants, thyme, my laziness. I fill up when I'm over there." As Catherine and I were driving, she had her radio on and she was singing along with an old French song she said her grandmother used to sing to her, "*Un Dimanche d'bord l'eau*," that is to say, "A Sunday beside the water," (sea). I thought it so sweet to have those memories of a grandmother. I had an adored, not one, but three grandmothers. The extra one a gift from my stepmother, Lucille, who came into our family after my mother and father's divorce when I was six years old, and my brother Jim, four.

I remembered with delight every mile of that drive south, having traveled it so many times before with my late husband. I loved the sight of mountains, the chaine de Massif Central, and the vineyards. Oh, the vineyards! The grapes had all been harvested by September, and the vines were all *jaune,* a sleepy and peaceful yellow; resting from their good work and the wine crop they had yielded. Outside our car windows there was the remembered immaculate countryside, its pretty little farmhouses, barns, manicured fields, the freshly turned earth's orderly beauty. And the familiar names of beloved towns rolled past on my tongue and on the road signs: Vaison-la-Romaine, Orange, Salon, Aix en Provence, Arles, Avignon, Nimes, and place of the heart: Marseille. It was the birthplace of my late husband, Andre, where he and I had spent many happy times.

Catherine was playing the *nostalgie* station on the car radio, and we listened to the Beatles' "Penny Lane." I thought of a Jacksonville Beach day so long ago when my children were little. We picnicked on a blanket, it was late afternoon, and our radio played "Penny Lane." Blue shadows were lengthening on white sand and the ocean kicked up high by a brisk afternoon wind. My husband's friend who shared our outing was swimming, engulfed up to his neck. I was fearful about the roughed-up surf, but he wasn't. He was really getting off on the fierce ocean and the beauty of the waning day. It was a glorious moment in the summer of my marriage. My children were young. There were the simple joys of beach, picnic, wind and the predictable life of a house in the suburbs with two small sons, a father who came home from the office, and a mother who stayed home. I was content as wife and mother, content to do the job I had signed up for. I had no foreboding sense, the same as any of us, of changes and dangers that were to come.

• • •

AFTER EIGHT HOURS of travel, it was early evening when Catherine and I arrived in Boulouris/Saint Raphaël, and our car rolled into the parking lot of the apartment building where Catherine and Jean had their two apartments. These apartments were to be found within a gated compound consisting of a fine multi-floor Italianate building, beautifully groomed grounds with all the usual vacation amenities: a large swimming pool; grassy little spots to sit and reflect, privately marked parking for the owners. Catherine and I unloaded her little Twingo, and we took our luggage up by elevator to the second floor of the building. I was shown to my very own private apartment, adjoining that of Catherine and her family. It was like the very best of accommodations for a luxury vacation in the South of France. I could hardly have afforded such without the generosity of my friend, Catherine. I slept that night the sleep of the privileged in that beautiful place under the protective watch of all the powers that be, and wondered what I had done to be so blessed.

Early next morning, Catherine set out to purchase what we needed in the way of provisions. When she returned, she and I had a lavish breakfast out on the terrace, and I decided, "Well, that settles it! I am never leaving!" At an eleven o'clock brunch for two, candles were lit on a table set with a cloth of blue and yellow colors of Provence. Catherine had set out all sorts of pastries including *chasson au pomme* (apple tart,) my old favorite *pain aux raisen* (a sugary wheel of pastry with raisins and custard) and in addition there were the huge Italian grapes I had always loved in Europe called *uve Italia Coperta,* so large and full of trapped sunlight they looked like they were plugged in to an electrical outlet. The bread Catherine had purchased was called *biologique,* utterly delicious natural grain bread coated with seeds. The terrace of the apartment was inviting with its chaise lounges facing the Mediterranean, a blue sky overhead, and sunshine seeming more August than October. Catherine remarked, "This is so rare in the Midi in October." "Yes," I said, "it's just for me."

On Sunday, we met Jean's train in town, and as soon as he brought in his bags and changed his clothes, we drove off for the marina where Jean kept his little cruiser. He couldn't wait to be out of Paris, and out on the water. When Jean, who was in the boat making ready for our outing, threw a tarp to Catherine who was on the dock, he suddenly lost his balance and fell forward into the water beside the dock dragging his princess along with him. Both of them, fully clothed, disappeared under the water. I suppose you could say Paris concerns literally fell from Jean into the sea. I was dancing about on the dock and screaming, "Au secours! Au secours!" when both their heads bobbed up to the surface and up they came, holding on to each other and laughing. Catherine returned to the apartment to change into dry clothes and bring some for Jean, and off we went after the mishap for our cruise in the open sea.

Now, I am a sailor who prefers a ship big enough to get lost in, and a traveler by air who likes a plane as big as the Alamo. Jean's little boat, while luxurious enough, was quite susceptible to what was happening to the substance on which it was traveling. Jean was an expert mariner, but even so on the return trip after buzzing Saint Tropez, seeing the magnificent villas in Fréjus' new port and the colorful houses climbing up the hills from the edge of the sea, there came up an extremely high afternoon wind. The sea became very choppy, and tossed our little boat up and down in a most alarming way. I was holding on to the rail at the back of the "bus," with all my might, and at one point, my heart in my mouth, I yelled out for Jean to slow down. "Stop!" It was all I could think of to shout, and he was so surprised, he immediately cut the engine. I don't think he had ever had a passenger as "squirrelly" as me. Little boats are for brave hearts, and I wasn't one.

• • •

CATHERINE'S DAUGHTER, Sègoléne, arrived several days later in Boulouris along with a friend, Marie. Jean again took us out in the little boat for a day trip to Saint Tropez. I remember how the two girls sitting in the prow of the boat and holding on to the rail as best they could, rolled around laughing and shouting as the waves knocked the nose of the boat up and down. The young court danger so easily! It brought to mind a time long ago in Atlanta when my family and some of our friends were rafting down the Chattahoochee River. We called it "rafting," the fashionable thing to do in Atlanta on a nice summer day, but it was not so much rafting as it was floating along in small canoes. My little son, Michael, was trailing along on a float tied to the back of our boat, and I watched with great anxiety, ready to catch the rope at any minute, visualizing my second-born floating away never to be seen again. Catherine was not a nervous mother, but I was!

The more I got to know Catherine's Jean Claude, the more I became interested in finding out about my host's history. His seemed to be in sync in a lot of ways with that of my late husband, Andre. One evening on the balcony at the apartments after supper, I quizzed him. Jean-Claude Houart was born in Brittany on March 15, the Ides of March. A Pisces, at home on the sea like my Andre, Jean remarked in jest that he was the reincarnation of Julius Caesar, murdered on that day. When Jean was twenty-five years old, he went to Algeria where Andre had been born. Jean moved to Saint Raphael in 1970 and worked for a company that constructed roads and bridges. My Andre also began his work career as a structural engineer for the Army Corps of Engineers. So many similarities! Jean then worked as a financial manager for land acquisition to build buildings for eighteen years in Marseille, Nice, Saint Raphaël, all of the South of France. He founded a company for international business established with Japanese materials, and he flew back and forth between Saint Raphaël and Paris. In 1989, he went to Paris for good, and in Paris he met the love of his life, Catherine: a lady of light in the city of light and a man of the sea. Both of them were older and wiser, had been married before, divorced, and had children of their own. It was an auspicious new partnership for the two of them, *c'est vrai!*

• • •

ONE MORNING, Catherine and I walked from the apartments to a little calanque, a protected inlet between cliffs with a beach for sunbathing where the sea was shallow enough for swimming. People spread their blankets on the rocky beach, and had their lunch while their children and pets played in the water. Catherine and I climbed up steps hewn from rock to reach the top where you could walk a long way along the edge of the cliff with no sense of any other person being present in the world. Just a sparkling sea, tall cliffs, a great quiet except for the singing of cicadas in the pines under the warm and healing sun. Heaven blesses earth in one of the most beautiful places on earth – the South of France.

What is another best moment of the day for the Kir Queen other than a walk beside the sea? Why, Kir time of course. What our beloved American President of my growing-up years, Franklin Roosevelt, called "The Children's Hour." My daughter-in-law, Sally, recently gave me a novel, *Evenings at Five,* by Gail Godwin. It was a strong tale of a marriage and love-after-death, which Sally said made her think, in many ways, of my own marriage. The husband of the novel, Rudy, announced Happy Hour each day to his wife with a telephone call from the Pope. "Rudy did the high Polish voice, overlaid with an Italian accent: 'Thees is John Paul. My cheeldren, eet is cocktail time." Catherine and I had Happy Hour on the verandah of her apartment, or if we were in town in Saint Raphael, the Excelsior Hotel was the place to sit out under the plantanes. I loved these plane trees, so common in France, which formed a graceful canopy over the terrace of the hotel, where one could sit in the shade of a late afternoon for a Kir and a dish of olives. One afternoon for a change of pace, Catherine ordered a Fernet Branca. I had no idea what that was. Try it, she said, it's good for the liver. The libations, dark brown in color, arrived over ice in a drinking glass. I took several tentative sniffs of the stuff before taking a small, experimental swallow. "It tastes like medicine!" I said in horror, and sat my glass down on the table for a braver taker than me. The Kir Queen prefers her champagne and cassis.

•

Watching the weather report on television one night in the apartment after dinner, Jean announced we were in for rain. "Catastrophic rain," he said as he went to pull his Jaguar automobile out of the parking lot into the garage under the apartment building. I went to bed that night expecting a downpour equal to that of Noah and his Ark, but when I awoke the next morning, it was raining only gently. On this day, we all went to the market where Catherine bought fish for dinner: twelve small *rougets* (you might call them finger fish,) and a large *loup de mer.* She purchased the whole fish, lying in a bin of ice with all its brethren, glassy-eyed and quite stiff in their specialized quarters. Fresh vegetables and fruits comprised the remainder of the purchases, and after they were delivered home, Jean took Catherine and me for a drive in the l'Esterel mountains, one of those terrifying ascents of a narrow, winding road with drops of thousands of feet over the side to meadows and fields below.

We survived the climb, me holding my breath most of the way, and it was worth the trip. I was shown the Pierre and Vacances Cap Esterel exclusive resort that was a vacation destination for many British and Italians on holiday. From the main terrace of the resort high above the sea, we had a spectacular view of red rock mountains ("A little Colorado," said Jean) as well as the breathtaking sight that is the Mediterranean Sea. Directly below a railing was yet another terrace with a rimless swimming pool spilling over into another pool on the level beneath. It was, I thought, quite a beautiful vacation sanctuary for the rich and famous, and being neither, it was a place to which I would never aspire except as an admiring spectator.

• • •

ONLY THREE MORE DAYS remained in my sojourn in France. As I showered before breakfast that morning, a knock at the door admitted Catherine, loose blonde hair falling over a white bathrobe, pretty as a flower in the dew kissed grass outside. She asked if I slept well and announced that my coffee was in the cup, "*Tu à bien dormi? Ton café est prêt.*" Oh, dear me, I was completely indulged by my adored Catherine.

My days in France had been indeed a beautiful dream, but I had not always slept well. A displaced unconscious was expressing displeasure through dream scenarios I was unable to interpret. It takes for me at least a week to get into the vacation mode although I did not think of France return as a vacation. It was a reverse homecoming, a search party, and what the search was for, had yet to be revealed.

Ségolène and her school chum, Marie, were on a school holiday which we do not celebrate in the States. Jean had said there were three major school vacation times: Christmas, Easter, and the Feast of All Saints. Imagine, honoring the saints for ten whole days! I guess they had a lot of saints to cover. Before we left Paris for The Midi, I noticed All Saints, as we know it, was on the way because there were the kind of Halloween decorations we know and love in the shop windows: pumpkins, witches and all the usual suspects. When I lived in Atlanta,

Halloween was highly celebrated by as many adults as children, adults who loved to assume for a night their favorite fantasy identity. It must have been Atlanta's favorite holiday. Driving very late one Halloween night with friends on a street near Piedmont Park, we saw a guy in costume, crawling on all fours at the red light, very much in character although there was no one around to see him but us in our passing automobile. Now, that is assuming another identity. But, the most memorable All Saints celebration was a Mass at a stone altar in the middle of Bosque Bello Cemetery on Amelia Island in the eerie silence and dark of night, lit only by candles and flashlights. The dead in their shoe boxes, and we, still on our journey through time, celebrating with each other the feast of saints. Where we were singing by moonlight and candlelight, my father lay in his grave some feet away, and had I but known at that moment, so sadly my Andre of Marseille and my beloved brother Jim were soon to follow.

• • •

TO PUT A FITTING END to one of my last days in the South of France, it was agreed we should go boating again – all five of us. The Mediterranean had been a glass mirror all morning. Joli Prince morphed into the Jolly Prince of the Sea who sang and made broad jokes, which set everyone in a good mood.

We spent less time in Saint Tropez than we had hoped, however, because storm clouds were beginning to gather. I remembered Catherine's letter to me which described a storm they faced on one of their boat outings. Here in my friend's charming English is a portion of that letter: "The way to go to Boulouris (here is our flats) has been a bit hard! Normally it's four hours and half of train, here I have been eight hours in the train I didn't know why, and nobody knows or tells us why we stayed stopped in the country among trees and posts but I had a nice supper to forget this, *"une bouillabaisse,"* it's a bit heavy as you know for evening… I have done NOTHING but breathe air, sea, wild plants, thyme, my laziness. I fill up when I'm over there. We took the little cruiser and went to St. Tropez just for a glance because my Prince Charming doesn't appreciate really the category of people, very often superficial and snob. We went in a lot of inlets. Coming out Agay bay we had a real little storm and I was completely terrified, saying nothing looking at the Captain who were really green faced… we were not in a liner and the hollow of the waves were about my height… So I had another nice supper *"lotte à l'Américaine,"* (Monkfish with tomatoes, wine and seasonings.) Good job when I'm stressful! Mediterranean can be treacherous and sly, you have to be prudent. I was tremulous and now I'll go only when I see as a lake under the sun."

So, you can see that I was in the mood to be prudent as well. There was a storm in the offing. Also, we were a little low on fuel and being October, many fuel stations were closed for the winter season when boat owners put their boats into storage until spring. We set out for home, stopping in Sainte Maxim, where there was a fuel station open. To my relief and delight, we disembarked for lunch where I discovered one of the prettiest little villages I had ever seen. Time seemed to have stopped as far as the 21st century was concerned in Sainte Maxim. We ate sandwiches from a little shop while strolling about on narrow streets, and came upon an open-air bazaar in a plaza by the sea where we would have liked to linger, but storm clouds were gathering in earnest. The wind came up, and it was a choppy ride home that had me clinging to my seat and the rail at the back of the boat. Poupette and Marie, however, on the deck of the prow were squealing with delight at being tossed about. I was calling on all the angels in the vicinity to get us home safely, albeit with great confidence in the nautical expertise of *Capitaine Joli Prince.*

•

We did indeed get to safety. All were welcomed home, safe and snug in the Boulouris safe harbor abode with dinner ready on the terrace. In the early evening, a Provençal red clay tile roof and cream-colored façade of the house underneath it peeked through the dark, green pines, their branches snarled and twisted into graceful shapes by the Mistral. The air was scented with the October perfume of a wood fire from someone's fireplace. I changed from sweatshirt to a warm wool sweater for dinner on the second floor terrace with my French family. Two more days in Paradise remained. The apartment complex was almost completely empty now. In summer, the apartments are filled with foreigners who own the apartments and come for holidays and vacation. Catherine had invited her friend, Anne, one of the few people who lived there year-round to join us for some champagne. We all gathered around the table on the terrace. Even the girls, Poupette and Marie, joined us for some bubbly. They stayed with the adults for the better part of an hour before retiring to the living room to watch television. They sat snuggled up against each other with the easy intimacy of French girlfriends that I found so charming. Catherine and I on our daily promenades walked arm in arm, *bras dessous, bras dessous,* in the way women friends don't particularly do in America. That kind of intimacy is not so easy for us North Americans.

Years ago as a girl of 18, I lived for a year in Caracas, Venezuela, with my stepmother, Lucille, and Bill Veech, the man she married after my father's death. I remember late afternoon evening promenades when girls would circle arm-in-arm in the main city park downtown under the watchful surveillance of their chaperones, while admiring young men on park benches checked them out. I could never get used to the Latin men on the streets who were so vocal in their appreciation as they passed a pretty girl. It was OK for a guy to cruise close and offer remarks of the most complimentary nature. Once I was out walking with Lucille's Trinidadian housemaid, Mercedes, and one guy got too close to me. "Rubia!" (Blonde) he breathed suggestively into my ear, since at that time I had a major peroxide streak in the top of my hair. He got a serious scowl from Mercedes, but undaunted, he went quickly on his way, mission accomplished.

•

When I came into Catherine's apartment mornings from my adjoining one, there would be the two girls lying comfortably close together in their nightclothes on the couch they shared as a bed, watching television before the family breakfast. Had I not been there that October, the girls would have had the second apartment for themselves. The generosity of my French friends who allowed me the privacy next door was really quite overwhelming.

There was only one time I ever shared sleeping space with a girlfriend.

It was after my father died, and my stepmother, Lucille, moved away from Amelia Island to join her second husband in Venezuela. He worked for many years for Westinghouse, traveling to the oil camps at Maracaibo, Barcelona, and to outposts in Colombia. My brother Jim and I remained in Fernandina in the care of foster families so that we might continue in school; I, in my senior year, Jim in his sophomore year. I had the happy circumstance of living for that year in the home of Bill and Jo Ritchie, and their high school kids, Billy and Joann. Joann and I shared a bedroom and a bed, and the entire household shared one bathroom. Here in these times of multiple bathrooms in everyone's homes, it would be hard to imagine such a situation as one bathroom for five people. But, we managed. During winter nights at the beach, Joann and I curled into each other's bodies for warmth, and never thought about the physical intimacy we shared. In the mornings, we dressed for school together, making our bed and tucking our nightclothes under our pillows, as Joann had been taught to do. I felt the difference between my motherless self and my girlfriend, brought up by a mom who shared traditions, even tiny ones like rolling up her PJs for another night.

•

My last, most important act, before leaving the South of France was to make a pilgrimage to my late husband's hometown of Marseille. I had felt a keen desire ever since his death to go back to the Church of Notre Dame de la Garde, high on a hill over Andre's seaport city. It was a church visited many times in the past, a church that had special meaning for us. At Andre's funeral Mass at St. Michael's Church, Fernandina, my friend, Wendy Philcox, made a keepsake handout for those who came. She printed out copies of my poem, "Marseille; My husband, the Count of Monte Cristo," and added a photograph of Andre and me, heads on our arms, resting together on top of a low wall on a balustrade at Notre Dame. What was said that day under the canopy of our arms escapes me, but the camera, and just maybe, the eye of God caught a grace note. Do not some primitive cultures shun the camera, believing it captures the soul? If I did not leave my soul at Notre Dame de la Garde, I surely left my heart. Whatever our intentions in that moment, the camera told the truth. It stopped in time and space a testament of a marriage, two bodies become one, made immortal by "Canon." Canon? How appropriate. Tenet, principle, law...

My mission in Marseille was to go back to Notre Dame, and light the biggest candle I could find for Andre. It was, for me, a completion, a closing that I needed for my peace of mind. And Catherine made it possible. On the morning before my return to the States, we set out from Boulouris with Ségolène and Marie in the back seat of Catherine's Twingo. I was pleased the girls wanted to come along. They entertained us with their chatter, and at one point when a police car pulled up alongside, they both scrambled to hook their seat belts. *C'est la loi!* It's the law!

It's easy to find the Cathedral in Marseille. It is built on the loftiest point of the city. We wound our way around the circular road leading up high to parking areas, crowded with cars and buses. Visitors come from all over to visit Our Lady. She's not the Statue of Liberty; she's the Statue of Mercy, Christ child in arms, calming wind and turbulent sea to bring home to safety sailors and seafarers. The great stone Cathedral walls, floor to ceiling, bear paintings of sailing vessels, along with plaques of thanksgiving from families for the rescue of loved ones. Along the sides of the nave, models of ships suspend from alcove ceilings—chapelettes where one may pause to meditate and pray.

In the great Cathedral's center was not the place I wanted to put my candle. Below, down a short flight of stone steps, is a grotto. There, you may purchase a candle as tall as a man to take its place among blazing masses of others, attended by a priest who will accept your intention and your money. It is a glorious sight. Andre purchased candles there on each of our visits, but the day of my mission, the grotto door, for whatever reason, was closed. It was necessary to regroup. Returning to the entrance of the Cathedral upstairs where there is a statue of the Virgin, and choosing a particular large candle in a clear glass container, I pushed it squarely to the middle of the table. Andre was home at the feet of the Blessed Mother, and his wife was at peace. My trip to France was a *fait accompli.*

Outside the Cathedral, stopping to breathe in the incredible vista before me, I said to Catherine in disbelief, "I can't believe I am standing here again." It is the Almighty's place in the South of France. It can't be bought at any price, yet it is free to the beholder. One cannot help but feel diminished here against endless azure sky; the Mediterranean stretching out forever, wearing her luminous little rocky islands like a string of pearls. The Château d'If only a swim away—if one were Johnny Weissmuller or Esther Williams, and impervious to sharks. Above all, there is the deafening hum of Marseille city bustle below. It is like the muted symphony heard from the deck on top of the Empire State Building. There, if you close your eyes, you seem to be falling, falling, into a gigantic whispering net, as if cradled in it you will never hit the ground. Stuff of infinity. In the center of this mighty surround of silence is an immortal moment when you hear the voice of The Other—that One who knows you, and is Known.

• • •

"Small wonder that still
in the invisible scrim of air
that delineates our separate worlds

your features sometimes press toward me
all silvery from the afterlife, woven in wind,
to whisper a caution. Or your hand on my back

shoves me into my life."

—MARY KARR, FROM HER POEM, "PATHETIC FALLACY"

Chapter Five

TO THE BLACKBIRD PERCHED ON MY ROOF WHO MIGHT BE YOU

Come back, come back, long lost lover,
come find me again with
your El Greco ardor, come kick
up the dust in Monet's peaceful garden,

drive with me until we run out of road,
tilt with me on a tightrope
over a bottomless gorge. I want these words
to come find you. I want to backspace

into time. I want to share your
last breath. I want to soar, winged
and gossamer as a dragonfly, mapping
the sun. I want to be as pearly as

October's secret opal, microcosm
of the rhythmic whale,
music written on the canvas
of the sky, choreographer

of cloud-speak over this contrived
world. Come back, come back,
Horus, hawk of my life, and claw
at my heart once more.

IF AS PSYCHICS SAY, I have been Egyptian royalty in antiquity, perhaps I had a falcon. Perhaps, of the deities of the day, my favorite was
Horus, son of Osiris and Isis, god of the sky, of light and goodness. "He
who is above." That would have been my bag: a god with the head of a
hawk and the body of a man. That's better for progeny than the cen-
taur's head of a man, body of a horse, but, obviously in mythology, all
things are possible. It is said after the creation of the world, Horus, in
order to rest, landed on a perch known as the djeba, which literally
translates as finger, which consequently became sacred. Horus, besides
being the Lord of the Perch, is the god of the Nile delta. Is that why,
after succumbing to the lure of a certain perfume in a pricey store at
Lenox Square in Atlanta, 80-plus of my scanty dollars went in the deep
pocket of Hermés for a lime-green bottle of a love potion called "Un
Jardin sur Le Nil?" A Garden on the Nile, that is ...

A blackbird is not a hawk, and the peak of my roof is not a djeba, but
the winged ones rule! Spotting an osprey in my neighborhood is a religious experience. On the island and its environs, we have a water and
wading bird paradise. It's not the Nile delta here, though we are surrounded by river, sea, and inlet. We have Neptune in residence, but do
we have a Lord of the River, mythological or otherwise? Probably not,
and not a single troll is grilling hamburgers under the island bridges.

• • •

EXACTLY IN THE MIDDLE of an azalea bush planted last year at the
back of my house, I was astonished one day to discover a single enormous sunflower growing there. The mighty head of the flower queen of
the universe had inexplicably sprung up among those lesser petals.
Where did it come from? I could not imagine unless its seed was in some
mulch from the bottom of an old pot flung at the base of the azalea, and
then forgotten about. Was the sunflower in all its bewildering beauty the
magic of the Magi at work, and it wasn't even Christmas? Indeed, it was
early summer when time was slowing down, and I was learning to live
alone, and not liking it. My task was to rediscover how to be a Me again
after a lifetime of being an Us. My husband was gone forever. I missed his
companionship, the male energy in the house that had been taken

blithely for granted.

My therapist suggested one solution: make the space in the house more mine, less "ours." Change things around, he said. The definitions of my living and dining areas were set in time and space. Furniture had to remain where it was because of the elongated room. I consulted my friend, J. D. Beck, the talented and visionary brains of "The Busy Bees" painting company. J. D. had repainted the walls of the main rooms of our house when Andre and I first moved in. We chose a pretty ivory to replace the existing nondescript beige. The former owner of the house must have been infatuated with that color because all the rooms in the house were evenly tanned.

After Andre's death, J. D. was my right arm. Not only that, he was my two strong hands and agile legs to climb a monstrously tall ladder when floodlights in my mansard ceilings gave up the ghost. Not to mention demonic smoke alarms situated in the very highest corners that beeped alarmingly, crisis or no. What did my friend not help me with in the unsought absence of the man of my life? The garage floor got a new makeup application of deck paint, the guest bathroom tub acquired sliding doors instead of an outdated shower curtain, and J. D. engineered installation of screens for the lakeside porch. Saint John Dennis Beck could do anything! It made sense what gladiator of the paint brush should be entrusted with my challenge to change, and paint was the tool of transformation.

Furnishings in my home are eclectic, varicolored, and if there is a theme, it must be past-life "All that medieval stuff!" declared my interior decorator daughter-in-law, Sally. Because of my inclination for a crowded, colorful environment, Sally's genius was the key that unlocked what color was best for my quest. "Yellow," Sally said. "It's the only choice." J. D. and I put our heads together, and pored over paint charts. After much deliberation we settled on two shades: a sunny yellow with one rich, buttery gold accent wall in the living room, the same deep color for the entire kitchen. I watched as J. D. began the transformation, my eyes as large as saucers, my heart in my mouth. It was going to be gorgeous!

When paintings, tapestries and furniture were restored to their original places, everything burst into life against the bright background. Sheers at the sliding glass doors were discarded to let nature be the star.

With an unobstructed view of the lake, it was like living on a house-boat—almost perfect. Yet, standing in my kitchen and looking toward the lake, something was missing. Eventually, there was a revelation. Not a painting, not an artifact, but lettering! My artist friend, Eliza Holliday, was called in for a consultation. I showed Eliza a French quotation by Chateaubriand, saved for some future purpose. Now I knew for what purpose. Eliza went to work on preliminary drawings. Before long, *"La poésie s'est le chant intérieur"* in navy blue script graced the space over the glass doors. Eliza's beautiful lettering, "Poetry is the song inside," and sunflower colors, interior and exterior, made my house sing. Paintbrush and stylus: the magic wands.

• • •

COMPANIONSHIP. I missed it—the male kind. Friends wondered why I didn't play the Russian roulette of internet dating games. My divorced hairdresser had met someone that way, and she said to me, "Why not? Go online and see what's out there. You don't have to do anything unless you find someone you'd like to know." I didn't check it out immediately, but eventually curiousity got the best of this cat. Talking it over with my therapist, we soon had a running joke about meeting "Mr. October." That was because a psychic told me at some point in my future; I would meet a younger man. "One who would be involved in something you are involved in," she predicted. To me, that meant writing, and writing meant the Amelia Book Island Festival which took place each October. Hence, "Mr. October".

Time passed. Mr. October did not ride up on his white charger, motorcycle or vintage Cadillac. I gave up. One day while sitting at my computer, I scrolled through the maze of faces on a dating website. Confections of men in a cyberspace shop appeared in the candy box of my computer screen. It was mindless fun. After that there were some contacts, a date or two, but hardly anything serious. It felt like high school again. Whipped cream, no substance.

But then to my surprise, I actually did find someone who interested me, at least on the monitor, but it had nothing whatsoever to do with October. After spirited e-mail and telephone conversations, exchanging photos and affidavits, we planned a face-to-face meeting. He flew into Jacksonville International Airport from his home in Carolina Beach, North Carolina, and I met him at the gate. We stopped for lunch after taking the scenic drive to the island, and I deposited him at his motel and went home to change. I had planned a series of entertainments: an art opening, dinners out, a tour of the island, a sightseeing trip to St. Augustine, Mass at my church. My friend Dickie Anderson opened her home for a cocktail hour, and invited others from our circle. It seemed a nice beginning. Then, I drove him back to the airport to catch a plane back to North Carolina.

Sometime after the visit, I e-mailed him. "Where do we go from here," I asked, and in return: an evasive reply. He was working on a book. Distance was not our friend. Hmmm. (?) I pressed for a more precise answer, and got more than I wanted. "We are not a match," he said. I was crushed—not his cuppa Cappuccino, not even his half-decaf. I turned to the indignation of friends for solace, and to meditation (ever my companion) to help me restore a punctured self-esteem. It took me weeks to quit brooding; even knowing this man had a complete right to say "No." Writers, by necessity, are obsessive, and I was no exception to the rule.

After a while, I recovered my balance. I reached into my meditation bag of tricks kept in the privacy of my bedroom, and fashioned a workable little visualization. On a giant blackboard, I placed the face of my nemesis; arch, cool, self-contained, Ivy League scholar, old East Coast elitist. No, no pins or matches; nothing dangerous—just a little white magic of the imagination. I stepped up to the blackboard in my ruby slippers with an eraser, and erased his face, saying the magic words (not "There's no place like Home,") but Cancel Cancel Cancel, the three C's, and making a giant X with my hands. Did my subject get the message? Probably not, but when I told my therapist, Dr. Ross, about it, he laughed, and then chided me for allowing myself to become so quickly invested. "I'm a rusty flirt," I offered, "do better next time!" "Get a bigger eraser," Dr. R. advised. Some time after this (after applying that bigger eraser) I got a letter from my friend from high school days, Elise Braun, "I hope you are not wasting any more of your precious energy on that unfortunate man," she wrote. Wow! What are friends and blackboards for?

In lines from the television play, *Elizabeth I*, the queen (played by Helen Mirren) says to her servants after she breaks down in front of them over the betrayal of the Earl of Essex, "One word of this, and you die!" Then, drying her eyes, chin up, her Highness says, and I couldn't have put it better, "Well—there's work to be done..."

• • •

EVERYTHING CHANGES for good or for ill. All we knew and loved: family, friends and place move out of our lives. The only thing you can be certain of is that there is no certainty. The poet Rilke wrote, "For there is no place that does not see you. You must change your life." Well, I have changed my life, and so has my hometown. The little island I grew up on in the 1940s is no longer recognizable in the grandiose and fashionable Amelia Island of today with its influx of the rich and privileged. I sent Elise Braun, who lives in Vermont, some articles from our local newspaper on the subject of changing times in our once small town. It prompted this response from Elise:

"The Fernandina News-Leader *was my first real job (I wasn't much of a babysitter) and my first opportunity to make enough money to buy some of my own clothes at Lynn's. Walking up and down the streets of the 'historic district' was hot work, gathering personals for the society page, and my favorite place in the newspaper office was the old cistern out back where the toilet was. It was always five or six degrees cooler in there, and a place to sit down. If I wax nostalgic it is to introduce a particular pain with which I live. You don't know how important and what a life-saver Fernandina was to me in those years and I certainly couldn't have explained it, then. If I could summarize what feeling living there gave me, it would be overwhelming relief. Relief from rigid Connecticut class-consciousness and the importance of place that flavored everything. In suburban Riverside of my first ten years, the street you lived on was the marker, and moving, within the town, indicated up or down. Because of the Depression, I'm sure half the people rented up or down, as we did, the nouveau pauvre who came from money—another confusion because my relatives were all so wealthy, Ivy-league, prep school, Martha's Vineyard.*

In New Haven, private schools, paid for through Mother's connections, was an embarrassment because I wasn't that good a student compared to the chil-

dren of Yale faculty, authors, artists, etc., but, when I survived, I surprised
Mother and Daddy by refusing to go on to the private high school affiliated
with the elementary school and went to the city high school—4,000 students,
split sessions, a tough place but anything to get away from four more years as a
fringe person in private school. Here, I was just a number and that was OK.

Then, when we moved to Fernandina, I never had to deal with all that
again—Nobody cared. We were just folks, together—the only marker, shame-
fully, was race, pretty much. Still, I finally found people who let me feel at
home with them." [Oh, yes. The Starhawks quote, "We are all longing to go
home to some place we have never been... Somewhere there are people to
whom we can speak with passion without having the words catch in our
throats..."] "And really, when I moved to Stowe, it was the same. I came with
a lot of newcomers who had very little money, minimal job prospects, but willing to do anything just so we could live here. Before Susan [her daughter]
entered kindergarten, I clerked in a store part-time and took in skiers. Half my
friends were native Vermonters and the rest, new, like us. And Susan had a
good childhood here, but even before she graduated from high school, the new
money was coming in and it has been a rolling tide ever since.

"All of this is by way of saying I am sickened by what has happened to the
two communities I have loved so much and which have been so good to me
and for me. Money, gentrification, upscale, showplaces. Connecticut Redux. I
seem to have had to get rid of all that. Hope you don't mind."

•

No, I didn't mind. My friend, Elise, spoke for me as well as for herself. The special joy of growing up in the isolated little fishing
village/mill town of Fernandina, where for most of us, nothing was terribly significant beyond the drawbridge, was a diminishing memory. But,
what a privileged childhood I had, and what special formative years
were mine with peers who were more family than friends in that first-
class, two-story school building on Atlantic Avenue which housed us all
from grade one to grade twelve inside its protective yellow brick walls. It
was a scholastic journey that predictably began with Mrs. Graham
downstairs in first grade, and when we reached exalted senior-class status, Mrs. Bennett's homeroom on the second floor was our destination

in Public School No. 1, Fernandina (lose the Beach) Florida. There were no drugs, alcohol, or kinky sex, at least none that I knew of. Cigarettes, lots of necking in the back seats of cars (if you were a good kisser, the news got around), slumber parties at the beach which boys were sure to crash—these were the occupations of choice when we all had pretty bodies and never-ending summer. Whatever else was happening in our lives, Old Fernandina High was the constant. Our classmates, our peer groups were our siblings. Teachers were stand-in parents when those at home let us down. It was a kinder, gentler world than the one we know today. Our lives were bounded by river, sea, and drawbridge, safe from the strange, big world Out There.

• • •

NAWLEENS! My friend, Julia, has been living there for two years now. She took early retirement from her big corporate job in Atlanta and realized her dream of a new life in the French Quarter. She bought two apartments on Ursulines Avenue and had been busily renovating and improving them ever since. A whirlwind of energy is my friend, Julia. She installed a little European-style elevator to take you to the second and third floors. Shades of those cramped and claustrophobic lifts in Paris with barely enough room to accommodate two persons! Along with her apartments, Julia got proximity to the Mississippi River, and the music of nearby passing trains. Perhaps the music of trains is negotiable to some people, but to me those organ chords as trains approach a crossing are the sound of America, of homefolks, of the one-time comfort and safety of small towns and rural villages. People living in harmony. People living in peace. Train time.

I made my very first visit to NOLA in May, 2005. At first I was a bit put off by the *Vieux Carré*. I thought it noisy, overrun by crowds of sightseers and tourists with music blasting everywhere, live and canned, from shops and restaurants, on street corners and even in the middle of streets at impromptu bandstands. It seemed dirty in the way Manhattan can be dirty: vagrants sleeping in doorways and sprawled on sidewalks, congestion, food, people hawking wares. I wondered what the attraction was, but it wasn't long before I was hooked. Like New York, New

Orleans had me by the throat next day. It felt almost a homecoming on those narrow, European-like streets. I felt comfortable among the mix of French Quarter dwellers: part affluent newcomers, part eccentric natives with their colorful clothes, air of entitlement and special command that comes from inhabiting a city so famous and old. Yes, my kind of place. The mysteriousness of shuttered windows and locked doors, old brick façades, and the reds, golds, and cream colors reminded me of Old Nice in the South of France. It was the secrecy that nailed me: teasing glimpses of private courtyards and gardens beyond iron-gated doorways. My late husband used to say an emphatic *Non!*, to the idea of visiting New Orleans, and so we never went. He said that, for him, New Orleans was McFrance!

•

What did I do in New Orleans? Well, *bien sur,* beignets at the Café du Monde was the first order of the day one early morning while musicians with guitar and trumpet serenaded us over café au lait and those famous powdery doughnuts. A couple at the next table was busily videotaping each other, devouring their beignets. Proof of purchase! Noise was the name of the game. Crowds were a given. Not a table was empty in the café that day, or any day probably. The trays brimming with beignets and cups of steaming coffee came and went. People stood up and dusted off their clothes before departing. "Wear white," Julia had warned, "or everyone will know where you've been!"

As we walked along a promenade beside the river after breakfast, I noticed a plaque that said New Orleans in large letters: "First sighted as Indian portage to Lake Pontchartrain and the Gulf in 1699 by Bienville and Iberville. Founded by Iberville in 1718, named by him in honor of the Duke of Orleans, Regent of France, called the Crescent City because of location in bend of Mississippi." My friends and I had thought to take a river cruise later than morning, bypassing the tourist steamboats with their garrulous calliope music and queues of people waiting to board. When we noticed the ferry on its way back across the river toward us, that seemed a better idea. While steamboats are patently glamorous, ferries have their own mystique, and it was a free ride (almost). We could say with pride we had actually been on the Mississippi. On the other side of the river, Westside it is called, we had lunch under an umbrella outside at the Dry Dock Café and Bar. Of course, it was not such a Dry Dock after the advent of Hurricane Katrina. When news came of that disastrous storm, I could not help but feel how lucky I was to have made it to New Orleans while it was still the New Orleans of lore. NOLA (not me, but abbreviation for New Orleans, Louisiana) and its French Quarter did not disappoint this particular namesake before catastrophe hit. Before Katrina, the party was forever in Nawleens.

• • •

BALLROOM DANCING. Good neighbors down the street from my house invited me to their house for dinner to meet a gentleman who was looking for a dancing partner—someone with whom to take lessons and go out for practice. Did I like to dance? Yes, I said, but it's been a while. Little did my neighbors know that in my youth, I dreamed of being a professional dancer. In high school in my little town, dancing was big. We had little recreation for teenagers, so everyone went out dancing at Moore's on the beach. Not to tango, samba, or foxtrot, just plain old jitterbug and slow dance: a fella holding you while you twirl around the floor. These days with the popularity of competition ballroom dancing, people swarm to these formal affairs. Dance competitions come complete with cash bars and banquet dinners. Women dance in sparkly, bright-colored evening dresses wearing the world's haughtiest expressions, heads tilted in proper posture, hands placed just so; it is alarming! I do not think there are sock hops in the school gymnasium anymore where even girls would dance with girls and no one thought a thing about it. I remember dancing with my girlfriend, Dolores Taylor. How dear she was, and what a good dancer. Did I think about sexuality? No, No, Nanette, er… Dolores.

I once wrote a piece having to do with a guy I was dating in high school. We were good together on the dance floor. "A born dancer." What I dreamed to be. In my little town in the 1940s no one thought about the possibility of becoming a dancer on a real stage. This was a fishing village and a mill town. There were secretaries and shop girls.

The artists came later, after the fact, discovering Amelia the way artists always find the unique and beautiful. Still, I dreamed of dancing. I performed my choreography to 78 swing records at parties for anyone who would watch, and the boys on the dance floor under the blue lights at Moore's whispered, 'Gee, you're a good dancer,' as we swirled to Artie Shaw and Tommy Dorsey. My special partner bent me backwards to the floor and said in awe, 'you know what I'm going to do before I do it! We could be professionals. We could be a team.' Oh yes. Fred and Ginger, LIVE!"

I wrote to Elise in Vermont about my experience of meeting the gentleman looking for a dance partner. She and I agreed about the importance of dancing in our high school days, those wonderful sock hops on Friday night in the gym at FHS, and how for so long, this diversion fell into disarray. She wrote me this in response: "I don't think there is anything better than dancing with a partner. In this post-feminist world no wonder it isn't done. A woman must surrender and follow a man's lead. That's the only way it will work, so the parties are equal—no one has an advantage or gets ahead. Better than most relationships and better than a lot of sex." Elise could always be counted on to hit the nail on the head, or the shoe with a sock.

• • •

ELIZABETH, my granddaughter, who lives in Atlanta, is nine years old. She is Capricorn, born the first day of January, one of several in our family born on a first day of the month. My birthday follows hers on January 6. She arrived on the island with her family, my son Anthony and his wife, Sally, for a week at their condo at Summer Beach. On a Saturday morning, I drove out to pick her up to spend some time with me while her parents attended a meeting. She buckled herself in the front seat of my car, a treat, because she is supposed to sit only in the back. It was nine in the morning. No stores were open for browsing downtown, so we stopped at The Dollar Tree which opened early. I told Elizabeth she had five dollars to spend. She did her shopping carefully. Her purchases, among others were a plush gray dolphin, a Barbie-type doll, and a ribbon that said "Number One." That means her!

At a nearby drugstore where I went to pick up a prescription, Elizabeth conned me into buying her a box of Coco Pops. Only later did she reveal that Coco Pops were not allowed at her house. She knows how to work Her Nola. "Her Nola," she calls me, and when she was smaller and had not found the L in my name, it was Her Noa. Occasionally we talk about alternate names for me that are more descriptive of my relationship to her. I offer "Great-Nola," but she turns it into Nola the Great. I ask her, if she can be a Granddaughter, why can't I be her GREATNola?

Elizabeth loves a shopping trip with me when she comes to the Island, or maybe it's that Elizabeth just loves shopping. She wants to go to the ice cream store first, not for ice cream, but for a candy stick (preferably colored purple) and a sample of chocolate fudge (free). Then, we begin our requisite tour of all the souvenir stores on Centre Street. This particular time, Elizabeth had a quest. She had been in a store, she said, where she saw a little box with purple flowers that had a bear in it. She wanted that box and that bear. I was amazed at the salespeople in the stores we entered, especially the women, how attentive and patient they were in helping a little girl. In the last store on our itinerary, someone remembered such a box as Elizabeth described. A search, however, among the shelves of merchandise turned up no box with a bear in it. In the process, Elizabeth picked up two items: a pink plush puppy and a princess doll. Elizabeth asked the price of each and deliberated about her choice. After some thought, and somewhat to my surprise, she chose the least expensive of the two, and we drove away with a pink puppy she dubbed Cherry Garcia.

Elizabeth wanted a bed for Cherry Garcia. When we got to my house, we went into my closet where there was an array of empty shoe boxes. She chose a bright pink box for Cherry's bed. Some flowered material became a sheet, made from a bag with cords that pulled to close it. "Cut the strings off, Nola," ordered Elizabeth, and then she made sure all the tags were removed from her purchases. Maybe it's a Capricorn thing, I thought. Tags and stickers must come off immediately in my house, especially ties on bread wrappers. Horrors! My cousin, Ada Geer, confessed to the same dislike for bread ties. Guess what? She's a Capricorn. As to the matter of pesky bar codes and those revolting stickers on fruit—Off with their heads! Then, I had a revelation. Elizabeth is an only child, and to see her interact with her toys and dolls is to see a little mama tending her children, a big sister caring for siblings. In Elizabeth's world, Cherry Garcia was reality, a real small friend, and there had to be no tags to spoil the illusion.

• • •

CONSULTING PSYCHICS? Yes, from time to time. I do not believe that science can explain all natural occurrences through cause and effect. There is a higher self, a spiritual world into which people with acute intuitive ability can tap to bring us guidance and information useful for moving forward on the earth plane. A psychic I met with in Miami when I lived there was Hans Christian King, an incredibly talented direct-voice medium who toured the world with his inspirational lecture series. We came together in 1995 during the time of my husband's first serious medical problems. Hans helped me in many ways, and he told me one particularly interesting thing. He asked me if I had lost a child. I said, Yes, there was a first pregnancy, which did not take. Then he told me, "There is a child in the spirit world that belongs to you: a little girl who goes by the name, an unusual name, a name you don't hear much, of Charlotte."

If you believe in ongoing life after physical death, regardless of how you personally conceive it, I do validate that. And, furthermore, I hold the view that those we have lost return in another guise. I know that contradicts the teaching of the church to which I belong. Probably a good scolding would be in order, or in the old days, I would be considered a heretic. Be that as it may, sometimes I have considered that my granddaughter, Elizabeth, might be Charlotte, returned to me. Here is a story Elizabeth wrote when she visited me for a weekend, all by herself. Her parents put her on a plane in Atlanta to fly alone to Amelia Island for the very first time. We did a lot of things during Elizabeth's visit; such as, taking a trolley ride tour (on wheels) of the island; having dinner out at an Italian restaurant, and on a Saturday afternoon, she and I sat in my office while I was working on the computer. She dictated the following story to me. I include it here because of the name Elizabeth chose for the companion in her story. So, in her own words, here is:

My Pony Adventure

Once upon a time there was this girl named Elizabeth and her friend Charlotte. They had ten horses, ten ponies, and a cow, and they had five puppies. They had to do all the housework themselves because they had so many animals on their farm.

They had a party, so they had to get ready for the party. They had to round up all the horses, the ponies, the cow, and puppies, and put them all in the den, except some in the stable. The puppies slept in the den. Then, they had the party and a pony got loose. The other ponies ran off to find her. A horse got loose and all the others ran to find her. They found the ponies and the horses. They were all gathered around to see that just the horse and the pony wanted to go live with another person because they loved her so much. Their family called up and said, you guys have to come and live with us in Fernandina Beach in Florida.

They had to sell the horses and ponies and the cow so they could buy a crate for the puppies. By selling the other animals, they earned $1,000. So they bought the crates, and had a little to spare. They bought a pony named Victoria. But, how could they get her on the plane, they wondered? So, they set her free, and she, Charlotte, Elizabeth, the rest of the ponies, horses and puppies lived happily ever after. When they got to Fernandina Beach, their Dad bought them each a horse. They moved to Atlanta, Georgia, and they kept their horse at Chastain Horse Park.

The End

Later, in Atlanta on one of my visits with Elizabeth and her parents, my daughter-in-law, Sally, shared Elizabeth's current progress report from her third grade teacher, Mrs. Kraft, at St. Martin's Episcopal School. Mrs. Kraft commented, "Elizabeth loves to write creatively. I enjoyed her description of her Halloween costume. She even used similes in the description. Elizabeth understands that paragraphs begin with a topic sentence followed by several detail sentences. Elizabeth loves to read anything in print to me." There was more in the report, of course, but I was interested in what pertained to my granddaughter's writing prowess. I have also been a witness to her pleasure in reading aloud. Elizabeth and I drove to St. Augustine one afternoon to attend a party at the home of my friend, Wendy Philcox. The drive from Amelia Island to St. Augustine takes a full hour and a half. Elizabeth, strapped in her seat belt in the back seat of my car, read to me entire chapters from a book, all the way to the front door of Wendy's house.

• • •

ANIMALS ARE STAND-INS FOR CHILDREN (or grandchildren) in
the dream state. Often in my dreams, I cuddle a cat that just happens to
have the gift of speech, or else, dogs figure in scenarios as intimate companions. And, for many people, they are exactly that in the real world—
not to imply that dreams are not real. They are. But, before I had a
grand-girl, I had a grand-cat: a beautiful lilac point Siamese named
Charlie Chan, raised from infancy, who became my child as genuinely as
my two sons. My heart still contracts, remembering the day I had to give
C. Chan away because I could no longer keep him. I put my confused
and frightened cat into the arms of the woman who would become his
new mother, and it was as if I had given up one of my precious sons.

Now, I have Kirby. Kirby is a dog. Kirby is the Perez's dog in Atlanta,
and he is one of the dogs I have loved in my life. He's a Portuguese water
dog, an important member of our family, and very secure in his water dog-
ness. To give you a sense of the priorities, my son Anthony has on his e-
mail address "Kirby is my dog, and Elizabeth is my girl." First things first.

I don't see Kirby that often, but he never forgets me. When I pull up
in the driveway in Atlanta, he rushes out of the house full throttle, bark-
ing his head off, but as soon as I speak to him, "It's me, dummy!" his
body language changes from vigilante to welcome home Nola.
I love how he likes to tuck his head between my knees and stands there
as long as I will rub his ears and nuzzle his fuzzy black head. Anthony
says, "My dog is in love with my mother." Once I was playing with
Elizabeth on her parents' big bed, lying on my back. Kirby jumped up on
the bed, hovered over me with delight as if to say, "Top of the world, Ma!
Top of the world!" He and James Cagney. Delusions of grandeur.

Kirby played more than a cameo in a reading in St. Augustine with
my spiritual advisor, Carrie, a psychic with the sweet face of an angel.
Carrie said to me, " I see this big black dog coming out from a swim, and
he is shaking water all over you." I said, "That would be Kirby, my son's
water dog." Carrie went on to say, "You and this dog have been together
before, and when you and he go home on the other side, you will see
him, and you will tell him you love him, but you did not appreciate his
shaking water on you."

The really funny thing is that when I left the room where Carrie held her readings, she shut the door behind me for a meditation of her own. Shortly thereafter, the door opened and Carrie appeared, shooing something out in front of her. "Get this dog out of here," says Carrie, "because he refuses to leave."

Another animal I fell in love with when he was only a small puppy was a cairn terrier named Jackson, newly acquired into the household of my next-door neighbor, John Givens. Sometimes forgetting this Toto clone's name (forgetting being common in my 70+ age group, *malheureusement*) I had to search my archives for the famous square in New Orleans to come up with Jackson. It's my hope these tricks will continue to work, walking down the road toward yet another age milestone. Jackson is a miniature Kirby, black and curly haired, and an incorrigible wiggle worm. When he sees me, his whole body squirms with pleasure. Was anyone—man, woman, or child—ever greeted with such affirmation for simply being?

My friend Wendy Philcox has a gorgeous golden retriever named Mia whose glossy red gold coat precisely matches her mistresses' red gold traffic-stopping mane. I love Mia for her beauty, and for greeting me with affection ever since I spent a night on Wendy's couch in St. Augustine. Waking often during the night, what a comfort it was that Mia chose to sleep curled up on the floor beside me. Each time I woke, and stirred, Mia would lift her head in the dark and the silence for me to stroke her head, as if everything, just everything was quite all right. Love between the species! Thank you, friends and family for sharing the dogs: all 321 bones and 42 permanent teeth of them. May they go far beyond their allotted years.

• • •

WHAT EVERY HAUSFRAU needs to know about cleaning her gargoyle. Mine came from Chartres Cathedral, purchased on one of my visits to that charming little French town and its cathedral, the main attraction on a cold winter day in February some years ago. After a long drive from Paris where my late husband and I were living, there was a comforting lunch by a warm fire and a glass of red wine of the region in one of the quaint restaurants surrounding the cathedral. "Tastes like strawberries," I told my husband and Jeannot, his nephew who was always interested in my pronouncements about the taste of the wine he ordered. Jeannot was visiting us with his wife, Nicole, on a very first trip to Paris. Jeannot and Nicole were from Marseille, and by direct choice had never before set foot in the City of Light. "The only thing wrong with Paris," Jeannot declared, "is there are too many Parisians there."

After lunch, warmed by wine and good food, we strolled the streets of Chartres with our coat collars pulled up around our necks. We braved the winter chill to examine the souvenir and gift shops which ringed the cathedral. Jeannot gifted me with a head of Bacchus which was also a shelf on which to place some small treasure. I fell in love with a stone gargoyle, and when I returned to our apartment in Paris, I hung it over the entrance doors where, presumably, he kept the devil at bay even better than a bouquet of garlic.

Years later when I returned to my island home of Fernandina, the gargoyle was hung over the sliding glass doors which opened to a porch beside the lake. On one of my habitual cleaning frenzies, good Capricorn I am, I noticed the gargoyle was beginning to blacken from the elements, much as gargoyles ornamenting churches in Paris become sooty from street soil. I dragged a chair to the glass doors, and Mr. Gargoyle, not London Bridge, came falling down and into a pan of water in my sink with a liberal dose of Arm & Hammer Super Washing Soda. None of those newfangled cleaning aids for me! Just my grandmother's familiar yellow and red box, "Pure & Natural Since 1874, 100% Fragrance & Phosphate Free." That arm has been pumping iron for ages! And after a half-hour immersion in the solution and much scrubbing on my part with an old toothbrush (didn't your Mom tell you to wash behind your ears, Mr. G?) he came clean, even if he didn't answer my question. Just his usual sullen stare, both hands clasped to his stony cheeks in a menacing attitude that freaked out my sister-in-law Sylvia when she came for a visit in Paris. "Pretend he's just got a toothache," I advised Sylvia who was averting her eyes and giving Mr. G. a wide berth every time she passed by the doors. I have to admit, he was an intimidating presence. After all, he had to keep the guy with the pitchfork away.

So after his beauty bath and the gargoyle was reinstated to his position on my porch, I decided to take Bacchus down from the wall in my kitchen for a good scrub, lest he be jealous of my attention to the gargoyle. I didn't want him to refuse to bless the wine harvest that year. Bacchus got his renovation, as well, I washed behind his ears, and he promised an exceptional Beaujolais Nouveau for at least several Novembers to come.

• • •

BONES! They are supposed to keep moving, but they continued to betray me. I didn't dream to cause myself more unwelcome trouble in the bones on a day I went with my friend, Iris Ward, to the ordination of a priest in my parish, St. Michael's Catholic Church, Fernandina. I had never seen such a ceremony, and I was excited at the prospect of pomp and ceremony, plus a visitation from our bishop who would preside over the proceedings. The priest to be ordained was a former Episcopal priest, and all his family filled the front pews of the church. Iris liked to sit upstairs on the balcony of the church, and picked a spot behind the balcony rail where it happened there were no kneelers. The ceremony was interesting and colorful, but I was on my knees on the floor for a very long time.

I was stiff when I started to leave the church, but had no idea what had happened to me during my devotions. First thing I noticed was pain in the right knee, the operated leg, of course. It couldn't have been the "good" leg. The pain got worse and worse, and finally got so intense, it sent me back to Dr. Tandron at Jacksonville Orthopedic Institute for a consultation. Well, my piety cost me, not an arm but surely a leg. X-rays showed two tears in the cartilage of the knee, and fluid retention in the Baker's cyst. Exercises Dr. Tandron recommended and icing the knee did not solve the problem. So, it was back to the drawing table, or an operating table at Baptist Medical Center for a little meeting with a radiologist who drained the cyst, and put in injections of cortisone and a long lasting anesthetic. This helped some, but not enough, so it was back to Dr. Tandron for three consecutive injections of a lubricant on three consecutive Tuesdays. "WD40 for the knee," said Dr. T. What the lubricant consisted of was actually the cockscomb, liquefied obviously, of a rooster. Jeez, back to nature in the medical profession! Now, I *know* I go to bed with the chickens, but this was ridiculous. I did not, however, crow at sunrise.

• • •

BIRD PEOPLE. I was one of those. Next to gentle, doe-eyed cows, nestling on the ground with their front legs prettily tucked under them like a contented cat; wild rabbits with soft, brown fur, and ducks of any size and color (especially those with iridescent green necks) birds are the Best! At the back of my house close to the deep lake, there were a couple of fine pine trees, a small enclave of marsh myrtles, and a fig tree that grew taller and more lush each spring since my husband planted it in the summer of 2001. The birds loved the trees that I fell heir to, and they entertained me endlessly with their darting flights and birdsong concerts.

How sad I was to find a common yellowthroat (anything but common with its brightly-colored breast, white head, and black Mardi Gras mask) dead in my driveway. I picked it up carefully, and held it cupped in my hands. It was still warm. Poor beautiful thing—no trash can for this baby! A box from my in-house collection lined with white tissue was the yellowthroat's coffin. I buried the box beneath my husband's fig tree, and over the mound I placed a cross of twigs. Who knows, indeed, how God calms yellowthroats when they die, or any of us living things, for that matter. As my doctor friend in St. Augustine, Walter Frady, once said, "We are only here for a short time." We want to believe our lives are of consequence, worth at least as much as the butterfly in the bottlebrush, the lark in the lantana, the yellowthroat in my driveway—precious in the sight of Higher Power, whatever you envision that to be.

• • •

"…and here am I,
not even born, and already a conservationist,
with nothing to assist me but the last
and most fabulous of beasts—language, language—
which knows, as I do, that it's too late
to record the loss of these things, but does so anyway,
and anxiously, in case it shares their fate."

—EAVAN BOLAND, FROM HER POEM,
"AN ELEGY FOR MY MOTHER IN WHICH SHE SCARCELY APPEARS"

Chapter Six

SOME QUESTIONS I MUST ASK

Was it dark of the moon
in your backyard that night. Or
was there light? Did she follow you
in trust, faltering a little
at the porch steps, holding on, holding on
to the arms that would never
let her go? You

were the easy part, second to leave
Captain Courageous, pistol in hand. Ahab,
waving adieu from the whale's back,
swelling the company of saints
by two, departing hand in hand, one always
as you were, and for eternity.
But what I want to ask

is not about the dark. The dark
and I are bedmates. I want to ask
about the light, if it came quickly
enough. Are the mystics
right—does the spirit depart its
body through the head, and did your
soul mate wait for you?

NOLA'S MEN, my big brother George dubbed the new wallpaper on my computer which he installed for me. It was a photograph of my two brothers, Jim and George, and my late husband Andre. Just their larger-than-life faces as they stood together on the porch of the condo in St. Augustine where my husband and I lived for two years. My brothers looked directly into the camera at me, smiling, but an unsmiling Andre looked off into the distance as if seeing his destiny there. And so it was. That was the summer of 1999. Little did I know all three of my main men would be soon be gone. First, my younger brother, Jim, an Ob-Gyn physician in Winter Haven, Florida, succumbed to a memory disorder in February 2001. Andre died of heart failure in the ICU at Baptist Hospital, Jacksonville, in June 2002, and George, gone by his own hand in February 2006.

When my husband and I lived in Brussels for two years, 1997 to 1999, my brother Jim and wife, Mary Ellen, came for a brief visit. Jim had just been diagnosed with a memory disorder at Shands in Gainesville, Florida. "Consistent with a diagnosis of Alzheimer's," the report said after an invasive cranial biopsy was performed. Jim arrived in Brussels with the right side of his head shaved, but ready to travel about in Belgium and Holland, and see London town with his sister and his best friend/brother-in-law. It was a good visit, in spite of Jim's obvious lapses into confusion.

Most significant in that visit was an afternoon walk with my brother to the métro station a short distance from our apartment. Jim and Mary Ellen were leaving the next day to return to their home in Winter Haven, Florida. When Jim's wife said she could use some time to pack without distraction, it left some time alone with my brother. Jim and I set out to catch the train to Woluwe shopping center to do some errands. As we walked together on the sidewalk toward the train station, we talked about his diagnosis. Jim said he had known I would take it well because "his sister was cool." I remarked that his belief in my strength meant a lot to me, but didn't think of myself as particularly cool. As far as any imminent departure of his was concerned for wherever we go when we leave this life, it was possible for me to be struck by a car tomorrow—be first to go. "Who knows," I said. Who knows?

When we got to the train station, there was an escalator to descend below. Jim stood hesitantly at the top of the escalator for a time, unable to make himself take that first step forward. "What's the matter with me?" he said, in dismay, before moving away and walking down the stairs beside the escalator. Etched in my memory of that shopping trip is when we walked through the mall at Woluwe and arrived at the grocery store. I busied myself with my purchases. When I looked around to find my brother, I saw he was browsing in the wine department. I stood there for a while and watched him, absorbed and happy, completely engrossed in the wine bins, holding up a bottle to read the label, selecting something special to take back to our apartment. It was such a small thing, but somehow such a sweet vignette of the things that make us happy. This is just one of those seemingly insignificant moments that in retrospect become infinitely precious small snapshots of a life.

•

Jim and I were more than siblings. We were left without a mother in the wake of a bitter divorce when I was six and Jim was four years old. The court awarded the children to our father Nolan, something unheard of for the times. It was the 1930s, hard Depression days in America and in our divided family. Our mother Burney left Fernandina with our half-brother George, child of her first marriage, further disrupting what Jim and I knew of home and safety. From then on, as big sister, I took on the mothering of my baby brother.

Happily for all of us, Nolan was able to bring George back in the family to grow up with us, the way it was meant to be. While Jim and I lost a mother through divorce, George was left fatherless by a father who committed suicide when George was just a babe. Nolan was the only father George ever knew. Nolan loved George as if he had been his own. Such a convoluted family history! Jim, George, and I were Burney's children, all three as close as any kids could be. George may have been a half-brother, but he was a whole brother to Jim and me. And there was mothering on the way for us siblings. We never lacked for grand mothering and maternal care. Burney's mother remained in Fernandina until long after the divorce to be near her grandchildren. Eventually my father remarried, and brought home pretty, young Lucille Clendenon, a schoolteacher from another small town, Blountstown, Florida, to be our stepmother. Then there was the constant: the loving ministrations of our housekeeper, Johnnie Mae, who had always helped care for us. My brother Jim was fond of saying whenever Johnnie Mae's name came up in family conversations, "We had good raising." To this day when a black woman calls me Baby, I utterly dissolve.

Recently when putting together my "Traveling Bag" (what I called the briefcase of important papers for my sons in the event of my death) I came across the only letter Johnnie Mae ever wrote me, saved lo these many years. When I lived in Paris on the eve of the Desert Storm war, I sent her a book of my poetry, and in her own words, this was written from Baltimore where she was living:

Dear Nola,

I received the book and happy to hear from my little girl. Also, very proud of you. You made my heart very happy to know that you still think of me. I am still getting around not as well as I use to. I am 76 years now. Will be 77 the 26th of July. Was very happy for the pictures of you and your family. I will always cherish them. George gave me some also when I saw him. We had quite a visit together. I will always love and keep you kids in my heart. Your mother gave you and Jim to me when you were babies. She would always say you were mine and I loved you that way. I am sending you some pictures of my daughter and her family. Also me. Give my love to Andre. I pray that I can visit with you both in the near future if there isn't a war. I pray that it won't be but it look very dim. I have a cousin that is a nurse. She had to leave her young kids. I pray that your boys doesn't have to go. I am enjoying reading the book. Keep up the good works. I will always keep you in my prayers. Write to me sometime.

Love always,
Johnnie Mae

• • •

FEBRUARY 2001. Andre and I had come up to Fernandina from St. Augustine to celebrate our wedding anniversary. We were to have dinner at Le Clos, an island French restaurant my husband vowed served the best lamb shank he had ever eaten this side of "the continent." A room had been reserved in a hotel across the street from Le Clos. We were on our way to our hotel when we got a telephone call from Winter Haven from Jim's caregiver. Jim had recently been taken home from the care facility he was in, and was not doing well. Then came the phone call soon after, this one from Jim's wife, Mary Ellen, telling us Jim had just died. It was nearly four o'clock in the afternoon and I fled to St. Michael's Catholic Church for Mass. Coming up for communion, I fell impulsively into the arms of the priest, Father Bob Napier, and sobbed, "Father, my brother just died." I was so distraught, all protocol was forgotten. The Church was the only place I knew Jim could still be found; the only place there would be help. As I fled up the aisle from the altar, handkerchief to my face, conscious of curious eyes upon me, Father Bob called after me, "What is your brother's name?" "Jim," I said through strangled tears.

•

MEMORIES. They are the only things we can keep, and the only things we take with us. To be deprived of them and have any sense of the loss must be living hell. In the end my brother Jim still knew me. I would make the trip to Winter Haven, about a four hour drive from Fernandina, as often as I could while Jim was in a care facility. Andre and I sat with him on the couch in his little sitting room. Once, he fell asleep with his head on my shoulder. He forgot how to walk, and I would wheel him around the corridors in his wheel chair. One heart wrenching memory was a day Jim wanted me to take him away, but he had no money. He was in his wheelchair. This beautiful man respected in his community for the fine physician he had been, this man who accrued a lot of wealth, was reduced to asking an astonished fellow patient if he could borrow fifty dollars. I will never be able to make peace with an ignoble finish that stripped my beloved brother of his dignity.

Toward the last when Jim was bedridden, there was a sign over his bed that said, "Keep Dr. Baker's head elevated." He who had cared for so many patients had been consigned to complete helplessness and dependence on others. One visit, as I bent over the bed to speak to him, it was as if he was in a trance, and, with eyes closed, he said to no one in particular, "I won't be here very long." And, he was right. He understood his condition, and he accepted it with grace. He was a graceful, kind-hearted man. His lifelong quest was for an all-consuming, all-embracing love which he felt he never found, that Jesus-love in the person of a woman, which for him was equivalent to the Holy Grail.

It's the most surprising thing. As my brother progressed toward his death, he became younger and younger, and he, one of the handsomest men I have ever known, was more physically beautiful than ever. How could that be? I remember my friend, Neil Gray, whose wife, Betty, died at home from Parkinson's, said the same thing. "She just got younger and younger, " Neil marveled. Perhaps for the bedridden person who has made a decision to die, or those who know they near the end of their journey, stresses and preoccupations of life fall away from the body. Perhaps they go so deeply within, that the spirit has already taken over. It is just that my brother in the last days of his life looked beautiful, peaceful, and rested, and the last time I saw him, I walked into his room with Andre's sister, Sylvia. When Jim saw us, although he was no longer speaking, his eyes grew huge with surprise. He knew us! I was joyous, and that was the last gift my brother gave to the Big Sister who loved him.

• • •

ONE YEAR LATER, in the summer of 2002, my beloved Andre was gone. I instructed George, the last of Nola's Men, "You are not allowed to go anywhere!" Little did I know what was in store. George's own lifetime love, his wife Corinne, had developed Alzheimer's, and was failing. George lovingly cared for her at home, and he kept close with me as much as he could. I would either drive to Jacksonville where he and Corinne lived (an hour drive to Riverside from my house in Fernandina) to go out for dinner, or he would drive to the island. Our favorite spot for lunch was Barbara Jean's on the marsh for crab cakes. George would have his one martini on the rocks with three olives, feed one vodka-flavored olive to Corinne (who always made a face) and I would have my one glass of Chardonnay. Then we would have our lunch, and help

Corinne to manage hers. George never lost patience with Corinne, even when she would mistake her napkin for food. He was always kind and loving, and of all the time we shared, I think this was the closest period of our lives together. After lunch, he would pull his big Cadillac into my driveway at Marsh Lakes, and help Corinne into the house.

Often, I had issues with my computer that he helped me with. He was interested in my writing, solved all those computer glitches I couldn't figure out, and put text into large print for aging eyes. George made sure I was never alone on holidays, and each Thanksgiving there would be a phone call to tell me I was invited to his daughter Jackie's house in Gainesville. Or, Easter, or Mother's Day, or whatever the special occasion, there was always an invitation to join the family celebration. I felt very nurtured and loved by my big brother George, but, finally, there came a time when Corinne was simply not able to move about comfortably. She was safe and happy only in her own home, in her own space, and my brother and his wife could no longer come over for crab cakes and martinis at Barbara Jean's.

• • •

GEORGE LESTER DERRICK, my big brother, was seven years older than me. When Nolan married Burney Derrick, he got a big bonus. He got Burney's son George, way before Jim and I arrived. George's father, in despair over his failed marriage to Burney, and the death of a subsequent young girlfriend from complications of appendicitis, committed suicide. When the girlfriend died in the hospital, George's father drove his car into the woods and shot himself. There is just so much loss a guy can take. My brother talked very little about the death of his dad.

George used to tell me he went out on Burney and Nolan's dates, or else he would pitch a big fit. After Burney and Nolan married and Jim and I arrived, George said he became the built-in babysitter. Not only that, he declared, "Nola, I used to change your diapers." Now, that was above and beyond the call of duty for any big brother, I would say! George, at 83 years old, had been in fairly good health except for the tuberculosis he contracted during his tour of duty with the Navy in North Africa during WWII. Later in his life, he had open-heart surgery, and other vascular problems. Decent health for George, as for Andre and Jim, was on the way out of the door. Little did we know what would transpire to interrupt our close relationship from 2002 to 2006, a happy time for brother and sister, in spite of Corinne's advancing memory disorder.

• • •

ROMEO AND JULIET. A great love story. That was my brother George and his wife. Their daughter, Peggy, in South Carolina wrote me this when her father was patiently caring for Corinne at home during their last days: "There must have been something in the Fernandina water for such enduring love to develop like Dad and Mom's, and yours and Uncle Andre's." Well, I don't know if it was the water. Sulfur water on the island in those days was pretty distasteful, or, wait a minute—maybe it *was* the sulfur!

George and Corinne fell in love as students in Fernandina High School. George tells how he was going down Centre Street with some buddies one day when he spotted this girl, walking on the sidewalk. "Wow!" he said, "Who is that?" Well, of course it was pretty, petite Corinne Hubbell dressed in her 1940s white slacks and white shirt, looking much like Katherine Hepburn in a vintage movie. George was no Spencer Tracy, but he lost his heart on the spot. He lost it for more than 60 years because they were married in the Presbyterian Church in Fernandina on November 8, 1944. George joined the Navy in 1941 (to avoid the Army draft, he said) and served during World War II until 1946. He wore his Navy blues to his wedding. In the only old snapshot I had ever seen of the wedding couple as they exited the church, Corinne had on a dark suit. Hmm, just like her future sister-in-law, Nola, who wouldn't have a white dress and a veil at her own wedding, and, furthermore, refused to pick out silver or china at the local jewelry store. What I liked was the store's Russell Wright stoneware, a table service that is now quite valuable. Some years back, I saw some pieces of this stoneware displayed in a glass case at the High Museum of Art in Atlanta. I liked being ahead of my time! Corinne entered the right family! We had traditions, but they were our own inventions.

In my case, I was only 19 years old when I married, and considered myself not bound to any conventions. I walked to a different drummer, or so I thought, and I was determined to be as different as I could. The truth of the matter was I didn't have a clue about what I was getting into. Corinne, on the other hand, was marrying her serviceman who was home on leave, and marrying him in a hurry. No time for satin and lace. America was still in crisis.

George's daughters were small when Andre and I were married. We lived away from them for so long, they scarcely remembered how their uncle looked as a young man. Peggy mentioned to me the family watched old home movies not long before her parents died. She emailed me these remarks: "Mom, Dad and I watched them all [the movies] last summer I think it was. I said, 'Holy Moly, is that Uncle Andre?' They said 'Yeah.' I said, 'Wow, he was drop dead gorgeous handsome!' And, that he was! I lost my heart for fifty-two years because of it.

George and Corinne had two beautiful young daughters. The only girls in our family. All the rest of us produced boys: two for me, four for Jim, and two for Andre's sister, Sylvia. No mixed kids in our family until the grandchildren came along, and helped us out with apples and oranges. It was a good life for my brother, George, and his wife, They lived in a modest little house on Wolfe Street in Jacksonville, the house they lived in all their lives, and the house in which, together, they spent their final hours.

•

Corinne's illness progressed to the point where George could do nothing else but care for her twenty-four hours a day. He would have it no other way, but problems became acute when his own health began to decline. He was in the hospital and doctor's offices more and more, and he could not leave her alone. He would not consider a care facility for Corinne. He told the family he would take care of her until he couldn't anymore. Only then would he talk about another solution. What happened next was that both George and Corinne were in the hospital at the same time. Corinne was released before George, and it was arranged for her to go temporarily to St. Catherine Labore home in the vicinity of St. Vincent's Hospital. As soon as George was able, he took Corinne home back to

Wolfe Street. He did not like the way she was being treated.

For a brief time after that, things were manageable. Then the news came that George had developed severe stomach pain that could not be relieved, and he was unable to eat. It became so intense, he admitted himself to the hospital for diagnostic tests, placing Corinne temporarily in a small, homelike place he had found. He felt she was comfortable there. I went to the hospital to be with George in his room while he had his tests. We spent this time just sitting together and talking, my chair pulled up to his bedside. George was continually anxious about what would happen to Corinne if something happened to him. A time or two, he talked about a plan he had. When the time came he could no longer look after Corinne, he would shoot Corinne, and then himself.

Once he broke down and cried while telling me this, saying "I know I can shoot myself—I don't know if I can shoot her." I never responded to George with any shock or reprimand. I knew I was not the only one to whom he expressed this. I simply listened, and asked him to let me know if he was going to do such a thing. We spoke about the suicide energy in our family: his father, our first cousin Harry Ryder's father, our mother Burney's numerous failed attempts. I joked that if following the family pattern for self-destruction, I would go into the garage,
start my car, set a lawn chair close to the exhaust, uncork a bottle of champagne and go find Andre. He laughed about it, knowing my passion for the effervescent grape.

•

I was in the hospital room with George when he got the results of his tests from his doctor. The diagnosis was a terminal vascular disease, and there was nothing that could be done. He could operate if George insisted, the doctor said, but he didn't recommend it. He doubted George would make it through surgery. It was so hard to know what to say. This was not the news anyone wanted to hear. George was discharged from the hospital the next morning, and went home to set up Hospice and make other necessary arrangements.

I was not able to get back to Jacksonville right away after that. I came down with a virus, and knew it wouldn't be good to be around George. I knew his daughters, both of whom lived out of town, were taking turns to be with him. On February 1, George sent me an e-mail. The e-mail read:

Dear Nola,

I am doing OK for now, liquid diet and getting my personal affairs in order since who knows how long. Hospice coming Thurs. to set up care I might need when necessary. Jackie coming up for meeting. Peg came last Sat. and Sun. and is coming back this weekend. Busy running back and forth taking care of things and then too going to see Corinne. Will have you come over when things get settled down a bit.

Love, George

On Monday evening, February 7th, I received a telephone call from George. Little did I know it would be our last one. He sounded relatively cheerful and said both daughters had been there. I should come over for a visit soon. "I wish we could go out and have a seafood dinner together," he said. I said we could still do that. He replied it would be no fun because he could not have any solid food. For the rest of his life, he said, liquids and liquid nutrition drinks. That was the last time I ever heard my brother's voice.

•

The year 2006 was destined to be full of grief almost from its onset. My brother George and I spoke about the presence of calamity in our family, the suicides that were a *fait accompli,* and our mother's many attempts to take herself out until her chronic alcoholism and throat cancer did the job instead. Our mother was good at cutting her wrists, but always seemed to get help in the nick of time. This was hearsay to me because only George was the player in Burney's life during this time. Either Jim or I were not there, or else too small to be aware. I have only snippets of memory of my mother. There are no memories of her ever touching me, except for a couple of cloudy images having to do with punishments. George remarked to me one time he was completely exasperated with being called home because Burney had attempted suicide. He said he told her, "For God's sake, if you are going to do this, do a good job!" Not said in seriousness, of course, yet our family was always quite out of the ordinary. Southern Gothic, even. William Faulkner would have had a heyday with us!

Because our family was so atypical, George's suicide talk was not taken seriously by me. It appeared to be merely talk, born of anxiety, not a plan that would be implemented. Our dark conversations of suicide took place mostly in George's hospital rooms when he would be at a low point, recovering from yet another diagnostic procedure. I remember there was a television soap playing one afternoon, *The Young and the Restless*. George remarked wryly, "Corinne and me, we're the old and the useless."

• • •

WEDNESDAY, February 8th, began just like any ordinary day. That is, until the phone rang too early in the morning. My niece, Peggy's, voice was on the other end. She said, "It's Mom and Dad, they're both gone." Fortunately, I had not seen the evening news. Police lines on Wolfe Street and the flashing lights of squad cars would not have been the way to get such heartbreaking news.

I learned later George checked Corinne out of the care facility for a visit in the morning, and when he did not bring her back, the administrator called his daughter, Jackie, in Gainesville. When the Hospice worker came to George's house about 8 P.M., she found the bodies of my brother and his wife in the back yard. George had shot Corinne, and then he shot himself. There was a note, too, explaining why. The police never divulged what was in the note, at least not to me. Much later, I tried to imagine how it must have been in that backyard that night. I imagined my brother, helping Corinne as lovingly and tenderly as ever down the porch step. She would never have known when he pulled the trigger. He would never have hesitated as she fell to put the gun to his own head because he would not be separated from her for even a moment. They left this world together, as close in death as they had been in life.

•

When the February 10th newspaper account came out about the tragedy, it was on the front page. A neighbor said in a statement that George had confided in him many times, "When the time came when he couldn't handle it any longer, he would do what he did. That was his way of making sure she'd [Corinne] be all right." The Times-Union reporter who wrote the newspaper account was unusually compassionate and perceptive in what she wrote. It could have been so sensational, so hurtful to our family, but instead it was, as my friend, Elise, later wrote, "Journalism to restore your faith." The newspaper headline read "Elderly Man who Killed Wife, Self, was Overwhelmed, Friends say." Funny, I never thought of George as being an "elderly man." I saw him as my handsome "big brother," just out of that Naval uniform. Elderly Man aside, the newspaper report continued, " She had Alzheimer's and he had been diagnosed with a terminal vascular illness. George loved Corinne for more than 60 years. He loved her in high school in Fernandina Beach. He loved her when he went to fight in North Africa in World War II. He loved her when they raised two daughters and grew old together. He never stopped loving her when her mind slipped away." She ended her write-up by saying George loved Corinne at the end. "He pulled the trigger."

After I got off the telephone with Peggy, I got into my car and went immediately to try to find my priest at St. Michael's Church. He was not there, so I sat with Jeanne Dean, our church secretary, in her office, and sobbed in her arms. She was so kind and loving. She made some phone calls, and then, I went into the church to sit. After a while, Jeanne came and prayed with me. Then, I was alone with my heavy heart and my chaotic thoughts.

In the following weeks, I kept close with my nieces, Jackie and Peggy. This is something Peggy sent in an e-mail:

Aunt Nola,

Sit down if you aren't, to read this one. First of all, you may or may not know, but Daddy gave my son his sporty Mustang

*the weekend before he died. J. D. never lets me drive it now,
but it has a CD hookup and my car doesn't, so yesterday
afternoon I asked him to let me take it to the store because I
wanted to listen to the "If Ever I Should Leave You" CD that
Dad made for me (the same one he had at the house that I
played for them that day) so J. D. said OK. I took off and put
the CD in and their song was #4 which he had recorded
again as #16.*

*Well, it was beautiful to listen to, as you can imagine, as I
had not listened to it since their death. I got to the store, and it
was now into song #5... I shopped for an hour and came
back and got in the car. I started the car up and as I backed
out of the parking place, "If Ever I Should Leave You" was
playing again. I said "Huh?" I had been on song #5. I looked
at the track number on the CD player and it said '16.' I started crying and crying, all the way home. I walked in and told
[my husband] and he said, 'That is their way of letting you
know they are OK... through the Holy Spirit and their music,
not to mention their car!*

•

It was some time later in the summer before we were able to gather
everyone for our private family ceremony. On June 24th, we met at my
niece Jackie's condo at Crescent Beach to celebrate George and
Corinne's lives. George left instructions that he and Corinne were to be
cremated, and there was to be no public service at all. Therefore, under a
tent on the beach in front of the condo, we had a little memorial ceremony, just our family, where some of us took turns speaking, and reading
scripture. Unsure about the suitability of sharing the poem that begins
this chapter, and not wanting to add any more sadness to the day, I consulted with my friend Elise. She replied, "I think your poem is so touching and beautiful, it would be appropriate for the gathering on the 24th."
And then she wrote (because she had just lost a beloved son-in-law)
"God protect our broken hearts, Nola, and keep us going."

I read that poem on the beach that day. Then each one of our little
family gathered two handfuls of ashes from the two containers, one for
George and one for Corinne, and we went down to the sea. I asked

George's son-in-law Allison which ashes were my brother's and which were Corinne's. He pointed them out, and he said "Corinne's ashes are so much lighter than George's. I don't know why," and I said, "There's a poem in there somewhere." And, perhaps there will be. As our loved ones' ashes went into the surf and out to sea, they joined Jim's ashes from a similar ceremony we had for him in 2001 on the beach at Fernandina. Now, the brothers would never be separated again, and forever a part of the Big Water, as Jim called "our ocean."

• • •

"DEATH is the middle of a long life," thus saith the Roman poet, Diogenes Laertius. Or, as the immortal Paulie Walnuts said in the last episode of the classic television series, "The Sopranos," "In the midst of death, we are in life, henh? Or is it the other way around?" I've been comforted in the years since Andre's passing by conversations with a couple of close men friends. These friends both had near-death experiences, but nothing really "near" about it. One of them was declared clinically dead, and his family called to the hospital.

I became fascinated with hearing about near death experiences because of my own flirtation with checking out early. There was a point after my brother and his wife's deaths when I suffered acute depression. It was in this dark place that I was also at a low financial point, and working on a loan application. Not only had emotions hit rock bottom, but my fragile finances plummeted. A double whammy, to say the least. One evening, I received a telephone call which delivered some sudden, unaccountably bad news. It doesn't matter what it was that devastated me, it's just that at the time it seemed the *coup de grace*. My well was overflowing like a gas tank, and spilling all over the ground. Interesting allusion in the light (or dark) of what I did next.

There was no bottle of champagne in-house. That should have told me something. The main ingredient besides me was missing. Nevertheless, I got up from the couch in my living room, went into my garage, plugged up all the air vents, turned on the ignition of my car, and set my lawn chair close to the exhaust. I was past ready to go find my guys. How long I was there in my lawn chair, I don't really know. Losing track of time, wandering in a mindless twilight time, it seemed like hours, but it was not hours. It was until a particularly insistent thought crossed my mind. The thought was, Do you really want to do this? Opening my eyes, I looked at the ceiling and realized that if I had to ask myself that question, I really did *not* want to do this. I got up from the chair, turned off the car ignition, replaced the chair in its accustomed spot, and exited the gas chamber. Two things were learned. (1) The more spiritual you are, the quicker karma kicks in, and, (2) God has a very large sense of humor.

•

The next morning it was business as usual, and I got into my car to run errands. The car said, NO. The engine would not even turn over. I hadn't killed myself. I killed the car... Thank God I have caring women friends who allow me to borrow their husband in an emergency. In response to my urgent phone call, my friend, Bob, came to my aid. He struggled long and in vain in what must have been 120 degree heat in my garage to get my car going. It did not. Finally, Bob mopped his brow and pronounced my car battery dead in the water. At least it wasn't me, dead in the lawn chair. Could it have been that I accidentally left my parking lights on? Bob mused. I didn't know, I said, and wasn't ready to talk about anything else. Not yet.

Bob got into his truck, went out to purchase a new battery, and installed it in my car. He was a lifesaver, in more ways than one. There would have been no new battery for this body. When I walked him from my garage out to his truck, thanking him profusely all the way, he didn't start up his truck and leave immediately. He sat there for a while and he told me a story. Bob's story was either simply on his mind that particular day, or else Spirit sent me metaphysical medicine. I chose to believe it was the latter. Here is what Bob told me.

Some years ago, Bob was in post op for a cancer operation, and he had been in the hospital for twenty-two days. Of those twenty-two days, he was critical for three days due to blood clots in his lungs. During the time he was on the critical list, he died. Bob related a sensation of his spirit lifting from his body and floating in the room over what was hap-

pening below him. There was great euphoria, and he was glad it was happening. He saw some great oak doors as if those of a cathedral or a
church, and around the doors, many bright moths were fluttering. The
doors opened wide, inward not outward, and in the doorway stood the
figure of a man dressed in a long brown robe like a Franciscan monk.
The man said, "Go back. Go back. We are not ready for you." Then Bob
had the awareness that he was back in his hospital bed. After his experience, Bob told me he would never be afraid to die again. When he said
that, it was like a valve opened to my sadness/illness, and the depression
flowed out of my body.

• • •

FRIENDS MEETING FOR COFFEE on a Tuesday morning. That was
our plan, but my main purpose was to ask my friend, Larry Dean, to tell
me again about a similar near-death experience. After listening to Bob, I
wanted Larry to recount something he had described in the past. Over
cups at the Kofe Hous, Larry, my friend since my Catholic instruction
days when he was one of the RCIA group leaders, sat in his motorized
wheelchair and retold me this amazing account of coming back from the
dead. At age 15 (and that was in the 1950s) Larry contracted polio during a huge epidemic in Ohio. The hospitals, Larry said were jammed with
polio patients. This was before Salk vaccine. His illness was so severe, he
was having difficulty breathing, and his doctors put him into an iron
lung. As a child, pictures of the iron lung filled me with horror. Larry did-
n't want to go in the lung; he fought hard against it, but it was a matter
of life or death. The doctors promised they would take him out as soon
as they could, and transfer him to a rocking bed. A rocking bed was a
regular hospital bed that undulated up and down and forced the patient
to breathe. It was during the time Larry was imprisoned in the iron lung
that he died—was pronounced dead by the doctors and his family summoned to the hospital. Larry said, just as Bob had, how he felt his spirit
rise from his body and he could see the medics working on him below.
Larry remembers a sky of a most intense blue color, and he felt calm and
peaceful. But like Robert, he was told to go back, it was not his time, and
he had the sensation of being back in his body. I have read a number of

accounts like this, and all of them have such striking similarities coming from persons who have not communicated with each other. One has to be a believer. I felt a great happiness knowing Andre, after expelling that long, last breath in the ICU at Baptist Hospital on June 7, 2002, must surely have still been with us, hovering over his family as we held on to each other in grief, crying and hugging. He was peaceful and happy, I do believe, but knowing my sweetheart, he must have wished he could have told us so.

• • •

I WAS HAUNTED by the knowledge that I needed to reconcile my reckless behavior, the loss of presence of mind that so thoughtlessly took me into my garage that night. Unable to bring myself to confession at church, I nevertheless realized how appropriate it was that the sacrament of confession is called Reconciliation. The aftermath of my thoughtless action was a sense of separation and a profound remorse stemming, as much as anything, from the realization that my circumstances were not that critical. They only seemed so in my already dark state of mind. In letters to Elise Braun and to Lise Goett, my confessors and my friends, I told them what I had tried to do, and pleaded please not to scold because I was already burdened with guilt. Elise wrote back that she could hardly scold me, especially in light of Bob's uncanny place in the healing. Elise wrote, "You did something interesting, and you learned something." But, I fretted ceaselessly, and, while seated in the church prior to Mass the following Sunday, I felt I would be unable to take communion. At that moment, the priest (not my regular pastor) appeared from behind the altar and walked toward the back of the church to change into his vestments. On impulse, I got up from my seat and followed him into the confessional room where he was about to robe for Mass. I asked him for a few minutes of his time. He listened gravely to my sorry story and was gentle with my spineless, "I haven't had a chance to go to confession." "You know what He wants you to do," he said. And when I told him about the car battery, he replied, "Better the car than you." His kindness was medicine for the open wound of my heart. Giving him an embrace, I began to cry and went back to my pew. A woman on her way back from the altar after changing numbers on the hymn board, saw my distress, and stopped to ask, "Are you all right?" "Yes," I replied, "but I have just spoken with Father, and it made me cry." "Well," she said, "this is a good place to cry," as she continued on her way, unaware of her blessing in my life.

• • •

"What if I dreamed someone else's dream?
It wasn't mine at all!
Is there a short book I could read
that would make life easy?

No one knows how God
calms sparrows when they die.
They were given the sky for roads.
Surely there is a heaven for each of us."

—JULIE LECHEVSKY, FROM HER POETRY COLLECTION, DOLL

Chapter Seven

THE NIGHT VISITORS

They know how to jimmy locks when
I'm curled in utero, creep like cats into corners
where darkness is deepest, or by the edge
of my bed where, freed from sleep's fist-
hold, I find them in the silence

keeping watch like winged messengers
of Biblical times. But, they do not
bear tidings or pronouncements
in rhymes. They are silent by definition,
and sure of their mission,

you see mouths moving though no sound
is made, as when one of their company
snuggles close to my body like a lover in bed,
whispering wordless secrets
left better unsaid. Embodied,

but faceless, my nocturnal guests
come as close as we get to that Stygian
scythe. They are ghosts in the garden,
rehearsing their deathwatch when
I leave this life.

THEY DRIVE BY NIGHT is a famous film noir movie, which starred George Raft, my favorite gangster of the old days. True to the classic lamentation of my age group, they don't make movies like that anymore. Joan Didion famously observed the seductive power of movies to teach dreamers how to live. We high school girls growing up in Fernandina in the mid-'40s studied under the seductive tutorship of the enchantresses of the Silver Screen. Or, at least, I did. Rita, Hedy, Betty Grable, I wanted to look like them—wanted the smolder, say, of Barbara Stanwyck or Gloria Graham. That caused me to spend a lot of time at the cosmetic counters of the Five & Dime. My allowance went for Max Factor pancake makeup, false fingernails, and Blue Waltz perfume in its distinctive small glass bottle with the corona stopper.

They Drive By Night played at a movie house in Tallahassee, Florida, when I was a freshman in college. Wearing a blue mohair sweater that was supposed to show off my breasts for the entertainment of my then-boyfriend, we sat close-up and personal in the darkened theatre. The sweater shed like a Persian cat. My boyfriend snapped (don't ask what we were doing) as he plucked strands from his coat, "Where did you get that sweater? In a Cracker Jack box?"

Well, surely poets are dreamers, inspired by demons and angels, driven by night dreams and imaginings. Especially night dreams such as mine, complex and intriguing scenarios starring not only persons in my life, present and past, but those invented in the mind's eye. The home folks often behaved in ways they seldom did in real life. Sometimes they resolved problems I wish could be so readily solved in daylight. Some dreams were so satisfying, I awoke smiling, happy all the way through morning coffee. Such wonderful personal appearances!

In regard to personal appearances, there were sometimes visitors in the night who seemed more real than Real. They challenged the border between dream and reality. I wrote descriptions of my current cast of characters in a letter to Lise Goett. She, in turn, talked about this with a friend of hers, and when speaking of my ghosts, he had a slip of the tongue and said "goats." Lise and her friend had a good laugh over goats, and in a reply letter she wrote, "Nola, you have goats in your garden." Goats or no, after sometimes being initially startled by them, my visitors were not unwelcome. There was never an answer to questions, though.

"Who are you?" and "What do you want from me?"

Let me describe these guys who lurk in the twilight zone, practice their art in the wee hours of the night. Immediately upon awakening, I found them standing beside me, at the end of the bed, and sometimes, alarmingly, in my bed. They were real, and like old soldiers, they did not die, they simply faded away. By degrees, even. Probably the most interesting visitors were those beside me as I slept. At least they had the good sense to be men. One of them sported a ponytail, and propped up, facing me, he seemed to have been waiting patiently for me to find him. Ectoplasm lover? Maybe... Then, there was the figure of a man, standing on the right side of my bed. He was dressed in a business suit, head bent, speaking on a telephone. Asking directions out of the bedroom, no doubt! On May 23rd of this year, I awoke to find two female figures, standing side by side at the end of the bed. They wore identical clothing, a sort of costume with a headdress, and each extended toward me a large bowl. I didn't drop in an offering. The collection would surely come around again! It always does. Most often, though, these "goats" in my garden were shadowy women, cloaked in darkness, waiting silently beside the side of the bed on which I was sleeping. Once, as I turned to change positions, there was a woman next to me on the pillow, propped up on her elbow, smiling. She was so real, I reached out to touch her, and as she faded slowly to blackout, there was only the empty pillow.

They keep coming, these night visitors. Not every night—only some nights. Until I blink myself awake, they, like the ghost of Hamlet's father, simply keep a wordless watch. A psychic once said that my mother came to visit me while I was sleeping. Only once was there a sense of my mother, or any known person for that matter. These benign spirits, meaning no harm, bringing no messages, are welcome in my nightlife.

• • •

THE MOTHER. An unknown dimension. Having been one myself, a mother to two sons, I learned a little more about mothering than I understood in the first 31 years of my life. Thirty-one was a late-life mother in 1961, when my first child arrived. Not so today when women of 40 years of age and beyond conceive and bear children. It seems, though, there are many more Caesarian procedures than ever before, as if natural childbirth is becoming less and less do-able. My first child took 24 hours in his passage, womb to waiting arms, and he came feet first. Although this arrival was not that much fun for me, I hoped it meant Anthony would always land on his feet. My second child, Michael, wasted no time in getting here. If our car, driven by an anxious husband, had stalled on the Fuller Warren Bridge on the way to St. Vincent's Hospital, Michael would have been a bridge baby.

When searching for a photograph of my Uncle Bill Sheffield to accompany an article being written about him in "O. C. White's Journal" by its editor, Carol White, I had a dilemma. After the death of my brother George, there was no longer access to treasures in his attic. Many of our precious family pictures had ended up there. When I was visiting George in Jacksonville, he could always be cajoled into bringing down photographs. Some, he gave me; others were taken home to be copied. But there were none of Uncle Bill in my archives. It occurred to me that my cousin Harry Ryder's wife might have one in their albums. Then I realized it was likely that my cousin's wife, Mary Lou, had never gotten the news of George's passing since there were few in the family left to tell her. I wrote a letter to Mary Lou, enclosing all the spin-offs surrounding George's death—newspaper clipping and other artifacts, along with request, if she had one, for a photo of Uncle Bill. Mary Lou telephoned me immediately upon receiving my letter. She had not known about George. She promised to go through the family albums to look for a photograph of Uncle Bill. And to my astonishment, she told me something I had not known about the circumstances of the death in 2003 of my first cousin, Harry Ryder.

Soon after our telephone conversation, Mary Lou sent me a packet of old photographs. In the packet were pictures of Uncle Bill, but there were also some important ones of my mother, Burney Sheffield, in her younger days. I enlarged them, and pored over the pictures as if they might contain clues about the mother, missing from my life since I was six years old. There was a photo of my grandfather Sheffield, my mother Burney, and a family friend, all of them crouching on a sidewalk, watching toddler George who is just learning to walk. My mother's body language is mine. Her expression, her flyaway dark hair, her pensive expression, and how she is dressed, sweater thrown around her shoulders against a cool day—all were mine. I spent a long time with these images of my mother. She had happy moments, a smiling girlhood with her sister Lillian in a photograph at 15. In 1922, she holds baby George in her arms. She actually touched her children. At least she touched George, I don't know about Jim and me. She was twenty-two years old. In a picture dated 1927, she stands in ankle-deep water in a bathing suit, protectively holding both of George's hands. My beautiful mother before I arrived to complicate her life, surrounded by loving family and friends. She was not tragic then. It was only later that life did not work for her. Alcohol and cancer claimed her at sixty-one. Who she was is a sealed book to me, never to be opened. The photograph of my mother, kneeling beside her father, Bill Sheffield, on the sidewalk, her chin in her hands, watching her small son take a few steps, sent me to bed in tears.

I slept fitfully an hour or so, and awoke abruptly to find a night visitor. A shadowy woman who had been standing at the end of my bed ran toward me with outstretched arms. I startled upright in the bed, and then she faded. My mother? My daughter, Charlotte, who never made it to term? I do not know. Only a woman on leave from the outer reaches, and when I rose for bathroom trip and a sip of water, I said, Please—no more tonight.

• • •

FRIENDS bring you gifts in unexpected ways. My longtime Fernandina friend, one of a select few who have kept close since high school days, Iris Ward, is married to Drew, one of three brothers in the Fernandina Ward family. All of these guys as young men were wildly good-looking (and have kept their looks.) They were physically beautiful, tall and rangy, along with what travels well: wit, perception, and intelligence. For as long as I can remember in high school, and some time after that, one of Drew's brothers was my heartthrob. That first love, that unrequited young love stands alone. He knows who he is.

The Ward parents, Frank and Grace, were admired by me. They seemed such strong, independent people who walked to their own beat. They set an example of a free spirit for me of which they would never be aware. How could they, worshipped from afar?

One evening at Iris and Drew's house, Iris showed me a note the boys' mother, Grace, had written to them on a long-ago Mother's Day. I can't remember the occasion why the note surfaced, but I fell in love with what Grace had written. Iris made me a copy. Grace Ward was some kind of a Mom. She was someone really special, and, to that end, the note Iris showed me must be shared:

TO MY CHILDREN on Mother's Day

The love I give you is a free gift. It is not given from a sense of obligation, therefore entails none. The toil and anxiety of rearing you has been mine by choice, and I exact no payment. I, despising fetters, have never used my maternity as chains with which to bind you. To each of you, there will come a day when a voice more compelling than mine will call to you, and I shall understand that you must answer. That is as it should be. I shall walk beside you to the door and bid you Godspeed. And leave the door ajar.

—Mother

I was struck by the way she signed herself: Mother, not Mom, not Mama, nor any of the maternal diminutives. Although the mother I never knew well was always "Mother" to me, it was a name that was formal and distant. There was nothing but compassionate love and the desire for her children's freedom in Grace Ward's message signed Mother on that long-ago Mother's Day.

In my entire life, there was only one letter my mother ever sent me. Written on onionskin, yellowed and frayed with age, it is in my family folder. My mother was ill with cancer when she wrote the letter. I was pregnant with my firstborn, a child she would never see. After this letter, a silver cup arrived in a package for the baby-to-be. Years later when Anthony was grown, the silver cup he used as a child was returned to him. "It belongs to you," I said. From my mother and his grandmother, who will always remain a mystery to us both.

• • •

HERBOTH STROTHER RYDER was a strong man with a strong name. He was my favorite first cousin, Harry Ryder: German to his toenails. Proud of his father's Germanic origin meaning "master of the army," he was equally proud of a Prussian heritage from our maternal Dantzler family. We shared a grandmother with a grand name, a royal name: Theodosia, grand matriarch of our entire clan. Engineers were in our family, and Harry's father was one of them. My husband, Andre, was one of them. My brother George's father was one of them. Harry's father, an engineer with the State Road Department, built many of the first hard-surfaced roads in Florida's Panhandle. His father died of a gunshot wound at home under unexplained circumstances. It remains an unsolved mystery. Gunshot wounds—a presence in our family.

Harry was born a child of Mercury, according to astrological lore. Believers in the Zodiac consider the traits of character and personality are influenced by our sign. I (Capricorn, double Leo and Leo in Mars) am a believer. "Children of Mercury are smart. They are fast talkers, quick thinkers, and sharp dressers, whose minds are always racing ahead of the conversation." A thumbnail description of my cousin Harry.

So, how is it that I took Harry, son of my mother's sister, Lillian, for my favorite cousin? No mystery there! I always thought he was the only one in my family who was anything like me. He was different, walked to a different drummer, and indeed he was an accomplished drummer in his younger days. He had a chameleon personality, and, along with a subtle sense of humor, was also a master of the practical joke. A friend tells this: "One of Harry's favorite tricks, remembered well by former Circuit Judge Charles H. Scruggs, III, who served with Ryder. It worked this way: Harry would conceal a telephone in his coat pocket prior to getting on an elevator. A device to produce a sound like a ringing phone would be in another pocket or package. When the bell began to ring, Harry would pull out the phone and appear to be answering it. Them he would say to whoever was standing next to him: 'It's for you.' That stunt invariably produced guffaws." This, of course, was obviously before cell phones!

Another account of a zany stunt comes from a partner in Harry's law firm. "From time to time, Harry and I would have breakfast before showing up at the offices. One of our favorite spots was The Old Meeting House on Howard Avenue. Occasionally, we would leave the restaurant and head south to Bayshore Boulevard, Harry in his car and I not far behind him.

Upon reaching Bayshore and turning left to head downtown, Harry would signal me; he was pulling over on the right side of the road. He would get out of the car, walk to the seawall and begin staring down into the water. I would stop abruptly, leave the car door open and hurry to the seawall to join him. We would both be looking into the water and pointing vigorously. Within a few moments, other cars were pulling over and stopping, at which point we would get back into our cars and drive off, make a complete circle and return to the scene. There might be as many as ten cars pulled over and the drivers all looking into the water...at nothing!"

Harry's music was terribly important to him, as it was to his first cousin, my brother Jim, and later to Jim's son, Jamie, whose bass guitar now forms the foundation of a rock band. My brother Jim often said if he had known in college what he knew later, he would never have played football—he would have become a musician. Harry was not into participating in high school or college sports. Instead, he was an accomplished drummer. He bragged he played in the Orange Bowl for the University of Miami in 1946. What position? "Snare drum," he would answer. He had won a music scholarship!

•

Harry transferred to Florida State University where he graduated with a bachelor's degree in journalism in 1950. Harry and I were in Tallahassee at Florida State at the same time. I was not yet a published poet, but Harry was already a scribe. Harry held several editorial positions with *The Florida Flambeau,* the FSU newspaper, including serving as editor-in-chief one summer. He also worked after graduation as a reporter for the Panama City, Florida, *News-Herald.* During the Korean War, Harry was in the Air Force. Just as Andre did in the Army during the same time period, Harry spent time in Germany. He was assigned to the service's counter-espionage unit in Berlin at the height of the Cold War. He married the sweetheart he met at FSU, Mary Lou Muster, in Dahlen, Berlin, on September 17, 1954, in a German civil ceremony in German language.

Harry graduated from University of Florida's law school in 1959 on the very same afternoon as Andre received his degree in Civil Engineering. It was a big family day. He worked as a field attorney for the National Labor Relations Board, assistant Hillsborough state attorney, an associate in a law firm and then became a partner in another. His I. D. card issued September 1, 1961, pictured a newly appointed Assistant State Attorney, Height: 5 8 , Weight 145 lbs. Harry and his first cousin, Nola, were the exact same height, exact same weight! A good package! Governor Reuben Askew appointed Harry to the bench as a trial judge in 1971 and to the appellate court in 1977.

Ernest Hemingway wrote "Journalism is about the facts. Fiction is about the truth." My cousin Harry was a real person whose life would have made a fascinating work of fiction. When speaking to Harry's wife on the telephone with the news about my brother George, how he had taken his own life, Mary Lou said, "He went Harry's way..." I was taken by complete surprise by this revelation. My thinking at the time of Harry's death was that he died of complications from an accident, a compression fracture of his back, which resulted in his being hospitalized. Harry had been diagnosed with Parkinson's, and because of an internal urethomy, he had to perform self-catheterization four times a day for the last five years of his life. He was in severe pain from the compression fracture. Mary Lou said, "I know the pain was just the last straw." The newspaper account of Harry's death stated "Herboth S. Ryder, 74, long-time appellate and Hillsborough Circuit judge and one-time Berlin spy (Yes! Harry was in counter-intelligence) died during the weekend of a self-inflicted gunshot wound at his home."

As in the case of my brother George, Harry's death was deemed an act of courage, respected and admired by everyone who knew them. Besides bravery, there was another significant connection they shared. At his annual Fourth of July parties, Harry had guests stand and read the Bill of Rights, each person reading a different amendment. "To the revolution!" he would shout, hoisting a toast! And, George was the backbone of the Florida American Legion. The cousins were passionate patriots.

When my friend, Dickie Anderson, dropped by my house for a brief visit, I showed her Harry's picture from the memorial booklet of proceedings at the Hillsborough County Courthouse, April 11, 2003, to honor the Honorable Herboth S. Ryder. I said, "All my men, Dickie, all my men…" and she said, "We have to be the survivors."

• • •

"Think of it,
my name, no longer a portion
of me, no longer inflated
or bruised, no longer stewing
in a rich compost of memory
or the simpler one of bone shards,
dirt, kitty litter, wood ashes,
the roots of the eucalyptus
I planted in '73.
A tiny me taking nothing,
giving nothing, and free at last."

—PHILIP LEVINE, FROM HIS POEM, "BURIAL RITES"

Chapter Eight

NOON MASS WITH THE ARCHANGEL

Late for Mass, I crack the church door slowly
so as not to ignite the Boss Angel's ire—
hold up one finger for the usher who finds me a seat
even though the pews are packed (and I don't
tip the mâitre d' until the plate gets passed.)

We've got "Father Seinfeld" today. He's as Irish as
an NYPD cop. His homilies are one stand-up joke
after another. And, he sings! Dogma's parked at the curb
these days—everyone's laughing, but I'm distracted
by affection in a pew where a teenage daughter's arms

encircle her daddy's waist. A miniature of her mother,
she wears a flowered dress, and her hair falls down
her back like mom's at bedtime when the lights
go down. But the boy! He's two years old—(I asked.)
A heartbreaking amalgam of mischief and sweetness

in a lime-green shirt, he stretches on his stomach,
flipping gaily colored pages of My First Book of Saints
until consigning the saints to the dungeon
beneath the pew, he crawls into his mother's lap.
At the Peace, he blows me a kiss, and I think how precious

these moments are in childhood's brief hour,
remembering my firstborn. How he fell feet-first
into life, his legs splayed out by design gone awry.
I see him in his birthday suit, fitted for a brace, amusing
all when the cold table caused his upright tinkle.

In time, these bones have righted themselves
through shoes with metal bar at bedtime—walked miles
and miles from mother love, childhood fears. A boy
disappears, but never his footprints—
regardless the years.

ST. MICHAEL'S CHURCH is where I go to Mass in Fernandina. St. Michael the Archangel has always been a huge presence in my life, anywhere I go. I lived two years in Brussels, the City of St. Michael, where he guards over his domain as a statue atop city hall in the *Grande Place*. I lived on boulevard St. Michel near St. Michael's Church, Brussels, and its accompanying St. Michael's Academy. When living in France, I was often at Mont St. Michel where the archangel lifts his sword toward the sky on the top of its highest point. One of my sons bears the archangel's name. I took "Michael" for my holy name when I was received into the Catholic Church. A saint's card bearing the archangel's likeness rides with me in my car, and he is all over my house in icons and in spiritual presence. I firmly believe he has saved me from any number of possible car accidents. I told my friend Iris Ward that when I get to the pearly gates, God is going to deny entrance because I loved his archangel too much. Iris doesn't think so.

At our church here on the island, we do not have a nursery during Mass. All ages of children appear at Mass with their parents. Most are well behaved; some are not, and heads will turn in the direction of a too-talkative tyke. I was at a service once in Normandy at Abbaye Saint Wandrille where the Benedictine monks sing glorious chants. During the homily, a youngster was disruptive. One of the monks came by the pew and merely stood and looked at the child. He had such a silently warning presence, the child was immediately quieted. We need this monk sometimes at services at St. Michael's.

I love the physical affection and closeness so evident in many families in my church. When I sent this poem that sets the stage for this chapter to my poet friend Lise Goett in Taos, she e-mailed me this: "Thanks for the poem, dear heart. I love the part about 'flipping gaily colored pages of *My First Book of Saints.*' We've all been there, seen this boy or some clone of him at Mass, been more entranced by the interplay between parent and child than what's going on at the altar. Once I was sitting behind a little girl and her parents, and when the host was being consecrated and the parents told her that God was in the bread, she said: 'Is he going to pop out?' Now, that would have been something."

Of all the motivations I have for getting myself to Mass, the affection I feel among families is a big one. That, and something Elise Braun said to me years ago. She said, in essence, there is just something gratifying about all those people gathered in one place all doing the same thing at the same time. Yes, there's a lot of power generated in numbers.

• • •

THE UNEXPECTED GIFT. There are no flowering plants in my Marsh Lakes yard except an occasional azalea planted when I first moved into this house. On each side, neighbors have a glorious hedge of azaleas against the side of their houses. In bloom time, these are riots of color, announcing their season with trumpets, not flutes. There are only modest spaced-out (like the lady who lives here) rows of spiky, green plants running the length of my house. I did not plant them. She who lived here before me, and built this house chose the flora. It was not especially to my liking, but then she never knew me, nor I her.

What I planted, other than the scant azaleas, were two bottlebrush and an elm tree. These have grown tall. The elm, which my yardman topped off in early spring, went haywire with growth, and I loved it. It burst out in all directions with long, snaky tendrils, graceful and free, that blew in the wind with the glory of new life. The fig tree near the lake, which my late husband contributed to the flora of our little universe, worries me sometimes. It aspires to take over the world, rising to dramatic heights, just as Andre did. Small wonder he loved the fig. To my complete surprise between the bottlebrush and the ligustrum which grow at one side of my driveway, a lantana bush sprang up. It blew my way on the shoulders of the wind from my neighbor, Donna Givens' yard. It was a wandering offspring from glorious masses of lantana, climbing rose, daisies, and all manner of colorful blooms. Flowers love Donna. They reward her loving, giving, nurturing nature with their abundance.

I watched my unexpected gift grow tall in the space between the bottlebrush and the ligustrum. The lantana began to challenge its neighbors for space, to demand, since flowers rule, they give way. It insinuated itself into the heart of the ligustrum, thrusting its strong stems up between the spiky green leaves to make an imaginative and unlikely bouquet. When Donna exclaimed over its growth, she said, "I don't even have that color in my yard." As new owner of this fierce hybrid flower, it has inspired me to follow its lead: to reinvent myself, expand, and grow, to bloom where I have landed, blown to new soil, new life.

• • •

NEW YORK, NEW YORK: It's a wonderful town, as the song goes. I tell my friend, Julie Pietri, who lives there that she is living my life. Julie and I met years ago when we both lived in Atlanta. Our common interest in French language brought us together in an *Alliance Français* class, and we have been friends ever since. Julie has been in New York for fourteen years now. It was a bit of a stretch, coming from the Deep South to live the big city, but Julie did it admirably. Not only that, but she reinvented herself after a divorce, enrolled at the New York School of Interior Design, got her degree and made a new life as an interior designer. She is one of my heroes. She has a tenth floor apartment in a co-op building on East 49th Street. She has a doorman and an awning out front. She has a rooftop garden. She knows her way blindfolded around a complex and endlessly fascinating city that I love.

In mid-October '06, I had more than one reason to go to New York and visit Julie. A poet friend I had not seen in years, Lise Goett, would be visiting there from her home in New Mexico. It was a chance for girlfriend time I simply could not pass up. I boarded a plane on a Friday morning with great anticipation, and Julie met me at La Guardia Airport.

•

Julie Pietri is someone I love to visit. Never mind that she lives in one of the cities I most love in all the world, she is effortless to be with, and I can live in her space in complete comfort, as if in my own home. It's the nature of our relationship to find ease in each other's company. What are the marks of a special friendship?—Walking side by side together in the cool, gray, city-sidewalk light on our way to a matinee movie, riding in a taxi along the East River or to the Meat Packing District for supper at a French bistro. Last, but certainly not least, sharing companionable silence over breakfast table coffee while reading *The New York Times* from cover to cover.

For our Saturday evening meeting with Lise Goett, we had reservations for dinner at a restaurant so quintessentially New York that I think of it as Our Place. It is the Union Square Café at 21 East 16th Street. I feel 21 again, walking through the door of the Union Street Café, sitting at the bar with my friend Julie: she with her cocktail, me with my signature kir. I feel 21 again, free, and completely in my element. A New Yorker by adoption, by temperament and by direct choice, I am happiest there than anywhere in the U. S. of A.

When Lise arrived, looking more movie star than poet, she plucked us from the bar for hugs and exclamations before we were seated at our special table by the window. It is the only window table in the restaurant, looking out into the city street outside, passersby peeking in at the busy bar crowded with happy people. There is the buzz of animated conversation in the air like bubbles in champagne. In the company of two of my dearest women friends in all the world, my head is exactly where my feet are without a single desire to be elsewhere. It's a miracle! I wanted the clock to stop there, in that very moment, but, of course, it didn't. Little did I dream that my visit to New York would finish on a less joyous note.

• • •

ST. PATRICK'S CATHEDRAL: I wanted to go to Mass there on my Sunday in New York. I had seen the Cathedral before, years ago when Andre and I were on a sabbatical in the city and it happened to be Saint Patrick's Day. We watched that awesome Saint's day parade from the steps of the Cathedral, glad to be among the hordes of people lining the street in front of the Cathedral. I fell in love with bagpipes and the NYPD, but isn't falling in love the occupational hazard of the poet? By profession (and confession) poets are resigned and reserved to the prisoner heart, where both animate and inanimate objects are forever trapped —the heart always in its crock pot, stewing away in its own juice.

I did not make it to the Cathedral that Sunday, and Julie needed to remain at home to prepare for a gathering in her apartment that evening. Julie made me a map to the nearest Catholic Church, the Church of the Holy Family at 315 East 47th Street. I managed to misinterpret her good directions in typical poet fashion, and made several false turns on a very cold morning when I should have already been warmly seated in a pew. My errant compass took me all the way to the East River in the wrong direction, but I finally got it, and got myself, thoroughly chilled, nose running (if not my feet) to the Church of the Holy Family. What was best about my detour on the way to church was being able to observe weekend New Yorkers about the business of Sunday. People were walking their dogs, young women jogged on the sidewalks with ponytails flying, a guy returning home from morning errands had *The New York Times* under his arm, and a sack from the bakery. Fresh bagels? With cream cheese and jam? I wanted their Big City lives, wanted to knock on the doors of their brownstones and enter, ask to stay. Pay the price. Do the Do. Do anything but windows. Ah! New York for this besotted Southerner!

The church was worth the walk. It was October 15th, the 28th Sunday in Ordinary Time. There was nothing ordinary about that church. It warmed my heart, cold hands, and feet, and felt like home. It is heart-warming to know wherever you go; there you are, as the saying goes. There is family, not to mention Holy Family. You are never a stranger in a strange land. In this often-times disheveled life, there is at least one hour of harmony to be found at liturgy in the nearest sacramental church. The Church of the Holy Family, by the way, describes itself as The United Nations parish. I did not, however, see any United Nations there. What I did see was a gorgeously modern, spacious interior stretching forward like a long ship from entrance doors to steps of altar. One wall almost entirely of stained glass was a mosaic of gold, green, and blue fragments, filtering beautiful, muted light. Running three-quarters the length of other side of the room were Stations of the Cross unlike any I had ever seen: a continuous bas relief sculpture of enjoined ivory blocks, depicting Christ's journey to the Crucifixion. The colors in the church were pewter, gold, and silver except for a black marble altar set in the center of a platform of black marble. The three steps down on all sides were also black marble. In the middle of the bottom step directly in front of the altar was a gigantic, pewter-colored pot, rotund as Buddha's belly, filled with mauve and amber hydrangeas, their huge blooms as big as balloons. It was a church, it was a museum, it was a place of harmonious beauty—a respite by the East River in an often-as-not discordant universe.

•

The *coup de grace,* the whipped cream and cherry on the top of my visit, however, took place that Sunday afternoon on the top of Julie's building—a 12th floor roof garden of lofty delight. They say "See Naples and die." I might apply that to Julie's roof garden! Up under the pristine blue skies over New York City, puffy white clouds drifted by on their way to paradise. It was as close to Higher Power, whatever you perceive it to be, as you get on this earth. At least, that is how it felt to me. The sky was not occluded, since the tallest surrounding building was probably no more than 50 floors tall. It is a blessing to see Blue in NYC! It was spacious up there, and looking down, you could check out other city dwellers' rooftop play space. How sweet it must be in summer to sprawl out in one of the lounge chairs and, Yes, get a suntan as surely as beside the sea. Who needs St. Tropez! Manhattan Beach high in the sky at 235 E. 49tth is available for a price. I'm afraid to ask Julie how much!

From city streets below came the muffled, steady, slow hum of traffic, a gentle static, unobtrusive and comforting. It is a rolling current, a muted roar like the white noise, and sleep-tonic of ocean breakers. It is energizing to have around you evidence of so much life, and more than that, it is a religious experience I felt the very first time I stood on the top of the Empire State Building. Never had I been so high in the sky, and over the greatest city in the world. Maybe not the best, but New York City is unequivocally the greatest. I heard the roar of the city, its streets like veins of a great heartbeat, the center of the world, MANHATTAN!

In Lex Hixson's book *Coming Home*, he wrote this, and it pertains to "The Ox" as a metaphor for Higher Power, or The Source: "The Source cannot hide because it exists through all forms though they differ in structure and appearance as sun, nightingale and willows. [Or pines, I might add.] The noise of city traffic is the Ox bellowing. The Source omnipresent not in abstract contemplations but in direct experience." The concept of The Ox works for me. The beast roars in New York City where His voice stops your heart 102 stories in the air atop the Empire State, and the beast roars in my own backyard: a place "Where the Fear Drowns."

All is so still you think the wind has made an exodus
like the entire city of Paris in August.
There are no messages except the larger one of silence.
Not a head stirs in the hanging basket of periwinkle,
transplanted from their habitual, grave stance
at our family cemetery. Grateful for summer storms,
they are electric in a burst of proud purple.
The lake's a-shimmer, satisfied for now, to travel
nowhere, reflecting light at each shoreline, dark
in the middle where the fear drowns, as becalmed as
a ship with lowered sails. The pine tree in its sexual
multiplicity, unlike a human counterpart denying yin-yang,
is both male and female. It spawns this marvelous mix,
this towering behemoth of myriad parts, thrusting needle-
topped heads over a perfect half moon of prayerful arms.
And, when the wind comes, finally, of its own volition
(wind bows down to no one) the small and youthful branch,
and beneath him, the mother lode, larger in concept—
two cones strategically placed like Madonna's
breastplate—will become the voice of The Ox who
roars in the wind for all to hear because soon enough,
soon enough, needles will turn brown, tatting
falling embroidery to cushion beneath The Source
of all who asserts in His immediacy, You too,
You too, will fall to earth.

•

I am not in my own backyard, however. I am in Julie's backyard, where looking down on varying levels of rooftops like stair steps to terraces, there is a hammock sans occupant in this October chill, a glass garden table, a charcoal cooker on green-grass carpeting, chairs emptied of their occupants. Dark green plastic arm chairs, once-white arm chairs soiled from exposure to the elements circle each other in silence while beneath them, fire escapes crawl the sides of their buildings.

In my line of vision there is a glass tower 30 stories high which reflects in its multiple bright squares the blue sky and rippled clouds. Mirrored facades of a facing building reflect images, which become, in distortion, images like Oriental temples; hieroglyphics spelling coded messages, strange faces with disassembled features, open mouths, staring eyes. I imagine a strange world on the other side of the looking glass one might fleetingly inhabit; such as, when lying on your back, the ceiling becomes unfamiliar territory, taking you to no rooms you recognize.

On this roof garden floor, there are climbing roses, yellow nasturtiums, and pale trumpet lilies. Two iron ornamental figures, one standing, one kneeling, decorate a neatly pebbled area surrounded alternately by board-walk and concrete block. All manner of potted flowers abound: blue morning glory reaching for the sun, miniature black-eyed Susans, and lantana far removed from salt. Ivy climbs a trellis, and lovely pink blooms, cousin to hibiscus, crawl with glossy green leaves around a rail-ing, giving a semblance of the subtropics. Bending over the railing at roof's edge, I wondered how far I would have to fall before dying of fright. Or, as in a B movie, be the body crashing on someone's cocktail table, uninvited for Happy Hour. I thought of a friend of mine who com-mented he could never stand at the edge of a cliff because he always had the urge to jump. Jump, I did not, but the clouds began to darken, taking the sun behind them. It turned very cool, and someone was grilling a city rooftop supper, the aroma of which brought backyard barbeque aromas my way, sending me down again to Julie's warm and welcoming tenth floor digs.

On this final night, Ms. Julie hosted what we later pronounced a liter-ary soirée, and a successful one to boot. Although two of Julie's invited guests were unable to come, we unholy three: Julie, Lise Goett, and I;

Mary Pat (another writer friend) and her visiting mother; Julie's friend, Wendy, from the building, and Henry Grinberg, my poet friend Suzanne Noguere's husband, gathered in Julie's living room. Suzanne was out of town that evening, but she was nevertheless a presence. In a few private moments, Henry spoke to me about his Suzanne with heartfelt love and admiration. This, after many years married is the mark of a keeper and an Aquarius—to me, the princes of the astrological world! Henry's new novel, *Variations on the Beast*, was forthcoming in December, published by The Dragon Press, NY.

Julie, as always, surpassed her reputation as a consummate hostess. There was a bottle of champagne in a crystal bowl of ice, good red wine from Julie's cave, and goodies to eat from our earlier excursion to the Whole Foods, Union Square. Julie had some reservations earlier because her only other invited male guest, other than Henry, was unable to come. Henry would be the lone man, and Julie thought I should alert him in advance. Some men, she thought, might find being the fox in the henhouse an uncomfortable position. I said, "You are thinking of how some ordinary man might react." What I knew was, Henry Grinberg didn't have an ordinary bone in his body.

So ended my visit to Manhattan on a happy note. There was no way to know in the hubbub of good food and conversation in my friend Julie's uptown-uptown New York apartment that next morning's scheduled departure would be anything but uneventful.

• • •

DURING THE LONG WEEKEND I was visiting in New York, a construction company was at work at the entrance of my friend Julie's co-op apartment building on a sidewalk repair project. The sidewalk was to be replaced and structural steel supports and vault ceiling underneath were to be repaired. The area between the entrance of the building and the sidewalk had been excavated, and there was a six-inch drop at lobby entrance, then a six-inch step-up at the sidewalk. Workmen had a wooden plank in place to pass over the excavated area from building to sidewalk. On Monday, I was to fly home to Amelia Island after my mini-vacation in New York. Julie called her limo service to take me to the airport around noon to catch my flight. The limo came on time, and Julie and I took the elevator down to the lobby of her building. She walked ahead of me, pulling my rolling bag. The doorman was at the curb talking to the limo driver. There was no plank in place that morning to cross over the area dug out from lobby to sidewalk. This fact didn't really register to me because I was focused on my imminent departure, and not keeping the limo driver waiting. At the step-up to the sidewalk, I tripped, and fell. I was completely out of control, and pitching forward I reached out for the doorman's back, hoping to break my fall. I couldn't get a grip, and fell to my right side, badly wrenching my neck and shoulders, landing on my back on the sidewalk. There was sudden excruciating pain. My immediate thought was of a neck or spine injury, but for sure something unfortunate had happened to my body. A woman passing by yelled, "Don't touch her, don't move her—call 911!"

An ambulance came, and paramedics talked to me a long time, asking me questions. Then two of them got me to my feet, and examined my neck and back. They determined I had an unexplained knot at the back of my neck, and said I must go to the hospital. The nearest one was Columbia/Cornell University Hospital. I was taken by ambulance after my neck was secured in a brace and I was strapped down to a board. Julie went with me in the ambulance, and never left my side until I was released from the emergency room around five o'clock. Julie had her camera with her when we went downstairs at noon to meet the limo because she wanted to take a photo of me as I was leaving. She took photographs of the accident while I was lying on the sidewalk, and was almost ejected by hospital security for taking pictures of me in the ER. I was grateful we had this good documentation of my New York accident.

Julie maintains I am a "detail" person—that I notice so many things that she passes over. When I went up to the roof garden on Sunday, I wrote the account of all I saw there. When I returned to Julie's apartment, she asked to read what I had written, and she said, "I have lived here for 14 years, and you saw more in the roof garden in a couple of hours than I have in 14 years." For instance, the tip of the Chrysler Building's spire is visible from Julie's roof garden, and she had never noticed it. Nevertheless, no matter what she says to the contrary, Julie is a very astute observer, and she wrote the following detailed notes of my accident from the time it happened to the time we left the hospital. Here are her notes in their entirety—a word mosaic of our day:

NYP EMT, New York Cornell, October 16, 2006:
EMT on back of blue shirts – emergency room, New York
Cornell. Fall at 235 E. 49th, 11:55 P.M., going to meet
Mirage car for flight to Jacksonville. Fall on Doorman, Franz
– on sidewalk – Pain – "Don't move," woman passing by,
"Don't move her – call 911." Mirage driver calls. Emergency
comes – good guys. John asks driver to go to Lenox Hill. Not
equipped. "What are choices?" Bellevue and Cornell are trau-
ma hospitals. Julie picks Cornell. Excellent hospital over the
other one. In ambulance on way to hospital, Nola answers all
questions clearly and precisely. Can't get blood pressure
because of all the belts holding Nola in place. We arrive
12:45. Changed to bed on wheels and placed in hall. Julie
goes outside and calls, reaches Sally who will call Anthony,
Iris and Delta. Julie calls Mona to cancel phone appointment
for career coaching. Comes back in. Emergency room gets full.
Nola still has not been taken for X-rays. They must not think
it is catastrophic. Crying person comes in – old man with very
gray skin. Ninety-eight year old woman comes in – moans
when lifted from stretcher to bed. Paramedics, navy shirt,
white pants, red and black badge, "Paramedics" on back of
shirt. 1:55 – Nola said, "Do you think they have forgotten
me?" We are still in hallway, not in a room. Nola does medi-
tation and falls asleep. Pain is subsiding a bit. 2:05, Nola and
Julie discussing that ambulance person was comforting and
reassuring. "Lucy" is Nola's nurse – she is leaving for lunch!
Oh No! We are waiting for X-ray person to come and get
Nola to take X-rays. Poor woman (98 years old) keeps moan-
ing and yelling "Ma-Ma" over and over. 2:20, Lucy has gone
to lunch. Nola has requested the pain medication offered earli-
er. It is Vicadan by mouth. Nola would not take it – probably
better not to. The moaning woman continues. EGAD! We're
going nuts. Have called Sally again and gave her the "no

*update." Saint Lucy came back from lunch. Thank Goodness!
She is going to save us from the nut house. 3:40 – Nola finally in X-ray room. Saint Lucy saved us! 3:50, Nola in X-ray
room. Nola had to take off silver earrings prior to X-ray. I put
them in Nola's business card case. I am not thinking ahead –
what can we have for dinner? Better yet, what can we have
for a drink? Too bad I took champagne out of refrigerator.
There is a little chilled white left, and some red. How about
vodka & tonic?? 4:00, X-ray finished. Cute X-ray tech? –
doctor? They finally take Nola's info for insurance. 4:10, Julie
takes pictures and is practically arrested for taking pictures in
the hospital. 5:15, finally leaving Cornell. Freezing, waiting
for cab. Advil – take with food and water…*

The remainder of Julie's notes reflected phone calls made in the hospital to family and friends, hers and mine, and a request from her building manager for a written account of the accident. There was much to do
when we arrived back at Julie's apartment to make arrangements for my
flight back to Amelia Island next day. The airline was not supportive of
dismissing a penalty in light of my accident. Instead, there were addition-
al monies to be paid for another ticket home. This added unhappily to
the denouement of my New York City trip. Nevertheless, I Still Love
New York.

• • •

"*Normally when I'm insulted*
I drive to Wal-Mart
And sit outside with the flowers.
But when an artist talks like that
There is little that flowers can do.
You just have to lean back and let the paint clot."

—JULIE LECHEVSKY, FROM HER POEM, "ODALISQUE"

Chapter Nine

RUMINATIONS IN THE PARKING LOT

Why are the sea gulls shopping here,
if not for White Stag, No Boundaries, or Faded Glory?
Is there some other story? Coffee, Tea or You,
or just practicing beach and gray-sky calls
over concrete, carts, and Handicapped Blue?
This turf is for blackbirds of the piercing cry, haughty
strut and beady stare. It's not for you to straddle
halogen in your evening wear of dove-gray,
black tie in this car-lot of no swells,

no breakers. What lures you, displaced
gracefuls—calls you from rides
on a rogue wind, pushing lace-topped tides
to stock minnow meals in pellucid sloughs?
You've paid your dues, and dour land birds
are the parking lot denizens. Surely you harbor
an unnatural appetite for hors d'oeuvres
that do not swim or paddle, though you buzz
pedestrians on stony reaches as when
dive-bombing the deep, or cruising

the beaches. For whatever draws you
to the superstore, super birds, I pray you reap
the sea god's pardon as you vie for the rail
over the holy grail of the WAL-MART sign

where no whitefish, black fish, shrimp
or snail, no fiddler crab scuttles for safety.
And may our God absolve us our sins
of the past—our ever-advancing
tsunami of concrete, steel, and glass.

NOVEMBER, and the saints came marching in—each and every one of
them on one of my favorite church calendar holidays. In my town,
women say as they take leave of one another, "See you at Publix." Sooner
or later, we all turn up at the Publix, which is arguably the most accessi-
ble grocery store in town. I know its aisles like the back of my hand
(although there are not as many freckles there) and I find myself at the
grocery store almost every day. Maybe this is a holdover from Paris days
when I fell into the European habit of shopping each day for fresh foods
for dinner.

On November 1, All Saints Day, I went into my Publix to buy flowers.
They were destined for Bosque Bello Cemetery here on the island to
ornament the graves of my father, my husband and in memory of my
brothers, George and Jim. I took my time choosing the bouquets, just the
right colors for each of my important guys.

As I was checking out at the counter, the checker (a young man hardly
out of high school, and not someone you would think cared a lot about
flowers) remarked that he liked my choices. I told him I was on my way to
the cemetery with them. His face clouded up, and he said, "Oh, I'm
sorry!" I explained that the flowers were for family graves because it was
All Saints, or All Souls Day, and then because he had a puzzled look, I
added, "Halloween, you know." He said, "I forgot that." As he rang up my
purchases, he asked me if I liked dragon snappers. "Dragon Snappers?" I
asked. A woman behind me in the line stepped in to say, "snapdragons." I
couldn't help but laugh, not at the young man, but at his quirky misnomer
for the flower. He proceeded to tell me how much he loved snapdragons—how he planted them in his parents' yard just for the pleasure of
looking at them. I was so touched. I don't suppose I will forget this young
man and his dragon snappers. I prefer his graphic misnomer. I will never
think of snapdragons again without a smile on my face.

• • •

THANKSGIVING DAY, November 2006, was unseasonably warm. It was like that around the country, mostly. Global warming. One of Elise's recent letters had this comment in it: "My friend Betsy and I planned to go see Al Gore's An Inconvenient Truth last night, and decided we were too hot to go. Something ironic there—" Elise could have been a stand-up comedienne. And then, "It was so warm in Massachusetts last week, people were walking around in T-shirts, and the day I got home (to Vermont) it hit 70 degrees in Burlington. You think our new Congress can deal with reality? I am relieved it is now reasonably cold and even a dusting of snow."

• • •

REMEMBERING what it was like to be a child. Some people never lose the child within. My son Michael is one of these. At Thanksgiving this year, a Thanksgiving unlike any other we've had, Michael watched our friend Wendy Philcox's little three year old, Andrew, walk around with "his marshmallow." We were to roast those sweet, squashy treats at the end of our feast. Andrew played with his marshmallow with reverence. Introducing it for everyone to see, he was completely obsessed with the marshmallow. Think about that word! Marsh Mallow. Marsh, squash, mush. Mallow, fallow, swallow. It's seductive. Michael remarked, "To Andrew, that marshmallow is God!" He remembered so totally what it was to be a small boy.

My memories of being a child escape me—good ones, anyway. There is only one snapshot of the her that was me. It is of a solemn little girl with a big bow in her short dark hair. She is standing on the pedals of her tricycle outside her Aunt Myrtie Burgess' house on Sixth Street in Fernandina. She does not smile for the camera, and she looks like the weight of the world is on her shoulders. My memories have been repressed until after age six, which is when my mother disappeared from my life. I don't remember her leaving. I don't remember much of anything about her, actually. The child, me, accepted her absence without question. There was a moment, waking at night, alone in a house some-where we once lived. I was frightened. I got out of my bed and picked up a telephone receiver, but help was not there. There was only a buzz in my ears. That must have been the genesis of a lifetime of feeling helpless. Then, miraculously, the "others" came back. I had been left momentarily, but didn't know that. Then, there is a vignette about being in a walkway beside a house in the rain. It was gray and dreary, rainwater, pure and crystalline flooded down from a drainage spout, and. if my mother was near, I didn't know where.

• • •

WHAT WAS DIFFERENT about this year's Thanksgiving? My son, Michael, returned home from several years of making his home in Houston. He came home to bunk with me while he worked on getting his new life in Florida in order. Our diminishing little family gives thanks he's out of Texas, and closer to us. So this year was special, "plus one," making community at my house again, and the two of us were invited by our extended family to spend the holiday with them. The Philcox/White clan from St. Augustine and Jacksonville gathered on the Island in Wendy and Chris' luxurious RV which was parked at the Fort Clinch beach campground. It was warm, happily, for a walk on the beach—just the slightest hint of chill in the wind. Our holiday feast was set out comfortably in the RV, an amazing vehicle large enough to accommodate our eight bodies, after which we gathered around a camp fire outside to roast marshmallows, followed by apple pie and ice cream. As darkness gathered up its skirts and folded us in, those of us not staying overnight at the campground, drove home at the end of a warm-in-every-way Thanksgiving holiday.

• • •

NEW YEAR'S EVE, ISLAND STYLE. The ultimate New Year's experience, I suppose, would be to be in the mix at Times Square, celebrating as that fabled ball descends to mark both an end and a beginning. The year's final hour, for me, has always been a bittersweet moment of mixed emotions. It comes with a taffy-twist mélange of joy and sadness so married to each other; it's difficult to separate them out. Though I have never been in New York City on New Year's Eve, there was an absolutely ecstatic first trip to Manhattan with a long-ago boyfriend. To explain my excitement, understand that an island girl can readily be a Gotham girl by adoption. New York, New York, was my dream town, and when I finally spent a week there, my boyfriend took me to Times Square at nighttime. I stood alone on a median traffic island, facing that famous clock in a dazzle of bright lights as cars raced around me on all sides. It was a perfect, unforgettable moment when I was so in the moment, I never wanted it to end.

•

Now, far from the glitter of New York, my days are spent a few grassy feet from a lake large enough for the navigation of small boats and canoes. The "big lake," as we call it, is surrounded by a mix of pricey mansions, and smaller, less pretentious houses, and by salt marshes. I live on the modest end of this development called, not surprisingly, Marsh Lakes. At holiday times, I can look across the lake at my neighbors' docks, gaily decorated with garlands of sparkling colored lights.

When the occasion warrants it, firecrackers pop and sizzle in my neighborhood, not to be compared, of course, to the grandiose pyrotechnic displays of our Ritz-Carlton Hotel. A New Year's Evening, Ritz-style, goes for $250 a head, but the fireworks are for everyone—no charge. This year a gathering of island friends organized a "Low Country Boil New Year's Eve." This reminded me of the philosophy of like souls of the Lop Lop Café in Brussels, where I lived for two years. The café's manifesto is, "You have just found the centre of the leisure, chattering and drinking classes in Brussels (read Amelia Island.) Here you will find writers, painters, stage and film people, opera stars, sculptors, geniuses and cretins, aristocrats and beggars, buggers and bankers (and bandits and blackguards.) Here is the raw stuff of Shakespeare: all the characters for a play. But you will not find the grey men."

Therefore, in the spirit of the Lop Lops, dress code for the Low Country Boil was rhine-stones and denim and the pass for the party was enough shrimp for you and yours, plus one other ingredient for the pot. Although electricity was not available at the pavilions, lights from offshore ships gleamed romantically in the distance. Power was run for the party from one of the automobiles with a power inverter for festive lights, music from an I-Pod. The first batch of delicious food: lovely pink shrimp and assorted veggies were spread out on tables for the hungry partygoers. Dessert was not crème brulee, but marshmallows roasted over a gas grill. There was candlelight, noisemakers and sparklers to join the midnight fireworks that the Ritz so graciously provided. Little did the revelers on the hotel's great lawn suspect that ours was a feast to match any *Bonne Annee* celebration on the Riviera. Alas, no Cary Grant or the once and future Princess of Monaco kissed in a convertible on a cliff as the sky over the South of France exploded, but our island-style New Year's Eve was glamorous, nevertheless.

• • •

CHRISTMAS IN ATLANTA. Christmas and year's end came so fast. Only yesterday, it was Thanksgiving in an RV. Now, Michael and I were to join Anthony, Sally and Elizabeth at their home in Atlanta. It has been summer-like on the island all fall and winter, so what to pack for Atlanta? I didn't take the right things, and had to borrow covered-up shoes from my daughter-in-law, plus socks for my cold feet. I'm a barefoot girl from a barrier island, and when I lived in Paris, so many times Michael (who camped with us for a spell during our sojourn overseas) would say to me. "Where are your socks?" Where, indeed!

One of the cool privileges afforded us by our Stafford-in-law family in Tifton, Georgia, was to sometimes hitch a ride to Atlanta in the Stafford family small business plane. This year, Anthony phoned us to say if we could be in Tifton by ten o'clock in the morning on the day we were to drive to Atlanta, that we could fly on the little plane with Sally's Mom and other members of the Stafford family. That we did, and it was worth the extra effort to get up early and get ourselves on the road.

When we arrived at the Tifton airport, I somehow managed with my unerring faculty for doing the wrong thing to drive between two buildings right out onto the runway instead of parking at the back of the Stafford hangar. The pilot of the little plane came out, and was surprised to find me rolling my little Saturn Vue right up behind the aircraft. Gentleman that he was, he simply unloaded our baggage, and then drove my car to be parked properly behind the hangar where it would remain during our time in Atlanta.

It was always a revelation to me to be able to fly confidently, considering I was a classic Fear of Flying candidate for years. As a 17-year-old just out of high school, along with my brother, Jim, I flew to Caracas, Venezuela, for the summer to visit our stepmother, Lucille, and her husband, Bill Veech. I have never been so terrified in my life that first time on an airplane ever. The stewardess (not called a flight attendant in those days) took pity on me, and in simpler times when such would be permitted, she gave me a tour of the airplane, and then took me to the cockpit to meet the pilots. That would be unheard of now, but my brother and I were two teenagers flying alone for the first time, and it was scary. Her kindness didn't reassure me, though. I was trembling in my seat in abject terror when the plane took off.

I was troubled with flying fear for a long time after that. Years later, when living in Atlanta and facing a first overseas flight over the North Atlantic to Paris, I found myself in a therapist's office, working on my phobia. As I learned the hard way, the only way to overcome fear is to stare it down. It was not even courage, just sheer dogged will power that got me through, and then Paris was the prize! How is that for a proper carrot at the end of the stick? My only genuinely frightening flying experience came much later when flying into a Washington, DC airport from Paris to join my husband for an FAA conference. It was a horribly turbulent descent into DC, and just as we were about to set down, the pilot suddenly took off skyward again. The passengers, especially me, were extremely anxious and confused, as no explanation came from the cockpit for some time, and then it was not really an explanation. The pilot said we would be making another landing, and in a lame effort to be jocular, he said. "Well, you will be able to see the monuments twice this trip." The second descent seemed more turbulent than the first, and the gentleman sharing my seat row who had obviously had a laryngectomy, breathed into his speaking tube upon our bumpy landing, and said to me. "That was quite an experience." Fortunately for me, I shared my space with an extremely calm person. He had survived a life-threatening disease and a difficult operation, which required learning a new way to talk. He was armed for out-of-control challenges! As for myself, I just grasped the beautiful red and green Christmas rosary my priest had blessed before I left. If I was going down, I was going down with my beads!

• • •

TWO in the house makes a family. It was different, it was an adjustment for both, but it was good. How was it good for me? I tempered my need for obsessive order in the house. I ceased being judge and jury, critical of how things looked: if the beds were made, if the rugs were free of snarls from repeated traffic. I have traffic. There's no other way to get around. Traffic is good. It means we are alive and well on Amelia Island. My personal space heaves a sigh of relief because I let go the need for perfection, for "just so," because that military voice in my head belongs not to me, but some master sergeant in the past I no longer need to obey. Whoever it was that expected me to be perfect, I took them to court, divorced them, and Michael was my counsel. I am reminded of some affirmations which have been useful to me. I say them again for the changing times: I am not my body, I am not my mind, I am eternal, immortal, and infinite. I am the force within. Today is my day, and all that I pull to myself for my highest evolution and growth. Thank You, Lord. You have many creative ways of freeing this woman from her unhealthy attachments.

• • •

ENCOUNTERS of the close kind. I haven't had any in my living space since July of 2002 when my husband lost his valiant battle with failing health. When you are a young mother with growing children, you don't question their ongoing presence in the house. And, when they leave, you mourn. When Michael went off to North Carolina School of the Arts as a dance major in the mid-1980s, I wept into his sweaters as I packed them for his year away. We had never been separated since he entered the world March 24, 1963. He had always been a constant in my life. We were so much alike that Michael used to say there was no use in our fighting with each other. No one ever won!

Now in his early 40s, Michael was again a resident in my house. He spent five years in Houston where he got his MFA to add to a Masters degree from Florida State University in Tallahassee. Then, Houston simply did not work for him anymore. There were medical issues and financial issues, and our dwindling little family (Anthony in Atlanta, assorted nephews and nieces) were more than ready to welcome Michael home. He had a new life to create, and Anthony and I were his cheerleaders.

•

At first we two solitary people accustomed to living alone tiptoed around each other, adjusting to our new circumstances. Then, we began to become accustomed to the face. I had arranged the house guestroom for his needs: a desk where he could work at his computer, an armoire for his socks, ties, and unmentionables—used furniture found during my bargain hunting at resale stores. New lamps were purchased for better lighting, and the closet emptied of my summer clothes to make room for his permanent collection. Because Christmas was nearing, I purchased a large clock-cum-CD player for his bedside table. It had a bright blue light even on the dim selection, but it was handsome indeed. Unfortunately, neither Michael nor I could figure out how to program it and make it work, even to set the time. Like mother, like son. Both of us are technically challenged, and of no use to each other in that regard. We called on my competent friend, Iris Ward, who brought her grandson to Michael's room to give us a lesson on how to use the clock.

After a while, I began to find the clock face down on the floor, or peeking out from under the bed. Replacing it on the bedside table, I again found it on the floor, lighted side down. I replaced it on the bedside table. Not a word was spoken for some time between my son and me in regard to the Battle of the Bulge, er uh, clock. Finally I bought a simple five-dollar alarm clock with a dial that lighted when touched, and only required one operation to set the alarm. So much for how my son and I negotiate our different opinions these days! Well, it works, and we give up on complicated toys.

Next silent standoff was the plug-in room deodorizer. Men's rooms smell differently from those primarily occupied by women. This insight pointed out to me by Nan, a poet friend in Atlanta, whose long-distance boyfriend moved in with her. A writer friend of mine of some note told me that he thought people were attracted to each other, Yes, on the basis of appearance, but part of the allure was olfactory, as well. An actress who shall be nameless who was once married to Cary Grant caused a stir years ago by remarking to an interviewer on television, "I dig your smells." Maybe she was just ahead of her time! My husband and I shared a room, of course, and our essences mingled in more ways than one, and the two small boys of our creation—their rooms smelled of sneakers and soiled jeans on their way to the washing machine.

In an effort to give Michael's room a competing aroma, I purchased a plug-in room deodorizer, being very careful to choose a scent I thought would be pleasing to the male species. A day or so later, I found the device had been unplugged, and placed on the floor. I plugged it in again. Again, I found it on the floor. After a bit of musing, I plugged it in under Michael's desk where I hoped it would escape detection. It was not to be. The plug-in was on its side under the desk beneath the electrical outlet. I didn't give up. I went on the search for a plug-in that had no scent. Life has simpler challenges these days.

• • •

GOOD GRIEF, CHARLIE BROWN! Michael was accepted to teach as an adjunct professor at Flagler College in St. Augustine, fall and spring quarter, '07. I was so sure he would be hired, that while he was interviewing at the college, I went into the nearby Cathedral and bought him a congratulatory present. Of course, at the same time I lit a candle and got down on my knees, just in case. When I went back to the college to meet him, he was walking on air. He got the job. So now, in preparation for this life change he has gone to work at the Super Wal-Mart to save money for the move. He is in Shoes: the shoe department, that is. Since being employed at Wal-Mart, shoes have been coming into the house in droves. He had to buy a basket for all his new flip-flops. I have five or six, and still increasing pairs of sandals in my closet to bring my collection of shoes to the Mrs. Marcos' level. I calculate I will have to add five years to my life in order to wear out all these new ones. Michael has a way of presenting presents. I have found two of the pairs he bought for me napping on my pillow when I pulled back the covers at bedtime. Last night when opening the refrigerator to pour the Chardonnay, I found a brand new shoe popped up against the milk. Cold as it was, it went on my foot along with its companion while I hopped around the kitchen in delight, and hugged my funny son.

• • •

WAL-MART (or "Wally World," as one of my son Michael's friends put it)—Did I ever, ever, shop there before Michael became one of their "blue shirts?" Well, politically correct, incorrect or whatever, it's a place I rarely frequented. Now, I am addicted to their shoes. It's one of the tragedies of life that I was never able to afford designer clodhoppers. No Manolo Blahnik, Jimmy Choo, Moschino, or Sergio Rossi for me! Be that as it may, Wal-Mart does have some sandals to die for. Good leather and comfort can be found in their Dr. Scholl's and their Earth Spirit brand.

One of the reasons I will always remember the shoe aisles at Wal-Mart has nothing to do with shoes. I was wandering through an aisle, checking out choices, when a child's voice addressed me. "Do you go to my school?" There before me was a precious small boy, 6 or 7 years old, his questioning big brown eyes looking directly into mine. "No." I replied, "Do I look like someone at your school?" "You look like the principal at my school," he said, "She has yellow hair." I have been a card-carrying brunette all my life now, but maybe caramel-colored highlights pass for yellow when you are 6 or 7. "Well," I said, "I would like to meet someone who looks like me." He promptly took my hand in his, and was energetically leading me up the aisle to go to his school when his mother stopped trying on shoes, and intervened. The mother said, "She doesn't really want to meet your principal. She was only kidding." I wasn't kidding. That would have been a fun excursion, supervised of course by the Mom in charge. The little boy was so undeterred, however, that I had to gently extricate my hand from his, and guide him back to his mother. Then, knowing he was defeated, he asked me my name before his mother marched him off. We exchanged names, he solemnly shook my hand, and he said as he was making his way down the aisle, "Come back to this same aisle and wear those very same clothes, so I can find you." I said I would. "I will miss you," he called back over his shoulder. "I will miss you, too," I said. And I did, and I do. A few minutes on my path, but in my heart forever...

• • •

"Now that she's ashamed of their ancient burls
and gibbous knobs—
'Don't be ashamed!' I helplessly cry—
I find myself staring at the raw matter of their
decay, nails crumbling to the opalescent grit
of their lunulae, liver spots speckling the blue dorsal vein
with its throbbing blue limbs, as if the leopard,
symbol of lust in Dante, lay panting, enfeebled,
in the dark wood."

—DAVID WOO, FROM HIS POEM, "MY MOTHER'S HANDS"

Chapter Ten

SOLILOQUY AT SEVENTY-SIX

This is the year I give up on the perfect body, its
creamy breasts, flat stomach, and shapely legs men praised.
This is the year I cease to grieve about lumps and bumps,
which unlike Elvis will never leave the building.
This is the year when crinkly arms, I've learned,

are no less loving, less able to embrace and comfort.
Exit stage left with a flourish, I say, to flawless skin, so
recklessly sacrificed to summer sun. Surrender
with a close-up, toothpaste-commercial smile, Mr. DeMille,
that perfect staircase descent I thought I would make forever.

Those mornings in the youth of my old age, how proud
I was to leap up, turn on the coffee, and race
back to my lover, raised up on one arm in our bed,
amused at my naked, shameless self. Nothing to lose
those mid-life days, the bedside clock ticking

time out; the car, idling in the parking lot while I
lingered for that glow carried into the workplace
(and never explained.) I'm letting go of reruns this year:
I've made my peace with old. And, imagine this,
it's not so bad. I'll head out, trailing good history,

pure, lacey, and as voluminous as a bridal veil, toward
that bony groom with the big grin. I'll pull down
my hood and fade to black, absolving him of guilt like
executioners of old at the guillotine. It's not his
fault—he's just the one who drew the duty.

THE POET'S PRUFROCK bemoans the lost years, as T. S. Eliot and I
concur: I grow old...I grow old...I shall wear the bottoms of my trousers
rolled. Shall I part my hair behind? Do I dare to eat a peach? As for me
(Mrs. Prufrock) I grow old...I grow old...the sun I asked for gold gave
back tenfold. Get ready for sun damage, folds and furrows where you do
not want them. The sapphire light of youth has turned to fallow lamp
light in which I sit to share this lament. In the small, sleepless hours of
the night, it's easy to fall prey to darkness. Kitchen table light where I
write draws tiny flying insects swarming from the dark to the illuminated
window pane. They want the light, scramble toward it, batting their
small black bodies carelessly against the glass. In their frenetic desire,
they bump each other, fall away, but come back doggedly to the light. It's
cold out there at the edge of night.

Pretty phrases from the past bat like insects at a windowpane: "Nola
always had beautiful legs," and, "Did she keep her looks?" "You were my
brother's first love." O, the wispy insect wings of the past, their dry whis-
pers of Gone, gone. Her name was Lola, she was a showgirl...
Just give me one more chance at the feathers, g-string, and rhinestones.
I'll do it this time. Rhinestones? I'll make them shine like diamonds.

• • •

DECEMBER is a time of finishing. The imminent end of a troubled year
was upon us. Christmas and family birthdays came and went with mine
to follow in January. An anticipated American Legion event to honor my
brother George and his wife, Corinne, was to take place on December
9th, 2006, which would bring closure of another kind. Our family had no
idea about the nature of the dedication, but we were excited to be invited to the upcoming ceremony. George's daughter, Peggy, received a letter
from American Legion Post 137 on San Juan Avenue in Jacksonville,

Florida. My brother had lived in Jacksonville for many years, and had been very active in the Legion. When George and Corinne came to Paris in the summer of 1991 to visit Andre and me, one of the first things George did was take my husband to Post No. 1, Paris. He signed Andre up as a member of the Legion, and paid his dues for a year.

The letter my niece received from the commander of Post 139 read as follows: "I am writing to first extend the Post's warmest regards to you and your family, and to invite you to the dedication service of the memorial for your mother and father. It is my pleasure to officiate the dedication ceremony on December 9, 2006, at 12:00 P.M. It would be our pleasure to have your presence at the general meeting providing me the opportunity to introduce you to the membership. I am sure there are many members that knew and respected George and Corinne and some you may remember as well from your visits to our Post."

It was a wonderful and unexpected invitation, and all our family intended to be there. When Corinne first began to show symptoms of her Alzheimer's condition, she and George were still able to attend the out of town Legion conventions they so much enjoyed. Eventually, Corinne became more and more disoriented and uncomfortable away from home. George decided to resign his work with the Legion to become a fulltime caregiver, and have as much quality time with Corinne as possible. When he could no longer take care of her at home, only then would he look at other options. The other options did not turn out exactly as any of us expected.

•

On Saturday, April 1, 2000, the American Legion Department Headquarters in Orlando hosted "George Derrick Appreciation Night" for his many years of dedicated service to the Florida American Legion. It was a huge affair for my brother who officially stepped down in mid-winter after serving for fourteen years as National Executive Committeeman, and had also been State Commander in 1977/1978. Andre and I attended the dinner and the ceremonies at which Roy Stone, Jr., Past National Commander was the speaker. I was proud to be introduced as George Derrick's sister! My heart swelled to be part of his family.

My big brother George was passionate about the military and his country, echoing our first cousin Harry Ryder's zeal for the USA. George joined the Navy in 1941 and served during World War II until 1946. He received letters of commendation from his ship's commanding officer for his aid in the evacuation of the wounded, and bringing the vessel in port after torpedoing on June 22, 1943. The letter noted his behavior reflected great credit upon himself and the Naval Services. And, in another letter written in September, 1943, his commanding officer wrote, "As a member of the crew of this vessel during the invasion of Southern and Northern Sicily and during the period when this ship was disabled by enemy action, you exhibited great personal courage on carrying on your work in a manner in keeping with the highest tradition of the Naval Service." Oh yes, I was proud of my brother, George Lester Derrick. He was not only a Naval hero; he was my hero. And to think, he used to change my "nappies!"

•

On December 9th, Michael and I drove to Jacksonville for the Legion's ceremony for George and Corinne. We had no clue where the post was located, so I made a phone call. The legionnaire answering the phone said they were in the middle of the meeting. I replied, "Well, we won't be able to get to George Derrick's dedication ceremony if you don't give us directions." He was not the best guide on the planet, and it required several stops for directions from much more helpful filling station personnel before we arrived at our destination. A filling station is more than a place to buy gas; it is my personal road atlas. I do not read maps, and/or suffer safe combinations gladly, and, I am, furthermore, completely unapologetic. Being born without a sense of direction is not the worse affliction in the book, only if the man you're living with thinks so. Mine didn't.

While living in Brussels, I admired a unique pocket compass small enough to go on a key chain that belonged to my husband's friend, Mike Galvan. Mike was visiting us from Madrid where he held the FAA CASLO position, the same job Andre had for the Benelux countries. Mike purchased the compass in Spain, and had given several of them as gifts to friends. Andre joked about my notorious lack of direction ability, so when Mike returned to Madrid, he sent me a compass. This, at my expense, ensued between Mike and my husband—Glory Hallelujah! To have been the impetus for this exchange:

> *From Andre Perez, 12/2/98: Mon cher Mike, I received your compass which I promptly passed on to Nola. Yesterday she left early in the morning to go shopping in some distant land totally confident she would find her way back, relying, of course, on her new guide, 'The Compass'. As of 3:00 today she has not returned home. She called me this morning and told me that she was lost somewhere along the North Sea coast! Where did you buy this compass? At Sears and Roebuck?*

> *From Andre Perez, 12/4/98: Subject, Looking for a Lost Wife. Breaking news!!!! The Norwegian coast guard found a woman stranded near the North Pole. When rescued she was asked what she was doing there. She replied, 'I followed the red arrow on my compass as told by Mike Galvan!' The coast guard confiscated the compass and agreed to return her home. Thanks, Mike!*

> *From Mike Galvin, 12/4/98: So glad you got your bride back. See, she does know how to read a compass... she followed the red arrow to the North Pole. By the way, did she happen to see a little old fellow in a red suit? Glad Nola liked the compass! In Viet Nam, they used to say that the most dangerous thing was a second lieutenant with a compass and a .45 pistol. Don't give Nola a gun!!*

And, so it went—my character being bandied about by two magnificent men. Here's to you, Mike Galvin, St. Michael of the Compass, wherever you are now.

In Paris, when setting out with a girlfriend for a guided walking tour of Paris (I needed guidance) I stopped to ask directions at shops along the way. My friend got out her map, and I said, "Don't bother with that—I'll get directions." She said, "You like to ask for directions, and I like to read a map." They didn't put that bone in my body! We got where we were going, using all tools at hand. After all, it's not the destination; it's the journey, as they say.

•

When Michael and I arrived at the Legion Post in Jacksonville for the dedication (and we did arrive) my niece, Jackie Folds, her husband Allison, son Bradley and daughter Derek met us in the parking lot. There were hugs all around, before the post commander took us into his office to explain what the ceremony was about. We were overwhelmed to learn that this Post community was dedicating the park beyond their swimming pool and recreation area to the memory of my brother and his wife. There was a large stone marker beneath the flagpole that read:

DERRICK PARK
DEDICATED TO THE MEMORY OF
GEORGE AND CORINNE
DERRICK
DECEMBER 9, 2006

A large gathering of the Post community was in attendance, as well as an honor guard at attention with flags and rifles. It was an impressive display. The commander made a speech, and Jackie and Allison addressed the group. Taps was played as everyone stood at attention. Photographs were taken of our family, standing in front of the flag pole with its marker. I sent these pictures to family and friends who could not be there for the dedication. My friend, Elise Braun, wrote this: "Michael's unmistakable body attitude was his father's. It was Andre." "He has your face," but his body language is Andre's." Michael loved it, and I loved it. Yes. The power of family!

When my niece Jackie returned to her home in Gainesville after the dedication service, she sent this to the commander: "Saturday was so endearing to me, and I want to thank all of Post 137 for dedicating the Park to my mother and father. As per his (George's) wishes, their memorial service was family only at the beach. It was so wonderful to hear all of you say a few words about what special people they were. Since my Dad never had sons, he took my sister and me to everything he liked: cars, fishing, hockey, and so on. I wasn't much on these, as I am a bit girly, but I cherish all the time he and my Mom spent with us. My Aunt

Nola adored her two brothers, and always loved my Dad very much. I am so glad she got to be a part of this, as well as my cousin, Michael. Thank you again."

Meandering past the park is an inlet which flows to the St. John's River; therefore, beside the grassy little park, there is the necessary water. We must be near water in this family. The ashes of George and Corinne, as well those of my brother Jim are part of a larger body now. The Atlantic Ocean they loved has received them into herself, and I will join them one of these days.

• • •

A POET GETS A POEM. Imagine that! I have only received one poem that was written especially for me. On the morning of January 6, 2007, I put my feet on the floor of my bedroom and walked barefoot into my office to find paper and pen. It was my birthday, and on that birthday morning, I wrote "Soliloquy at Seventy-Six." I e-mailed it to Walter Griffin in Atlanta, and in response he sent me the following. He said he wrote it in ten minutes. "But it is heartfelt," he commented. It is not only heartfelt, but I would like to see something he spent some time on, and I have in his book collections and his poems in countless literary magazines. There is not a poet in this country any better published than Walter, and thank you, dear Walter, for deleting a few of my years in your ten-minute jewel.

For Nola Perez on her seventieth birthday

AND DEATH WILL BE JUST ANOTHER ONE OF YOUR LOVERS

Come and lie down with me
in the weeds and beneath
curious stones. If I should

feel awkward, it is because
I am not used to your bony
touch, your cold kiss upon

my lips, the steel blackness
of this strange place. But I
will learn to love the peace,

the lack of pain in your
arms, hold me like a young
girl, let the darkness enter

me like a virgin on her bed
of satin, her eyes closed,
the alien bone entering.

• • •

LOVERS? Good grief! Lovers haven't been thought of in years. The gentleman callers who crossed my path along the way? Above and beyond physical attraction, they were my teachers. If I had not connected with one, a man who especially validated and encouraged my writing, the road to getting my work "out there" would have been a much longer journey.

There were a couple of interesting dynamics held in common by each of the men in my life. With only two exceptions, these guys came from other countries. I suppose you could say that a Jewish man of diverse talents could have been thought of as being from "another country." He had a brilliant scientific mind, was an inventor, and conversely, had performed in musical comedy on the New York stage. To a small town girl raised Protestant who had always had one eye cocked toward the white lights of Broadway, these attributes seemed exotic enough to seduce her.

The other exception was someone as Southern as the famous hot dogs from his little town of Macon, Georgia. However, though Southern from his birthplace, his maternal grandparents were of Russian descent. He was pure caviar, and just as hard to digest, but my poetry advanced because of him. Everything is a tradeoff of one sort or another.

I am not sure what these choices had to say about me except there's always been a taste on my part for something different. "She likes something odd," an acquaintance once observed. I do not mean to suggest that men I have known in the Biblical sense were like peas: too many to be counted. *Au contraire!* They were only as many as the number of days in a week, and select—the most select, being, without question, the beautiful man I married. So, there you have it: few, far between, carefully chosen, Grade A all the way, luxury-class cruises, making waves, large and small on my sea of emotions. Only one was a tsunami, almost taking me under. Even now, I wish him no ill, because he was a great teacher. Graduation was painful, but we got through—we got through.

Every man with whom there has been an in-depth relationship, be it a romantic attachment or simply good friend, there was also another common denominator. Each suffered the absence, or at least the major neglect of his father. What quality in me caused fatherless men to adhere to me like nails to a magnet? A sense they would find nurturance, perhaps, as healing for the love they did not get from the male figurehead in their family, or perhaps my proclivity for being a keeper? Years later, I told a therapist that he should be grateful if I did not love him, because it would be forever. He remarked with some amusement, "So, the worst you will ever do to me is to love me!"

• • •

HEREWITH, for any questions raised, and principally, a question along the lines of "Where during this period of other men in my life was Andre?" He was there, of course, but we were not at that time in a working partnership, or rather, it was working on some levels, but not in a conventional way.

It was Atlanta in the 1970s, and after forty years of uninterrupted marriage, there came a time when the relationship was in jeopardy. The problems were acute ones, and eventually resulted in a separation. Both of us went into counseling with a psychiatrist, and if you believe in miracles, you may be able to believe that a ten-year separation from marriage can ultimately result in creating a new connection so perfect as to be legend. A woman friend remarked once that in the course of a marriage, you are married to many different men, according to changes that the years effect. Not only that, but a wife may become someone other than the woman who said "I Do." I Do can become I Don't.

Andre and I chose each other in the infancy of our youth. I was nineteen when I walked down the aisle for a man waiting at the altar who was barely twenty. Neither one of us had a clue about the journey we were embarking on, but to this day I am convinced that we were drawn by our karma into a partnership meant to last a lifetime. That is exactly what happened, but not exactly in the expected way.

In the beginning, and there is always a beginning, my husband and I were like flotsam, floating in a turbulent sea, clinging to the life raft of each other, each coming from difficult backgrounds—his on one continent and mine on another. How unlikely was that in the first place! When Andre took up residence in my little hometown, he had many choices among the local girls who were attracted to him. He chose probably the most offbeat among them. That was me, and he liked it that way.

We were married in Fernandina on February 18, 1950. The Separation was not the only separation. We were two years apart while Andre was overseas in the military. We remained in Fernandina after his military service for several more years. I worked as a secretary. Andre commuted to Gainesville to attend the University of Florida. Since he was only "home" on the weekends, count this as four more years of living apart. Real time, 24-7, began after his graduation from college when he went to work at Cape Canaveral at the behest of the U. S. Army Corps of Engineers.

A year later, we were in Jacksonville, Florida, buying a first home, and raising children. The poet and Bohemian in me, more (or less) successfully embraced the role of suburban housewife and stay-at-home mother. It was my choice to be a Mom who stayed home with small children. I meant to do my very best for the two babies I brought into the world. There was a profound joy in mothering that mitigated my own lack of mothering. As the poet, Anne Sexton, has said, "Children are the big gifts."

I liked to hear my next door neighbor at our condo in St. Augustine refer to his grown son as "My boy." It seemed so endearing. "My boys," Anthony and Michael were, and are, my finest hour. Initially fearful of motherhood because of my lack of guidelines (the mother absent from my life since early childhood) I found, to my astonishment, that beyond fear lays great fulfillment and happiness.

When our family moved to Atlanta to begin a new cycle in our lives due to Andre's job transfer near Hartsfield Airport, I can only say that, along with all the other changes we faced, Andre and I seemed to be at odds with one another. We were, in fact, beginning to impede each other's growth. There were battles, often bitter ones, and we were unable to resolve our issues. My primary fight was for my personal freedom. I wanted to return to the work force when my children were in school, and Andre was adamantly opposed to it. All along, there had been certain parenting problems. I felt a lack of support from my husband at times when it was most needed: the anxiety of a new mother when a child was sick. For instance, when insisting that we take our young toddler to the pediatrician's office because he was running high fever. Andre thought it was overreacting. Perhaps so, but this assurance that my precious child was OK was needed by me, and when we leaving the doctor's office, Dr. Boothby said to my husband, "You are not much help to your wife, are you?"

At one point, Andre decided he needed to talk to someone. He chose to see a psychiatric therapist. This was hardly believable, since in the mid-1960s when I suffered an emotional breakdown accompanied by frightening panic attacks, there was a day I knew professional help was needed. I remember that day in our kitchen when my husband planted his feet and said, "Absolutely not! I cannot afford a psychiatrist." I said, "I am going to see a psychiatrist, or I am going to die!" In fact, I did not die—I spent four years in therapy, and it took a couple of those years before there was any relief from my symptoms.

For me, the resolution came in Atlanta when the patriarchal, misogynistic counselor Andre had been seeing, reinforcing already overbearing behavior, felt the problem was me. He advised Andre to get his unruly wife under control. "Tell her there will absolutely be no divorce," he told my husband. "You are the boss." It was hardly the solution I was hoping for, and after a particularly bitter contest in our kitchen; I decided it was time for a major Time Out. Therefore, the unruly wife became the catalyst for the split.

Andre moved out of our conjugal house into the home of close friends while searching for his own apartment. I remained at home with the children. Sometime later, I moved into the city from my house in suburbia into a midtown apartment near Northside High School. Andre moved back into the house while our older son finished his last year in high school. The reason I moved was to allow second son Michael to attend Northside School of the Performing Arts—his heart's desire. It was necessary to live in the school area in order to be admitted, or else there was a long waiting list, if a place would be available at all. Northside was the prime high school performing arts venue in the South under the baton of Billy Densmore. It had a prestigious Tour Show company made up of especially talented students. Michael was eventually accepted into the touring company, launching him into a ten-year dance career with Atlanta professionals.

There was no divorce. There was a legal separation, an agreement drawn up by a lawyer between my husband and myself, outlining responsibilities until such a time when there might, or not be, dissolution of the marriage. Living apart seemed to be the best avenue while we were struggling to find our necessary and separate reality, all the while taking care of the important business of the well-being of our two children. That goal was paramount for both of us.

During what turned out to be a ten-year sabbatical from married life, both my husband and I "saw" other people, under the guidance of our therapists. Andre and I met weekly for dinner at a restaurant to discuss our children, their needs, and what was to be done to meet them, short of moving back into a marriage that was temporarily derailed. During these ten years, we worked for clarity, for direction, for answers. We managed, even though we ended up sharing the same therapist, to keep the issues uncontaminated. The danger, obviously, in seeing other people was running the risk of an emotional involvement that would end the contract. This didn't happen. It was not meant to be. There is nothing I can say to detractors and those who would be critical of this period in our lives. I can only point to the outcome! I learned a lot about myself through other relationships. What I learned was that the bluebird of happiness, as well as Horus, perched in my own backyard. There actually came a time, and more than once, when my husband thanked me, painful as it was for both of us, for having been the catalyst of his personal growth through our separation.

What I did, most importantly, during this period alone was to embark wholeheartedly on a writing career, which until that point had been subjugated, and I might say, suspect, and undervalued, even by myself. I applied for, and received, publication grants from the City of Atlanta, Bureau of Cultural Affairs, and one from the State of Georgia. It so happened that a man I was involved with for a time in Atlanta was an entrepreneur, an artist and a Bohemian of the first order. Under his tutelage and guidance, I published my first book of poetry, and then another. He was my introduction into the artistic community of Atlanta's Little Five Points, and together we produced a poetry play at various Atlanta venues. He directed local actors in a play constructed from my work called "Fernandina and Other Images" at Seven Stages in Little Five Points, also a staged poetry reading by actors for the Atlanta Arts Festival in Piedmont Park, and performance readings at bookstores and art galleries.

I began to treat my writing with great seriousness. This man who launched me on the way came into my life for just this purpose—as catalyst for putting my feet on the writing path. If he had not believed in me, and been so insistent, I would have been much longer on my way. He helped me become the woman I came here to be. I am grateful for that, even though we had an erratic and difficult personal relationship. Even this had its *raison d'etre*. I had always thought I wanted a crazy artist in my life, and then I got one. Be careful what you wish for...

This was also a time when I worked on my craft with prestigious Atlanta poet, Walter Griffin, in his longtime important Poets Studio group. There were weekly workshops under Walter's expert baton in the homes of the writers, and in time, my first public poetry reading ever. There was even the honor of reading with Walter, my teacher and my mentor, at Atlanta's Callanwolde Arts Center. In terms of my marriage, I thought of myself as being in my Simone de Beauvoir period, because some years toward the end of our separation, awed by my husband Andre's commitment to me and his complete refusal to give up his "second time" courtship, Andre and I began to see more and more of each other. His therapist had advised him, "Forget about your wife." "No way," said Andre of Marseille.

When we met for our weekly dinners at one restaurant or another, Andre would say to me in parting, "Come back to the one who loves you." Soon, we began to travel together, my husband demanding nothing more from me than the pleasure of my company. It was awesome. "There is no one," I thought to myself, "who will ever love me like this."

It was at one of Fernandina's Shrimp Festival weekends that the inevitable happened. We drove from Atlanta to visit a mutual woman friend and her husband at their condo on the north end of the island. Little did our friend know that she would be held responsible in eternity for cementing a fractured marriage under the act of simply providing us her hospitality. It was at lunch that day in her home, when she and I were alone, that there was an occasion to explain that Andre and I were simply friends and traveling companions, no longer husband and wife. She would have none of it! When Andre and I went downtown to take in some of the afternoon Shrimp Festival activities, we came back to find a deserted house. My friend and her husband had packed up, and left us to spend the night at our own devices. It was a conspiracy! I felt compromised, and a little angry, but her strategy was not without its effect. Perhaps we needed someone to force our hand, and without being too graphic about it, for Andre and me that was a new beginning. We draw a diaphanous scrim across that night of nights, but it would make a good scene in a Neil Simon play on Broadway, perhaps to be called "Back Together Again!"

•

What we did after that (drum roll and trumpets) when we returned to Atlanta was to observe the status quo. That is to say, while adjusting to changed circumstances in our relationship, we continued to live apart but together, as did Simone de Beauvoir and her husband, Jean-Paul Sartre who though married to each other, occupied separate floors of the same hotel. We became, for a time "Apart-ners," living in separate locations, making appointments for intimate rendezvous. I would spend a night, often a weekend in his apartment. He lived at that time in the noble Pershing Point apartments, formerly a grand hotel at the junction where the two Peachtrees met. There was a great little restaurant downstairs with a terrace open to the street. Andre and I would meet for dinner, then retire to his bedroom on an upper floor where cars sped past on Peachtree and streetlights shone into his room. It was lovely. It was romantic. It was the idyllic courtship of adults, which we were too young to have enjoyed before our marriage.

Eventually the fine old Pershing Apartments were trashed to make way for a new building, in the way that many such wonderful historic edifices are sacrificed to "progress." I wrote a poem, which seems apropos to include here, as homage to the Pershing Point building where Andre and I were happily reunited. When the poem was written, he was away on a business trip to Paris, and he had said he would call to let me know he had safely arrived. The call did not come, and I was anxious. There is a price to be paid for loving someone. D. H. Lawrence wrote in a 1922 essay, "And it's more difficult than poison-gas. It is to leave off loving… Wives, don't love your husbands any more, even if they cry for it, the great babies! Just boil the eggs and fill the salt-cellars and be quite nice, and in your own soul be alone and be still…" Yes, you sacrifice being alone and still in your own soul when you love, because love takes everything we have, and brings pain in absence, as in

WRECKING BALL BLUES
It's raining in America.
You haven't called, and I wonder if
Paris is your mistress now.

You say that here
we have no sense of history.
We level old buildings
to raise up more commerce,
more beehives for our workers:

Intricate structures of concrete, steel,
and glass, reflecting clouds
and sky color. A small virtue
against such loss.

The old hotel where the two Peachtrees met
is leveled now, and with it
your corner room where taped forties'
tunes synchronized our coupling
amid lights from Peachtree, dancing
across your ceiling like some
sparkling ballroom globe, and I, again,
the girl you won in '49.

•

Andre was unwillingly displaced and un-housed, along with all the other occupants due to the imminent demolition of that wonderful old building. Fortunately, he was able to relocate nearby. We continued our weekend interludes in his new apartment until there came a time when our son, Anthony, returned to Atlanta from the University of Georgia with his girlfriend. They were getting engaged, they needed a place to live, and Andre turned his apartment over to them. Sadly, their engagement was eventually broken, and they both moved on, but it was at this point that Andre and I began physically living together as (not) any old married couple on the block. He moved into my middle floor apartment in a handsome old triplex brick house at 135 Terrace Drive in Peachtree Battle. It was the summer of 1985. End of separation, beginning of happily ever after, or at least, as happily as anyone gets.

Our next move was a dream fulfilled for both of us: Paris for four years, 1990-1994. "Marry me," Andre said to me in 1949 when he came to get me at Florida State University with an engagement ring already in his pocket, "and I will take you to Paris." Forty years later, he made good on his promise.

• • •

DAMAGE CONTROL from the separation was never, ever complete, however. There was residual scarring to this day for both our sons from pain caused by our break. There was residual regret on my part for having been the catalyst for it, even though my husband was adamant it was one of the most positive things that happened to him. He always maintained that without that experience he would not have been the changed person he became through therapy. None of us will ever really lose the impact. For myself, I can say this: I was the recipient of such a storybook commitment, of such completely unconditional love that it was beyond belief, and I was allowed by some sort of grace in this life to survive my own stumbling. The blinders came away, and I am still in the process of clearly seeing Andre of Marseille, wherever he is now, for the utterly amazing, quite extraordinary man that he was.

• • •

THERE WAS ONLY ONE PARTICULAR MAN of the several I met during my sabbatical (if you can call it that) who stands apart. Like Andre, he was a keeper with a capital K, as in his name, "Kauko"—not kept, however, because our disparate paths led elsewhere. Yet, he was a significant fellow traveler along the path, one of two who came in from the cold. He was from Finland. His snow-country counterpart in my life before him was from Denmark. How in the name of the gods and goddesses of legend did Aphrodite send a girl reared on collards and cornbread, these cool men with ice in their eyes? I don't *think* so. Though one was fair and one was dark, the glacial waters of fjords coursed in the veins of both. One was (God help me) an aristocrat and an elitist, but the other was of sturdy middle class stock, and rather more in my comfort zone. Both men, growing up, had the prerequisite absentee father. The father Kauko never knew was an Italian soldier who had his way with a pretty young Finnish girl. He abandoned her, leaving her to raise their son alone. Kauko's only legacy: a lovely Italian last name.

We met in an Atlanta disco club. I was with my gorgeous, statuesque blonde artist friend, Nancy Jones. Nancy's good looks were the main attraction anywhere we went. This cat was out to play! But, I was bored that evening. Sitting alone at the bar with a glass of white wine, SO ready to go home to book and pajamas, someone noticed. He came up and stood beside me, wanting to talk. I was cool and disinterested until hearing that accent—a different speech that always nailed me. Although he did not get much encouragement he was undeterred. He liked that I wasn't easy. I liked it he was not a homeboy. There was something about his serious demeanor, his European courtliness. He was clearly a gentleman who was not simply on the make. As is written in fairy tales of this sort, one thing led to another. He was in and out of Atlanta where I was then living, and when he came to town, he called me. Our dates were casual. I told my friends at work, "This man took me to a movie and bought me a hot dog and Fritos." How "corny" was that! The aristocrat who came in later would have thrown up. But, I liked it—it was amusing, and it was platonic for a time. My druthers. He did not press me with unwelcome attentions.

One afternoon late my suitor came over for a swim in my apartment complex pool, but first, he wanted to take a walk. We did that, single file behind my apartment buildings, and I noticed how purposefully he strode ahead of me, his backside fitting nicely in a pair of black slacks. For the first time, hormones began to rear up, buck and neigh. A few hours later in the pool, finishing our swim, we sat on deck chairs, facing each other. He had curly black hair, unusual for a Scandinavian. His eyes were blue, direct, and as honest as cornflowers. The afternoon sun was lowering as we sat there, talking. He became chilled as the sun went don, shivering in his wet bathing suit, suddenly looking vulnerable as a child. Stricken, I wanted to take care of him. He put on his shirt, wrapped up in a towel, and we drove in his car to a parking space at my apartment building. When he turned off the ignition and turned to me, the thermometer went up on kisses I had been cool to up to that moment. He leaned back and looked at me in disbelief. Then, I touched his beautiful man-hood— honored his birth, honored his death, honored the father he never knew, honored his mother. He understood, and he was astonished.

After that we went up the stairs to my apartment, arm-in arm. There was no lock on my bedroom door, so quickly and efficiently, he placed a chair against the doorknob. Off came our clothes, and into each other's arms we went, not noticing in our haste Saturday night revelers, enjoying a beer on their balcony across the way. We stood before my picture window, nude, oblivious to the world. Then, becoming aware of the voyeurs, laughing and pointing, I drew the blinds, closing out the world. The joys, the sorrows and/or what happens next, and the Finn and I fell into my bed.

•

When he was dressing to leave the next morning, I said, "It will be important that wherever you are in the world today, you must call me." Insecurity? I suffered a little— impulsiveness was not my nature. He said a lovely thing. "I am not a hit and run," and true to his word, he called. Neither he nor I had an emotional hangover. It was the right thing at the right time. My world recovered its balance, and we saw each other when-ever he was in town for a long time after that. It was not "salad days," it was champagne-in-a-silver bucket nights, ordered from room service.

All things end, however, in this impermanent world, and eventually, we parted company. Why was this one of my most memorable attachments to a man, ever? For one thing, he was a decent, caring human being. For another, it is the only time in all my history this wary Capricorn goat, innately cautious and suspicious of footing on the uphill climb, gave way to such abandon. Never such an existential moment of complete freedom, consequences be damned, all sails billowing in the wind. It was stuff of legend, stuff of dreams.

Kauko has a room in my heart, now, where no one goes but me. There is no need for a chair against the door, and here are some words I keep for him, "You showed me what was to be free, free as you were, O Aquarian. Our time together was not meant to be permanent, our time was meant to be impeccable."

• • •

THIS IS A NEW YEAR, WE HAVE A NEW LIFE, is the title of an old poem I wrote while living in Miami Beach. It was about a beginning, it was about the intrepid kudzu, growing beside the highway that takes over everything in its path. My teacher and mentor in Miami, Andy Glaze, pruned it to its lowest common denominator: "December, the roadside kudzu's seasonal sleep—like the mind at year's end low, from limb to limb plotting. Later, the greening surge will come. Now, overhead there's an aperture of light and occasional azure. It reminds us we are more than clay, and that many desires enter as passengers at many depots."
Desire! The streetcar named Desire (or rather, train) had not pulled into my depot for ages. What's more, no greening surge had come in a long, long time. It was past time, and this was a new year in which a new beginning was on the horizon from someone in my friend, Marie White's, family. Her cousin, Holly Brubaker, was getting married in Ft. Lauderdale, and Marie's husband Carol was not up to making the trip. Marie asked if I would like to accompany her. I welcomed a sojourn, however brief, to warmer climes. We were to meet Marie's daughter Wendy, husband Chris, and their three-and-a-half-year-old Andrew in Lauderdale, all of us attending the wedding together. The Howard

Johnson Hotel on the beach allowed Wendy and Chris to park their opulent RV in the hotel parking lot, provided they also rented a room. Therefore, Marie, Andrew and I shared the hotel room, Marie and Andrew in one bed and me in the other, while Wendy and Christ slept in the RV. Shhhhhh! All quiet in the parking lot.

Andrew kept his captive audience of grandmother Marie and honorary aunt Nola entertained in mornings after reveille. He is an inquisitive, exquisitely chatty child, and a well-behaved one, attesting to good parenting. Wendy has endless patience with her little one (not always... she said). Andrew was fascinated with the bucket of ice in our room, and with water in general. I said he was surely destined to be a chemist, because he endlessly transferred water from one plastic bottle to another, then into the bucket, watching the ice transform. "Water," he would tell us informatively, holding up a bottle of the interesting stuff. Who needs toys? Andrew had H2O from any faucet!

On the evening of our arrival in Ft. Lauderdale Beach, we were invited to the home of the bride, Marie's cousin Holly, for a post-wedding-rehearsal gathering. We met the groom, Dave Benefield, and many friends and family of the couple. Holly's home was so reminiscent of Miami, its tropical flora, coconut palms and varieties of citrus trees that it made me homesick for South Florida. Marie and I picked bagfuls of grapefruit from Holly's backyard to take home with us. Marie declared she would make grapefruit sorbet. I declared to add fresh grapefruit juice to a Spartan diet on my agenda when I returned home. There was avoirdupois to be reckoned with on the horizon (and around my waistline) from holiday indulgence. During the evening, Holly's brother, Tom, entertained guests with a surprise video. It began with the caption, "It's a Girl," and then on to "It's a Boy," comprised of home movies of the bride and groom as children, and then progressing to a charming account of their present-day courtship and engagement. It was a moving (literally) gift from a brother to his sister on the eve of her marriage.

The wedding took place next morning at 11:30 in St. John Vianney Catholic Church. Holly had as her only attendant her daughter, Ashley, a stunningly beautiful blonde college student. I loved it that the wedding was Florida laid-back with groom and groomsman in short-sleeved tropical shirts and wearing a single magnolia blossom in the lapel. Holly came

down the aisle wearing a beautiful smile and a pretty, short white dress
with an interesting asymmetrical hemline. She carried a bouquet of white
flowers. She and her groom looked incredibly happy, holding hands while
sitting facing the people in the body of the church while the priest spoke
his homily. Everyone applauded as the new husband and wife walked
down the aisle after the ceremony into a gorgeous, warm, sunny January
day under flawless Florida blue skies. It was a good omen.

•

Holly and Dave's wedding reception was held at the Howard Johnson's
Hotel in their Cadillac Jack's venue. It was a nightclub setting: dance
floor, performing stage with a starry Vegas-like backdrop, and romantic,
intimate lighting simulating evening, no matter the hour. Tables were set
with candles, flowers and white tablecloths. Food stations were strategically placed so that guests might easily serve themselves, and a long bar
occupied one end of the room. The room quickly filled to capacity with
wedding guests. An entertainment duo, billed as "When Buffett Meets
Sinatra" had been hired for four hours of entertainment. The music began
immediately, getting people to their feet for dancing. The duo was comprised of J. C. Unger, the Jimmy Buffett of the concept, adept at a number
of instruments including the violin, and Dale Williams, the sophisticate at
the other end of the spectrum, specializing in singing beautiful old stan-
dards. He looked as if he just stepped out of Frank Sinatra's Rat Pack lineup, and he caught the eye of this wedding guest, big-time. One look at
him, and I was cheddar in the trap. It was that quick.

J. C. Unger stayed seated at his low microphone during the show. He
was casually dressed, his hair in a ponytail, and he looked as if he would
be at ease on the deck of any Key West bar. Dale, in contrast, standing
with a handheld mike, was nightclub handsome in a black suit with crisp,
white shirt, open at the neck. He was the spokesperson of the two, easy
of manner, completely relaxed and superbly confidant with what he was
doing. A consummate professional. Ummmm!

On a trip to the bar to refill my glass of Chardonnay, I worshipped
from afar as he launched into yet another wonderful old Sinatra stan-
dard. "I've got you under my skin," he sang. He was under mine, or I was

going under—one of the two. A waitress passing by murmured about his good looks. I tripped her, and they had to call 911 (just kidding). The song took me back to my college days and my college boyfriend, Mike Brenner. We were besotted with each other, but I was promised elsewhere, and I left Florida State University to get married. When we talked on the telephone a year or so after my marriage, he said to me, "You will not be allowed to break my heart again." But, that is another story, and in Ft. Lauderdale Beach at Holly's wedding reception, I was simply having a déjà vu moment of how it felt to be young and in love. I was "falling in love with love again," and in that magical setting, daylight transformed to dark by the whisk of some magic wand, make-believe was the order of the day.

I made a decision. When I returned to my table, I announced my intention to ask Dale Williams to dance. Waiting until he was free while his partner played something slow and sweet on the violin, I screwed my courage to the sticking point (thank you, Will Shakespeare) and made my way to the bandstand. "Are you allowed to socialize with the guests?" "Yes," he replied. "May I have this dance?" I asked, extending my hand. He took it, stepped down from the stage, and into his arms I went. "I used to be able to waltz," he said, looking into my eyes with a smile. "You do just fine," I said, knees crumpling. We exchanged names. "I'm Dale," he said (as if I hadn't researched that!) I'm your soul mate, I wanted to say, but didn't. He asked me where I was from, and misheard "Ireland" for Amelia "Island." I didn't correct him. I liked the fantasy of being from the Emerald Isle. "Let It Be," as the Beatles said. "How long are you going to be in town," he asked me. My heart skipped a beat, maybe two or three (not long enough, that's for sure). Did he live in St. Petersburg? I asked. "Only a few years," he replied. "I'm from Detroit." I wanted to know everything, anything, all of it, his complete life history, but there wasn't time. It was only one dance, but it was Metro-Goldwyn-Mayer. Cameras flashed at us from friends at my table as I put both my hands on Dale's handsome shoulders, and moved in for my close-up, Mr. DeMille. For me, it was an immortal moment. For him,? just another day's work, but I hoped I had made an impression. We both turned out heads and smiled for the camera. It was Hollywood. It was the Red Carpet. It was better than being from Ireland.

When I returned to my table after the dance, someone remarked, "You got really close!" Well, I had felt welcome. Something about the vibes were all right, although my therapist has told me I have a much less inhibited sense of personal space than most persons. He thinks this comes from having lived abroad, where folks tend to get up-close and personal more readily than we Americans. To be sure, the space necessary for psychological comfort varies among individuals and people of different cultures. If I have become a kissy, huggy Frenchwoman of an *age certaine,* it feels OK. And, apropos to that, after I returned home from Holly's wedding, I pulled up on the Internet Dale Williams' website. It indicated his signature was a champagne flute. Auspicious! Toward the end of the reception in St. Petersburg, I ordered a last glass of bubbly from the waiter for which I said I had a special intention. When the time felt right, I made my way again to the stage, and I offered it to Dale Williams. As he bent to take it, I whispered, "Thanks for the magic." "You are a doll." he replied. Yes!

•

My close long-time poet friend and teacher during the Atlanta years, Walter Griffin, another of my significant men friends who never knew his father. In addition, like me, whose mother was not present in childhood (or ever), he was raised by a loving grandmother. The art of grand mothering deserves enormous respect and admiration. Grandmothers are heroines who pick up the pieces when maternal parenting is null and void. They are saints with big haloes who give us guidelines when there are none. To that end, thank you, Dosia Sheffield, thank you, Lucille Clendenon, and thank you, Susan Lilla Blalock Buchanan—"Miss Lilla" to the world, "Nanny" to my Walter.

•

Another dear man friend of mine, J. D. Beck, had similar energy in his growing-up years. No mother, no father. What is this pattern, of gathering to us unbeknownst, these people broken in the way we are broken? J. D. and I met when my husband and I moved to the island from St. Augustine, and purchased a house just off Amelia Island. When I was in R.C.I.A. on my quest to become Catholic, there was a young man in our little band of searchers whose name was Dennis Beck. He came to sessions in his paint clothes and cap, so it was easy to guess his profession. During R.C.I.A, I confronted Dennis at the church door one day to ask if he could do some painting at my new house. It was not Dennis, however, but his father J. D. who arrived at our doorstep to give an estimate for re-painting the living room and kitchen walls of our new house. Yes, we were surrounded by color: blue of lake and sky, emerald of pine and marsh myrtle, graceful grassy slope down to lapping water. Peaceful, lapping water, that is, until the wind blew hard from the sea, making waves, sometimes mini white-crested tidals, like its mighty mother, the Atlantic. But, we needed to make the walls of our new house interior "ours," and not a former owner's choice. We wanted our own expression, and, to that end, J. D. entered our sphere.

There was an immediate connection between J. D. and myself, and Andre liked him. This was important, because the Marseillais allowed few men into his intimate circle. He had friends all over the world, but only a small number got close. Our paint work commenced under J. D.'s expert hands, but more than that, during the long year of Andre's illness, J. D. visited often to sit with my husband. J. D. was a Catholic convert, as I was, and he brought his wife Betty and his sons Dennis and Chris into the church. Another connection was the discovery J. D. had been born the same day as Lise Goett. April 2, Aries—the Ram has been important in my life.

When Andre passed away, J. D. was there for me for crises, small and large, that arose in the aftermath. He and I would sit in my kitchen for an occasional Happy Hour when he was working in the Marsh Lakes area. While we solved the problems of the universe (would that the gods had been listening) he entertained me with vignettes about his life. He was a born storyteller. My door was always open for *un verre*, French shorthand for a glass of wine (and good conversation.) J. D.'s stories were so interesting; I thought they should be written down. He decided to col-laborate with me on a tale I liked best: how he met and married his wife Betty. Here it is, as I wrote it from his taped conversations: "Let me tell you a story, and we're going to call it 'Betty Lou's Man.' It's about a city slicker and a country gal, falling in love. It's about our little life story ..."

BETTY LOU'S MAN

*Short synopsis is, I was kinda running wild, and left
Jacksonville, Florida, going nowhere in particular and having
nothing to do. About the only smart thing I did was resign my
job with the post office so I wouldn't get fired. I knew one day
I might come back and renew that relationship and retire with
a good retirement, which is what I did. So, I wind up in
Lexington, Kentucky, for no apparent reason whatsoever, and
I meet this guy named Little Joe. Now, you gotta know Little
Joe. In my introduction to "country," Little Joe was one that if
you went to a bar, you sat with your back to the wall because
he's gonna hit somebody and start a fight, and you don't want
anybody coming up behind you.*

*Anyway, to make a long story short, we lived next door to
each other. He gets in trouble with the law, he loses his driver's license, so he can't drive to work, and they come and
repossess my car. So, Little Joe's got a car and no license, and
I've got a license and no car. He's working at a meat packing
house, and he says, "Why don't we go to Nashville? They've
got a packing house up there and we'll go to work there." I
say, "What do I care? I'm going in no particular direction,
anyway." So we get up there, and we go to work at the pack-
inghouse, okay? A lot of things changed for me after that. For
one thing, I became a Catholic. There were five brothers in
the business, a Catholic family, 50 kids, and they prayed
about everything. I'd been out of church for 25 years, and
they really made a big impression on my life.*

*Two weeks after I began working at the packing house,
Betty Lou walks in. Now you gotta know Betty Lou is country, and I'm city, and everybody in the country has got two
names: Betty Lou, Helen Sue, and so on, but anyway, this
gorgeous gal walks in with hair all the way down her backside, and I just fell in love with her. So, we wind up working
pretty much in the same department in the packing house, and
we are doing what they call a "hog cut". A hog cut is when
they kill the hogs the day before, they butcher them the next
day, and everyone is on an assembly line. The butchers cut off
this piece or that, for a ham or whatever—and they send it*

down the line and then people like me would take it off the
line, wrap it, weigh it, mark the box, and pack it away for the
truck drivers to take to the grocery stores. Now, Betty Lou is
upstairs on the next floor up, and she is making boxes for me.
We kind of got to smiling at each other, winking, and grinning,
and so on, and every day when the hog cut was over, I had to
push the boxes back up that were left. She took them up and
saved them for the next day so that when the washing-up was
done on the floor, the boxes would not get wet. One day, I
decided to write on one of the boxes, "How about Saturday
night?" I pointed to the box and I pushed it back up to her,
and she saw what I had written on the box and she gives me a
circle with her fingers, like OK, Good deal.

Now, I don't have a car, so we are going out on our date
in her car. She's got an Oldsmobile with no heater, no
defroster or anything. When you're driving and it's snowing
and icing over, you gotta get a can of de-icer, leave the window down and spray the windshield so it doesn't freeze over.
That is neither here nor there, but that's the way we started.
So we decided to go out, and we went out Saturday night.
We walked all over Nashville, then we went down to a place
called The Cellar which was in Printers Alley where the
nightclubs were. I get down there to The Cellar and I am in
blue jeans, T-shirt and a casual jacket which was all I
owned, and the guy says, "You need to have a dinner jacket
on to eat here." I say, "I don't own one." He says, "Well, I'll
lend you one."

So, we sit down at the dinner table, and the first thing I do,
(because I'm from the city and I understand all this) I ordered
a shrimp cocktail. Betty Lou thought that was something to
drink. She never forgot I introduced her to a shrimp cocktail!
We had a lovely dinner, and hit the late show at the Grand
Ole Opry. I spent my whole paycheck, and had to borrow ten
dollars from her to live the next week.

After a while, we're into the "Go meet my folks" phase.
Now, I don't know anything about "country." When I'm talking about country, I'm talking about the courthouse guys playing checkers on the square, a Dollar Store, an auto parts
place, a drugstore, and that was pretty much all there was to

it. People would come to town every Saturday just to ride around the square. Now, I'm a city guy, and I ain't never seen seen nothing like this, OK? Anyway, we go to see her dad, her step mom, and grandpa. Now grandpa (we called him Pa) he didn't like me a little bit. First thing he asks Betty Lou is, "You're not gonna marry this man, are you?" And she said, "No Pa, I'm not fixin' to marry him." And Pa says, "Well, I don't like his looks."

I thought, Oh Boy, I'm in deep poo-poo right now, and I ain't hardly got in the door! So anyway, I get into the house, we talk and whatever, and then it's time to go to bed. Pa's kind of like a dog I used to have, he was like, in-between me and her so I didn't touch her. He wanted me to keep my distance. He says to me, "You sleep in the back bedroom." Now, the back bedroom, it was cold. It had no heat. It's an old, wooden log cabin, and I got in there with a half a quart of Lord Calvert and got under all the blankets and quilts, and finally got to sleep. I'm good and sound asleep when Pa comes in to get me up for breakfast. He reaches and gets the covers to wake me up, and instead of the grabbing the covers, he got my hair and he pulled me straight up out of the bed. Now, this man is a replica of Abraham Lincoln, OK? He scared the bezoodles out of me, because I looked up and all I could see was this man reaching to the ceiling. He says, "Breakfast is ready," and buddy, I hit the ground running to the breakfast table. That was my first experience with Pa. Things didn't go well that weekend, but over the years, they got better.

The encounter with Pa wasn't the only thing I remember from that first time I went up there to meet the folks. Betty Lou was driving 65/70 miles an hour around those hills, and I'm scared to death. I'm used to driving on Florida flat ground, and while she's driving around those hills, she introduced me to a "holler." I thought a holler was when you yelled at somebody, but I found out a holler was a drop you can't see to the bottom of, and Betty Lou's going 70 miles an hour. When we got back from that trip, I got out and looked at the tires, and there was no tread on those tires. Next week, I borrowed her car and went out and bought four recaps. That was all I could afford back then. So, next time we went to the country, we had some tires underneath us.

Anyway, we progressed a little bit further along in our lives, and we got a '65 Plymouth Fury police interceptor. Pa was beginning to see that I was progressing a little bit in doing something for Betty Lou, so we broke our relationship down to a cordial thing. We got to a better place with each other, and he got to where he would say, "You got a little horn with you?" Now, if you don't know what a horn is, in the country a horn is a drink of whiskey. So, he'd say, "You got a little horn with you?" and I'd say, "Yep, Pa, I got one with me, and I'd like to have me a little horn." So, as time went on, things got better, and he could see that I was providing for Betty Lou, and so he mellowed a whole lot. It got to be where he would let me take him to town to pay his bills which was something she always used to do.

Betty Lou and I were out on the town in the Fury one night. I was pretty well crocked, and the manifold busted. I mean we probably woke up the whole town. The sheriff was right behind me, followed me all the way out to Betty Lou's daddy, Jesse's house. Next day, I have to go to town to get the car fixed because I can't drive it all the way back 80 miles and warp the valves, or something. I've got to go to Grogan's—the only game in town: one mechanic, one service station. So, I go to Grogan's and I've got to sit down and explain who I am and what I'm doing up there while they proceed to sit down in a circle and tell me who got married, who didn't get married, who was doing whatever. It's like going to John's Barber Shop, which is to say if John doesn't know it at the barbershop, "it" didn't happen. That's how Grogan's was— if they don't know it, it did not happen.

So, they are all sitting around, and Grogan finally tells me, "I can't fix the car. I can't get parts for it." I say, "Man, I don't need to drive this car back to Nashville and warp those valves because cold air will run in on the valves after I run that 80 miles. That's what's gonna happen," and he says, "Well, I can't get parts for it. I'm sorry." We sit around for two hours and I am listening to all the town gossip, and all of a sudden Grogan says, "Pull your car up on the rack." I did, and the mechanic comes over there, took his torch out, ten minutes later he has it fixed, and it never did break again.

That's part of what I was learning about country ways. It took two hours to get ready, and ten minutes to fix it.

Betty Lou and I made a trip to Detroit in that Fury, and her uncle had bought a Grand Prix—midnight blue, white vinyl top, four speed, Hurst transmission, all wood grain dash—the whole nine yards. The uncle's wife didn't like the car at all, so he said, "I need to get rid of the car. Do you guys want to buy it?" I said, "Yes, but I don't think I can afford it." He said, "Give me 500 dollars." "You have got to be KID-DING!" I said, and that is how we bought the car for 500 dollars. When we drove it back to the country, Pa was coming around, saying, "Well, maybe this guy is really doing something." Anyway, he is getting more proud of me. We're getting in like Flynn!

Next thing Betty Lou and I do is, we buy a "hippie van." The hippie van had horses all over it, a port hole on the side, shag carpet all over the ceiling, and a bed in the back. We're back in her little country town again (that's about four or five blocks wide) and they sure enough don't want a hippie van in town. Pa says to me, "I need to go to town just to pay a bill," so I say, "OK Pa, let's go." We head to town, and Pa says, "With this vehicle, you probably need to park on the square. He meant they weren't pretty much going to accept that vehicle in town. So, we park on the square. Five minutes later, here comes the sheriff. Pa's name was Fate Lee, and the sheriff says, "Howdy, Fate, how you doing?" and Pa says, "I'm doing good." The sheriff sticks his head in the car window, and he sees all that shag carpet, that bed in the back, and this country town sheriff, he wasn't ready to accept all that. He looks at me and he asks, "Who is that?" Pa says, "That's Betty Lou's man, and, now, he's a good 'un." And the sheriff says, "Well, that's good enough for me."

I probably could have spun circles around the courthouse, and nobody would have said anything about it after that. Fate was one of the most respected men in town, and if he said something was OK, by golly it was OK. And if I was Betty Lou's man, I was Betty Lou's man, and I could have done anything I wanted to. Pa was a great man, and a great person

to know. So, all the years I was with Betty Lou, all the years
we were married, Pa never called my name. I was always
"Betty Lou's man." That was good enough for me then, and
it's good enough for me now.

The End

Sadly for me, Betty Lou's Man and Betty moved away from the island. Not too far away, only to Jacksonville, also purchasing a modest brick house in the Tennessee mountains where Betty grew up. Betty, one of the most positive and courageous people I have ever known, had been fighting a valiant battle with cancer for years and years. I was happy for Betty's house in the mountains to which she could always go home: Home, capital H, where people are paramount in a place of healing, peace, and nurturance.

• • •

FEBRUARY, it seems, has traditionally been an enormously difficult month. Even with milestones such as my February 18, 1950, wedding, and my son Anthony's entry into the world, these happy occasions have been overshadowed by tragedies. My brother Jim died in February, as did George and Corinne. In February of this year alone, there have been five deaths of close friends. What is it about February, anyway? Research tells us January and February date from about the time of Rome's founding. When introduced, January was given 29 days and placed at the beginning of the calendar year. February was given 23 days and put at the end. Was there an insight; such as, February is consistent with endings? Ask someone who is Greek. They made the calendar, and God help us numbers-challenged folks, they created math, from which I run screaming in the opposite direction.

February is the second month of the year in the Gregorian calendar, the only month with length of 28 or 29 days. February, apparently, has to make haste to catch up with the rest of the months. February begins, astronomically speaking, with the sun in the constellation of Capricornus. As a Capricorn person, that points February directly to me, and it has an arrow with a very sharp tip. If in the old Japanese calendar, February is called Kisaragi, which means "the month changing clothes," I would say for me it means "the month changing my life."

•

So it begins again with yet another phone call. "She's gone," he simply said. February 15, 2007, around midnight, that black hour, J. D.'s Betty lost her valiant battle with liver cancer. I loved her, too. Until the end, you would not have known she was ill. She was bright of spirit, optimistic, and uncomplaining. She had a mountain woman's legendary strength, sense of place and people, and she was enormously generous. I knew J. D. for a long time before I ever met Betty. They were estranged at the time, though still living together in their home, and J. D. maintains that his friendship with me is what, in an odd way, brought about their reconciliation. An overheard phone call, a suspicion that J. D. and another woman were a little more than friends led to a demand for an explanation. No Way, she found out, and as she later told me, she wondered, "Why do I care?" But, she did care, and cared a lot. Loss, and sometimes even the dawning realization of what that loss would mean, brings clarity. J. D., Betty and I met for dinner shortly after that. Betty and I liked each other immediately. "Your wife is so pretty," I told J. D. And she was, even when past breast cancer, in remission, came back with a vengeance—this time in her liver. When Betty lost her hair to chemo, J. D. shaved his in sympathy, and two bald people appeared on their Christmas card that year.

Before her battle was lost, Betty invited me many times to her house for dinner. "Come have dinner with the Becks," J. D. would say proudly over the telephone. When we sat out by their swimming pool, Betty was the one who grilled steaks. There was always an invitation on holidays to join them because they didn't want me to be alone. Only once did I have occasion to make dinner for the Becks at my house. We sat out on my screened-in porch, shoes off and casual, discussing the state of the world. Betty remarked how she'd like to sit in my swing on the grassy bank which meandered down to the lake and have morning coffee. "Thoughts fly highest over water," someone once said. Ocean, lake, river, crystal streams over rocks—they are good conductors for prayers.

Once, J. D. and Betty took me to a dinner theatre in nearby Jacksonville. They were season ticket holders, and especially liked musicals. On another occasion, Betty called me from her office at Amelia Island Plantation, and asked, "Would you like to spend an evening with my husband?" She was not feeling up to the drive to Jacksonville for an outing to the dinner theatre, and J. D. really wanted to go. The Becks and I also attended Saint Patrick's Day celebration in the parish hall of St. Michael's church complete with music, singing, corned beef and cabbage, and, because we are Catholics: an open bar (no blue noses where the Archangel hangs out—maybe a few red ones). As we sat at our table, Betty said to me as she glanced toward J. D. sitting between the two of us, "Is he not the luckiest man in the world?" This wife made a generous place for another woman's friendship with her husband.

On the day after my `brother and his wife died, I spent the day alone in my house in complete silence. I was sitting on my porch, putting words on paper in the healing presence of the lake, the birds, my two pine trees. Betty Beck unexpectedly appeared at the screen door with a complete chicken dinner take-out. In sickness (hers) and health (mine), she was a friend for all seasons, all reasons. I told her as I accepted her gift, "You are the only person in the world I would have wanted to see coming around the corner of my house today."

Betty died at home with her husband and her two sons around her bed. They held her hands as she died. "Like us around Andre," I said to J. D., "Anthony, Sylvia, Father Bob, and Andre Ferreira." Passages. We share each other's lives; we share each other's deaths. I have no doubt Betty died as bravely as she lived.

• • •

THE MAN I THOUGHT I KNEW. Many longtime wives and partners (not Betty Beck, though) blithely assume that what they know about their husband is the end-all and be-all of who he is—that the marriage defines him. What is it that gives some of us the right to think we understand our partner within the limits of our relationship to him? I was with a man for 52 years, and only later began to understand how much was really not known. Marriage is a mysterious karmic journey to be continued on another plane because there is still so much work to be done. I believe it!

There is a whole life a husband (or wife or child or sibling) has in their personal interactions which we never see. When someone dies, people come out of the woodwork with revelations that amaze us. My friend Elise Braun remarked that when her mother died, a woman told her a complete account of her mother's wedding. Elise never knew her mother the bride! She would never have been privy if this woman had not had a relationship with her mother long before Elise arrived on the scene.

During an appointment with a doctor sometime after Andre's passing, he remarked how he missed the political discussions and opinions my husband shared with him when they would meet in the examining room during Andre's long illness. Andre had a lot to say about the turbulent Middle East situation. He was born in Algiers of a Muslim father and a Roman Catholic mother. It was his unequivocal opinion that peace would never be possible between Arabs and Jews. I miss watching the evening news these days with my husband sitting across from me in his burgundy rocker, listening to his wisdom regarding the unsettling events taking place in our world today.

• • •

MAKING ROOM in a drawer in my office the other day, I came across my husband's and my fiftieth wedding anniversary file. It contained a documentation of the anniversary celebration soirée in Fernandina, along with keepsake cards and letters. February 18, 2007, will be the 57th milestone marker of our journey together. One of us is here; one of us is not. It makes no difference in the sense that we are married for eternity—absence or presence, better or worse, sickness or health, richer or poorer—all of the above.

Last year, before going out to Bosque Bello Cemetery with flowers for my husband's grave, on the occasion of our anniversary, I spent time sitting in the stained glass light and musty silence of an empty church. In my pew at St. Peter's Episcopal Church, Fernandina, many past images presented themselves. Two seriously young innocents, dressed to the nines, knelt before the altar, as a seriously dignified Reverend Frederick Golden-Howes bound their wrists together with an ivory silk stole. In the highs and lows of ensuing years, they sometimes tried, always failed, to sever that bond. Who would have thought silk to be that strong!

On Saturday the 17th of February of this year of Our Lord, there was an e-mail from a man who was, and is, my husband's closest friend. Andre and Walter Wulff were men who carefully chose their intimate circle, but when they selected someone, it was ivory silk, all the way. They are February people, Aquarians by birth. Aquarian men are the salt of the earth, so saith this earth-sign Capricorn. Amen. It is no fluke of nature that Wally Wulff's birthday is February 18th, the day Andre and I was married. Among the innumerable gifts Andre brought me was my own special connection to his friend, Wally. Wally, an air traffic controller, was also an equity actor. He was in many theatrical productions in Atlanta, starring in a one-man show about Teddy Roosevelt called "Bully," and one about our mutual hero, Franklin D. Roosevelt. Wally lent his acting talents to interpreting my poetry. Along with Atlanta actress, Hanna Hamlett, he performed my work in such venues as an art gallery, a bookstore, and the Atlanta Arts Festival in Piedmont Park. Wally and his wife, Carol, a Capricorn sister, no longer live in Atlanta. They have retired to the paradise of Point Clear, Alabama. On my one visit there, I was struck by a similarity to Amelia Island. Andre and Wally, similar energies to the end: island ambiance and Capricorn women. Here is Wally's e-mail message:

Nola,

I always think about you and Andre on the 18th. It is a special date for me. I think of him often. He was more of a brother to me than my own. Convinced me to get out of Fairburn and move into downtown to pursue theatre. One of the best things I ever did. We had such memorable times, Atlanta, Paris, that I will never forget. I will always remember when I first met Andre in San Juan. We seemed to hit it off instantly. Me, in Air Terrific (Air Traffic) and he in Airway Facilities. Kind of an oil and water relationship between the two divisions. We liked each other instantly. Carol, Tracy, the dogs, and I were flying 1st class on our return flight from San Juan to Atlanta when Andre came aboard the same aircraft. He looked at us, the dogs, and said 'I always knew air traffic went first class while the rest of us peons had to fly coach.' I will never forget it. From then on, we were buddies. I truly loved him. I hope you are not sad on this day because I know he loved you. Be happy and think of the good times. Remember, we all had Paris.

One of the most valued papers in the 50th wedding anniversary file is a letter from John Cassady and his wife, Darlene— friends from the Federal Aviation Administration days in Brussels. Reading it again seven years after its receipt, an excerpt seemed more than fitting to be included in this book. This letter, while marking our anniversary, also addressed John's sentiments apropos to Andre's retirement after 43 years and one month of service to the American people:

"Taking the two main milestones in the order of their celebration, may we first congratulate you both on the occasion of Andre's graduation from the FAA. Andre, even as one as inclined to humility as you, you must be very, very proud of your achievement. Literally every one of the colleagues at FAA that we know considers you extraordinary, both professionally and personally. In an age of decline of likeable people, you are, understandably, one of the most widely liked persons I have ever known. Now, as to the matter of your 50 years of marriage: Aside from my parents (married 62 years this April) Darlene and I know of no couple whose mutual devotion is so noticeable. While you are in many ways a complementary match, your esteem for each other seems identical in its reverence. We love how you love each other, and it deepens our own commitment to each other."

•

John's letter was a love letter to the living. There was such an outpouring of heartfelt sorrow over Andre's death; it would take reams of paper to share. Here are some of the messages received from the world he touched beyond mine. If there were something I would say to those who one day face devastating personal loss, it is this: be prepared for the discoveries—be prepared for the revelations that will assail you day by day. Absence is a great clarifier. Bereavement will show you that person you loved with new, acute insight, as if you suddenly found yourself in a blaze of light. I, too, will have left a legacy, as did Andre. That graduation could come any day now. No one knows the hour. I look forward to it with the apprehension and uncertainty accompanying all new experience, but surpassing this, I have an enormous curiosity. There is the expectation of seeing in the light at the end of that tunnel many have described in a near-death experience, those persons loved in life, coming forward to meet me, led by Andre. After that, what else, what else? There's a book in there somewhere!

·

This book had its beginning with the question from someone wondering why I had not written about my husband's death. It seems fitting to end it with the demise of the year. The year of Our Lord, two thousand and six, disappears into history, even as my personal new year begins with my birthday, January 6th—Feast of the Epiphany, Feast of Lights, Dia de Los Reyes, Three Kings Day—all those designations for the Twelfth Night of antiquity. This month's old god faced opposite directions, backward and forward. Two-faced Janus came in riding an old star, one that guided shepherds and kings and gave an intense light all its own. We are here to give a light all our own—that is our mission which plays out in hundreds of different ways.

In the 76th year of life, it is my hope when my light flickers out; there will be a graceful exit on my part, leaving some measure of phosphorescence behind, like plankton in the sea. I give thanks for the intervention of all those in my cast of characters, those who entered, altered and illuminated my life. I would change no history along the way because how could it have been different? We all have regrets, and each of us knows well what those are. We are flawed human beings, but in the final analysis, we did our best. We were who we were, and we are who we are. God (however you envision him) be blessed for the journey. How good it would be to be remembered as having lived a life as well as Andre of Marseille. Here are some of the words from those who knew him in ways in which his wife had no part. A little bit of the legacy of lives he touched.

From an x-ray technician at Baptist Medical Center, Fernandina:
> I can't tell you how saddened I was to read about your husband's passing. It seems just last week that you two were in the emergency room. As I read Mr. Perez's obituary out loud to my mother, I realized what an incredible life he led... I think if I lived to be 200 years old, I could never imagine accomplishing all that he did... Even on your husband's worst

*day, I could still see the love he held for you in his eyes. My
life is so much more blessed because of your husband's presence in my life. I will cherish the memories I have of him for
the rest of my life.*

From Elline Lipkin of the late, lamented Paris Poetry Groupe:
*I will always harbor such strong and fond memories of
Andre's beautiful spirit, his warmth, his laugh, his fine mind
and heart... I grieve with you, as well, and will miss knowing
Andre is here, although he will never leave my memory and
my heart.*

From a novelist friend in Miami:
*I am so glad I got to know Andre. He knew so much about so
many things. The memories of the wonderful dinners we all
shared will always be with me.*

And from the novelist's wife:
*Andre was a remarkable man, so full of good cheer and spir-
it—we shall miss him.*

From a young man friend from Atlanta days:
*The passing of Andre deeply saddened me, but my feelings
were tempered with warm memories of a man who always
treated me—indeed all he met that I ever saw—with the
warmest of welcomes, respect and joviality. His genial kindness touched me time and time again. Andre was the first
adult I knew who treated me as an adult, and respected my
being gay without condemnation or coolness. I will miss him.*

From his Federal Aviation Administration Commander in Chief:
*Your Andre was a remarkably fine and patient gentleman.
What a calming influence he was on us all when the situation
became tense. Yes, grace under fire is the true mark of a
leader, and that was how Andre consistently conducted himself. I, along with his legion of friends who are in and out of
the FAA, and who valued his friendship will miss him dearly.
That he departed this life gently and with dignity was as it
should be.*

From a fellow worker from Atlanta days:

Andre is special to me for a lot of reasons. He was a true pro-
fessional, so knowledgeable, and always a gentleman. I came
to work for him in 1978 during an especially trying time in
my life. He was such a quiet support to me, and I have
always valued his friendship. He will be missed by many.

From Frank Anthony in Windsor, Vermont:

The times we were fortunate enough to be with both of you,
Andre's devotion (for you) was an example never to be wit-
nessed again. This memory is therapy for all of us.

Dr. Frank Anthony was born the same month and same year as my
brother, George Derrick. Connections He had a Ph.D. from Florida State
University, my university. Connections! He was Andre's look-alike and
admirer. He was the founder and guiding light of New England
Writers/Vermont Poets. RIP, friend Frank, 1922-2006.

From Elise Braun's brother, Sam Holmes, Sag Harbor, NY:

The other morning I lay in bed thinking about all the things I
had to do, and of course writing to you was one of them. I
thought of Andre and remembered his wonderful laugh—deep
with a few high notes. I could see his gleeful face laughing. I
think I will always be able to hear him and see him. Suddenly
I had access to tears, for the first time in several years.

From Willyne Blanchard, a longtime Fernandina friend:

Thanks so much for your beautiful words on the anniversary
card you gave us. We shall keep it always, especially because
you and Andre sent it. Thanks for the gift of yourselves on
May 2. Little did we know that would be the last we'd be with
Andre. You were magnificent at Andre's farewell, Nola. The
beauty and strength of your character was never more evident
than when you stood after Mass and spoke of the man of your
life. Saint Andre! What more could a man ask for?

• • •

RAIN, and morning blessing of a new day. It's not yet first light outside, only lightning illuminates the bedroom: God's flashlight, 10,000 watts. Lying in the warmth of my bed, I turn, pulling the comforter close, to face the windows. After night, there's always morning, or at least we've come to count on it. That works in nature, and in life. This is one of those moments, needing no companion, no other, except He who made the day and the night. Psychics pray to Mother/Father God. He's both, one in three persons, masculine and feminine. He is the One, throwing bolts around to lighten the dark this early morning, and, hopefully, will clear it with indigo and sunshine. We've come to count on it. His voice breaks open the sky to let us know the natural world is at work on His business. Whether it is clear to me, no doubt the world is unfolding as it should. There is light at the end of the metaphysical tunnel, and at the end of that one which will take us home. I'm not ready yet, please God. Time to put feet on the floor, untie the ribbon on this new day.

Stopping to open the glass doors to my porch, the world outside glitters with crystals of rain, and the rain music is soft, comforting. A single frog chirrups contentedly. The frog knows. There is happiness in the moment, and in the expectation of more to come. Look to the rainbow. Honor the lost. They have been found. Amazing Grace! Only the living feels loss. Pain means we are alive in this strangest, most mysterious of miracles called life. If you can think of at least half a dozen reasons why life is good, stay here, and do your best. Don't even think of checking out. If I had counted to six when I tried it, I would have thought of this: Early morning rain when you are snug in bed. It's dark outside, you can stay in, and the calendar's clear all day. Driving over the bridge to the island when it's high tide and the river is meandering out to sea under a gorgeous sunrise. A friend calls to thank you for just being you. Going to dinner at a nice restaurant with your son, the handsomest man in three counties, and just maybe, the world. You can't get past your bedroom window at dawn because the sky is painted purple, vermillion and gold, and if you blink, it will be gone. Shopping with your granddaughter at Publix, and she tells the checker her grandmother is a poet (and don't you forget it!) Helen Mirren as Queen Elizabeth 1 tells it like it is—there's work to be done. And, if you don't do your work, you are going to hear about it upstairs, downstairs, right here in this room, or wherever He hangs out when overseeing his handiwork. There are not more of us than he can keep his eye on. Onward and upward to the stars!

• • •

Epilogue

FAMILY. A word that binds with ivory sik those who have loved you, love you now, and who will love you in the future: "The procession of the loved." If there is one thing the Kir Queen has learned from her homecoming, it is that home is those who people it. As a child, a children's movie I loved was The Bluebird with an adorable, dimpled Shirley Temple. Little Miss golden ringlets cut the pattern for child stars in a story of the search for happiness. The moral was, happiness is found in your own backyard. I have a backyard, now, have learned that lesson. I am happy, more or less. If there was a kir for all the times something devoutly desired was searched for somewhere else, in astonishment found I already had it, I would be in rehab. *Ailleurs n'est jamais loin quand on aime...* The French have a phrase for it. Elsewhere is never far away when one loves. It's a matter of vision. Family matters. Family *matters.*

And just what is it about being born on a barrier island? Of a barrier island, the dictionary says, Noun: A long, relatively narrow island running parallel to the mainland, built up by the action of waves and currents and serving to protect the coast from erosion by surf and tidal surges. Key word: protection. In the growing-up years, we were separated from the "stuff" beyond the drawbridge by bodies—bodies of water varying in size: ocean, sound, river. It was purification. We had diversity. We had constantly changing environment, and even though our primary dunes have dwindled, still we have protection. Key word: protection. We were baptized with brine, marked with the sign of the marsh where the river rules and the ocean is the imperative. Home is in my own backyard.

I had coffee recently with a woman who lived away from our mutual hometown for many years. She is divorced, childless, and baffled her big city friends by returning to Fernandina to finish up. "Why in the world would you go back to that little town," they asked, "when you have all of these wonderful things here?" My friend said to me that what she missed was community. It was only a short time, she said, before she was seen—acknowledged by old friends and new, in a place where a circle opened to receive her, eyes brightened as she entered, and voices cele-brated her power. The poet Merie Kirby wrote in her poem "The Second Winter," "I didn't say it was paradise, I meant it was home."

This book of bones began like a cake with batter as thin as gruel. What would the ingredients be? The eggs were omitted. Nuts, dates, and lots of seeds were thrown in. The mixture thickened. I asked myself, who is this sole soul with pen in hand, a Me, not a We, stranger than any stranger, surviving losses, starting over. Home, it seemed, was the missing leavening to make the thing rise. These days have become seamless, one endless thread looped in the needle of life. Still sleeping on the wedding side of my body, hugging the farthest margin of the bed where the night visitors come, they keep their engagements—offer courage. They teach forbearance. As in lines from the television screenplay, *Elizabeth I*: "The hardest thing to govern is the heart." We need help there. The Kir Queen may be dethroned now, but she does not prick her finger, or take a bite of poisoned apple and fall asleep. There is no glass coffin. The shining knight has come and gone, shucked off his armor, laid down his sword, and His lady who trusted that words would save her has finished her book.

She ends with this from D. H. Lawrence, dying of tuberculosis in the winter of 1929-30. From his last book *Apocalypse*, these saving words: "For man, as for flower and beast and bird, the supreme triumph is to be most vividly, most perfectly alive… The dead may look after the afterwards. But the magnificent here and now of life in the flesh is ours, and ours alone, and ours only for a time. We ought to dance with rapture that we should be alive and in the flesh, and part of the living, incarnate cosmos."

Fin

Photo Gallery

Andre' of Marseille in his element – "Neptune" rising from the sea, Cassis, France, 1993

Happy on a Mediterranean beach just outside Marseille, 1993

A pensive Michael on a parapet of Notre Dame de La Garde Church, Marseille, overlooking his father's hometown

With Andre on our apartment balcony in the rosy days of North Miami Beach, 1995

With my brother, George Derrick, at his home in Jacksonville

With my brother, Dr. James Baker, at his son, Jamie's wedding rehearsal dinner in Winter Haven, Florida

Andre in Miami, recovering from his mitral heart valve replacement - 1996

Entryway to Casa Massalia, our new house in Marsh Lakes, 2001

With Andre in our living room

Becoming Catholic: With Bishop Snyder in the Cathedral Gardens, St. Augustine – 2001

With my brother-in-law, Vincent Ferreira, in Jacksonville, 1999

Revisiting my 1990-1994 Paris home at Daumesnil – 12th arrondissement

A sun-worshipping Catherine in the little cruiser on the Mediterranean

Catherine and her daughter, Segolene, in their apartment on avenue de Wagram, Paris, 2004

Catherine and Jean-Claude (Joli Prince) breakfasting on their balcony in Boulouris - the South of France

Catherine and Joli Prince take an unscheduled dive while preparing the cruiser for a trip to St. Tropez

With Lise Goett and Julie Pietri at Union Square Café

Ms. Julie Pietri

Julie Pietri's gorgeous rooftop garden at 235 E. 49th Street, NYC

Two Paris poets reunite. With Lise Goett at Union Square Café

Nola still loves New York!

After the fall on the sidewalk of New York

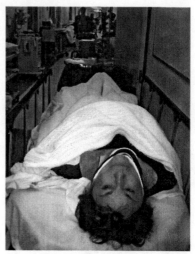

A scary day in the E.R. at Columbia-Cornell University Hospital – Julie in attendance

George Derrick Appreciation Night, American Legion Department Headquarters, Lee Road, Orlando, Florida – April 1, 2000. Daughter Peggy on left, daughter Jackie on right.

Honor Guard at the American Legion Post ceremony

The American Legion memorial

Our little family gathers at American Legion Post 137, San Juan Avenue, Jacksonville for the dedication of a memorial for George and Corinne. Left to right: Michael Perez, Nola, Bradley and Derek Folds (grandchildren) and daughter Jackie Derrick Folds- December 2006

George and Corinne on their honeymoon in front of the Capitol building, Tallahassee, Florida - 1944

High school sweethearts, George loves Corinne - Fernandina High School, 1938

Smokin' ! Best friends, Nola and Elise at Andre's going-away to the Army party, Moore's restaurant, Main Beach - 1952

My surrogate Mom, Johnnie Mae. "We had good raising!"

My Mother, Myself – Burney, crouching between her father, William Sheffield and an unidentified woman watches baby George, take a few steps

All Rise! The Honorable Harry Ryder takes some down time in the country

Frank and Grace Ward at their home, Fernandina

Iris and Drew Ward on top of the
Fernandina light house

Elise: Water colors beside the water

My favorite photo of Elise in her house in
Stowe, Vermont

Wally Wulff in character as Franklin
Delano Roosevelt

The awesome profile of Walter
Griffin, poet extraordinaire

J. D. (Betty Lou's Man) and Betty in the courtship days.

Betty's Man, Betty, and their baby son, Chris

Wendy, Andrew and Chris Philcox at Holly Brubaker's wedding in Ft. Lauderdale, Florida

J. D. Beck shaves his head to complement Betty during her cancer treatments

Falling in Love with Love Again? Dale, the Wedding Singer at Holly's wedding reception

With Julia at the Café du Monde, French Quarter

With Marie White, Julia Jessup and our waiter at Antoine's, New Orleans

In the wake of troubles. On board the good ship Melody, 2003

Romance on the High Seas. Kaloyan of Romania, our table wine steward aboard The Melody

They want to order spirits, but Kaloyan is distracted by my camera

With sister-in-law Sylvia Ferreira and the ship's captain. All dolled up for a gala dinner...

Miss Elizabeth Perez hugs a tree.

Sally and Anthony Perez show off baby Elizabeth.

Mellow Mia of St. Augustine

Kirby the Water Dog

Among The Rocks That Formed Him,
this most beautiful man, dozing peacefully
under a Mediterranean sun,
is forever in our hearts

Made in the USA